MEDIA
ADVOCACY
AND
PUBLIC
HEALTH

MEDIA ADVOCACY AND PUBLIC HEALTH

Power for Prevention

Lawrence Wallack
Lori Dorfman
David Jernigan
Makani Themba

Foreword by Michael Pertschuk

 SAGE Publications
International Educational and Professional Publisher
Newbury Park   London   New Delhi

For information address:

SAGE Publications, Inc.
2455 Teller Road
Newbury Park, California 91320

SAGE Publications Ltd.
6 Bonhill Street
London EC2A 4PU
United Kingdom

SAGE Publications India Pvt. Ltd.
M-32 Market
Greater Kailash I
New Delhi 110 048 India

Printed in the United States of America

Library of Congress Cataloging-in-Publication Data

Main entry under title:

Media advocacy and public health : power for prevention / Lawrence
    Wallack . . . [et al.].
        p. cm.
    Includes bibliographical references and index.
    ISBN 0-8039-4288-5. — ISBN 0-8039-4289-3 (pbk.)
    1. Mass media in health education. 2. Health promotion.
I. Wallack, Lawrence Marshall.
RA440.5.M427 1993
362.1'014—dc20   93-30314
                                                                            CIP

93 94 95 96 97 10 9 8 7 6 5 4 3 2 1

Sage Production Editor: Yvonne Könneker

CONTENTS

FOREWORD

Who among us does not rail habitually at the news media? Daily? Hourly? Pick your peeve: the more trivial the tale, the more commodious the ink; obsession with the sensational; pandering to advertisers; the sensationalizing of personal tragedy; the scrupulous avoidance of change-provoking analysis; the prevailing assumption that individual quirks rather than societal flaws are at the root of all tragedy.

Those who view American mass media with critical ferocity and disdain—both from the political left and from the political right—write of such failings with much wisdom and insight. But once their diatribes are played out, once we are told again and again how captive of dominant elites and unresponsive to democratic needs our mass media are, they leave us with little recourse but gnashing of teeth and despair.

This is a postdiatribe book. The authors reach beyond frustration to prescription. They understand very well why the media behave as they do. But they have addressed their scholarship and devoted their public health practice to seeking out the skills and strategies through which the new media can better be made to serve the greater community interest in social justice, especially the public's health.

It is also an empowering book. Lori Dorfman, one of this book's good authors, once gently rebuked an earnest gathering of academic policy professionals struggling with strategies for empowering communities. "No one can really empower anybody else," Lori observed. "The best we can do is help unleash the power that citizens already possess."

It is, finally, also a book for hopeful realists. Realistic in its unclouded understanding of the unadmirable forces at work to inhibit the media from serving society well; hopeful in recognizing that, with skill and luck, public health advocates can and do approach the media in ways that can seed the transformation of public policies in the public interest.

Take tobacco control. The realist knows that Phillip Morris and RJR Nabisco, with their food, alcohol, and other subsidiaries, deploy advertising budgets that dangle like diamonds before the eyes of publishers and broadcasters, quenching the already dim fires of investigative zeal and editorial outrage in pursuing tobacco company perfidy.

And yet . . . and yet . . . admittedly 30 years late, each day's news brings solid, even unrelenting stories, not only on the hazards of tobacco use but on the lobbying and the lying. We're experiencing a social revolution in this country, not just in our attitudes and behavior toward smoking but in public recognition that tobacco use is a primary public health problem and that tobacco companies' lies and lobbying are the primary barrier to sound and essential public health policies.

Make no mistake: That social revolution would simply not have taken place without responsive media coverage. And that responsible media coverage would not have taken place without media advocacy—the blending of science, politics, and advocacy—by advocates who knew what they were doing.

Some of them, their best stories, and the lessons they learned along the way, grace the pages of this book—along with the good and telling stories of their counterparts in alcohol control, AIDS, handgun control, and other public health initiatives.

These are the "experts" on whose wisdom and experience the authors rightly draw. Indeed, in media advocacy the very notion of expertise is redefined. Larry Wallack once observed to me, "Degrees may be irrelevant, but depending on the situation, hands-on experience can mean as much or more than academic training; creativity and quick insight can be more important than facts and figures. What is necessary is the ability to intuit and communicate the human meaning of data."

Physicians can be media advocates, victims can be media advocates, cancer volunteers can be media advocates. Lawyers and professors of public health, if they escape pedantry, can be media advocates. Politicians who still care can be good media advocates. An alert and articulate 10-year-old can be an awesome media advocate; angry parents and grieving survivors can be fierce media advocates. A straightforward and informed citizen, saying his or her piece on a talk show, can be a more effective media advocate than a corporate executive trained in public relations and earning six figures when arguing a morally compromised case. You can be a media advocate.

The authors call media advocacy a blend of "science, politics, and activism." They are right. They also would have been right if they called it a blend of art, drama, the love of words and images, and passionate commitment to public health.

There are two foundation pillars of media advocacy: (a) deep understanding of what moves the news media and (b) realistic hopefulness.

The authors have probed deep under the skins of the journalist, the editor, the producer, the publisher. They understand better than most of these actors themselves what real stimuli they respond to and how and why.

They have also drawn on the real-life experience of a new generation of public health advocates who, faced with resistance to accountability and reform by politically potent adversaries such as the tobacco and alcohol industries, came to understand that the news media, however flawed, could still be tapped to reach an attentive public with the sunlight of knowledge and exposure that can transform the political equation.

So this is a book for the hopeful.

"Hope," wrote the great psychoanalyst Erich Fromm, "is neither passive waiting nor is it the unrealistic forcing of circumstances that cannot occur. It is like the crouched tiger, which will jump only when the moment for jumping has come."

The successful media advocate is a crouched tiger. And, with this book under his or her belt, the public health media advocate will surely be an awesome jumper!

MICHAEL PERTSCHUK
Codirector, Advocacy Institute
Washington, DC

PREFACE

I was skeptical when I received an invitation to attend the Surgeon General's Workshop on Drunk Driving scheduled for December 1988. It promised to be another large consensus meeting with little impact other than a report that would be quickly forgotten. This meeting, it would end up, was different. It changed the alcohol field in several fundamental ways, establishing a new legitimacy for policy-level approaches to alcohol-related problems and prescribing a new set of skills for using mass media to promote those policy approaches.

The surgeon general's meeting took on substantial importance not only because of the great status and respect that Dr. C. Everett Koop commanded but because drunk driving was likely to be the last substantive area he would address while surgeon general. Equally important, however, was the controversy generated by the planning of the meeting. The alcoholic beverage industry and the National Association of Broadcasters boycotted the meeting, and then some industry groups raised the stakes by seeking a court injunction to stop the meeting. Up until the last minute no one could say for sure whether the more than 100 people who had come to Washington to participate would ever meet. In the end we did meet, consensus recommendations were developed, and the landscape of the alcohol world changed. This book has grown out of that early experience.

The surgeon general's meeting contained the basic stuff of public health—science, politics, advocacy groups, and corporate agendas focused on bottom-line considerations rather than health and well-being.

It had drama and conflict and, for the alcohol field, was to result in the first application of an emerging technique called media advocacy.

The purpose of media advocacy is to use the media strategically to apply pressure for changes in policy to promote public health goals. It provides a framework for moving the public health discussion from a primary focus on the health behaviors of the individual to behaviors of policymakers and corporate executives whose decisions structure the environment in which individual health decisions are made. It is intended to make explicit the conflict of values and the political nature of public health that color issues such as alcohol and drug problems, tobacco-related disease, AIDS, and violence.

The 1980s was a difficult time for many who were concerned with social and health issues. Across the country community groups and local agencies, in an effort to accomplish more with less, became increasingly innovative and adventuresome. Media advocacy is one of the products that has emerged. No one invented media advocacy, rather it evolved when people realized that other media approaches were not meeting their needs. Media advocacy is a tactic for community groups to communicate their own story in their own words to promote social change. It is a hybrid tool, combining community advocacy approaches with the strategic and innovative use of media to better pressure decision makers to change policy. In this book we have tried to put a framework around the experience of media advocacy to make it more accessible to others. Most of our examples come from the alcohol and tobacco fields, but we recognize that there are many other areas where these skills are being applied. It is our hope that readers will be able to generalize from the principles and examples used here to their own areas of concern.

LAWRENCE WALLACK
Berkeley, California
February 1993

ACKNOWLEDGMENTS

There are a great many people who contributed to the material in this book and who deserve recognition. More than any other person, Michael Pertschuk, codirector of the Advocacy Institute, is responsible for popularizing the concept and practice of media advocacy. Robert Denniston, director of communication at the Center for Substance Abuse Prevention, has been a strong supporter of this approach and has been instrumental in facilitating its evolution and application. Phil Wilbur from the Advocacy Institute contributed the case study on Nicotina in Chapter 6 and is a leading media advocacy trainer. Rene Durazzo, Linda Nettekoven, and Charles Salmon reviewed the draft manuscript and provided excellent suggestions from which we, and you the reader, have benefited. Maria Kerschen expertly copy edited the final manuscript. The S. H. Cowell Foundation and the L. J. Skaggs and Mary C. Skaggs Foundation granted financial support for parts of the book. The Marin Institute for the Prevention of Alcohol and Other Drug Problems provided general support for work on the book, and in particular, the staff of the Resource Center provided invaluable research assistance.

The Pojoaque, New Mexico, case study was adapted from a longer report commissioned by the Marin Institute and written by Juana Canela and Marilyn Aguirre-Molina of the University of Medicine and Dentistry of New Jersey with support from the federal Center for Substance Abuse Prevention. Garen Wintemute provided background for the case study on handguns described in Chapter 6. The case study on MADD was adapted from *Lobbying and Influence Alert* ("MADD Gets Mad," 1991), which is no longer being published. It is used with permission of Lobbying and Influence Alert 1991 (© Global Success Corporation). The Sea World case study was adapted from a much more extensive piece commissioned from Cheri Pies. James Baker, Pamela Rahn, and others provided interviews and background materials for Pies's study, and their contribution is greatly appreciated. The cooperation of Tom Sheriden was essential to the Ryan White case study, and Charyn Sutton's participation made the Uptown study possible. For other contributions to the Uptown, St. Ides, and PowerMaster stories, we want to acknowledge Robert Robinson, the Reverend Jesse Brown, and the Reverend Calvin Butts. Also, Terrence Herron, Sylvia Castillo, Karen Bass, and Andrew McGuire provided background material and other information about their media advocacy efforts. We would also like to acknowledge Ann Marie O'Keefe for her insights on the use of paid advertising, and Lisa Aliferis for sharing her experience in the newsroom.

Lawrence Wallack would like to express special thanks to his colleagues professors Meredith Minkler and William Vega for their ongoing good-natured and valuable support.

Overall, we would like to express our appreciation and thanks to all the people who are working to make things better. Some of these people are discovering the power of media to develop voices for change. We hope this book will support them in this task and help others to make better use of the media.

If you don't like the news, go out and make some of your own.

—Scoop Nisker, news commentator, KFOG radio

1

PUBLIC HEALTH
AND MEDIA ADVOCACY

Woody Allen once said that the world is facing a fork in the road that is more important than at any other time in history. One path, he explained, leads to alienation and despair. The other path leads to total destruction. "I pray," he said, "that we have the wisdom to make the right choice." Some people feel this way about public health. They perceive public health problems as intractable, with alternatives leading only to dead ends.

The Institute of Medicine Committee for the Study of the Future of Public Health (1988) report suggested that the public health system has fallen into disarray and must be reconstituted if it is to address threats to the public's health effectively. There is ample evidence to support this bleak conclusion. More than 35 million people have no health insurance and thus little, if any, access to health care in the United States (Fein, 1992). Inner cities seem almost lost to epidemics of violence, alcohol and other drug problems, and perhaps most important, a sense of alienation and despair prevails, leaving little prospect for a bright future. HIV infection, nutritional deficiencies, infant mortality, and a resurgence of tuberculosis are just a few of the increasingly severe public health problems that tax our ability to keep things from getting worse, much less to create social change to make things better.

Yet, despite the massive public health problems facing the United States, a great deal of energy to stimulate change persists, and change is happening. All across the country, diverse groups of people are gathering to organize and promote policy development on strategies to gain access to health care, limit exploitive and unhealthy alcohol and tobacco marketing, prevent violence, stimulate environmental protection, and combat homelessness.

Some of this energy stems from the cross-pollination over the past decade between the public health community and the consumer interest movement. As public health and consumer groups work together more closely, the political and social issues underlying health problems and the strategies needed to address them are becoming clearer. For example, the work of Center for Science in the Public Interest has helped to define alcohol advertising as a public health issue needing regulatory and legislative relief. Numerous antitobacco advocacy groups have similarly highlighted and made salient to public health professionals key political issues such as excise taxes, advertising, health warnings, and product availability.

Consumer groups have been effective in getting these issues on the media agenda, the public agenda, and the policy agenda. This has been a critical determinant of their ability to promote change. They have become sophisticated in advocacy, grassroots organizing, and using the mass media in innovative ways.

The mass media are a powerful force in our society. Gerbner (1992) has noted that if you can tell a nation's stories, you do not have to worry about who makes its laws. "Today," according to Gerbner (1992), "for the first time in history, most stories are not told by parents, schools, churches, communities, or even native countries or cultures, but by a handful of business conglomerates that have something to sell." Television, in fact, tells most of the stories to most of the people most of the time. Television, our dominant medium, forms the mainstream in which issues are identified, discussed, and responded to (Comstock, 1991; Gerbner, Gross, Morgan, & Signorielli, 1986; Gitlin, 1980; Postman, 1985). The mass media's ability to set the public agenda and amplify and lend legitimacy to the voices and views of our nation's political debates render them essential participants in social change of any kind.

This book is about an innovative use of mass media—media advocacy—as a strategy to promote public health. Media advocacy can be a significant force for influencing public debate and putting pressure on policymakers by increasing the volume of the public health voice and, in turn, by increasing the visibility of values, people, and issues behind the voice. This book is about the skills public health advocates need to amplify the voice of public health and ensure that the stories being told reflect basic public health goals and values. Succeeding chapters of this book will provide stories of how people are using media advocacy skills and what they are learning about social change, the media, and the future of public health.

Public Health Stories

Media advocacy is, in large part, about making sure that the story gets told from a public health point of view. The power of media advocacy to make a difference grows from the specific fundamental principles and values underlying it. It seems appropriate, then, to begin by telling a few stories that illustrate these principles and values. The first story is about the political context of public health; the second highlights the tension of values underlying public health; the third illustrates prevention, the primary mission of public health; and the fourth emphasizes the importance of community participation and self-determination as a strategy for change.

Who Came First?

The first story involves three people who meet in a coffee shop and start discussing a wide range of topics. Finally, they come to the topic of the world's first profession, each claiming that their profession is worthy of that distinction. The first person was a surgeon who argued that surgery was clearly the world's original profession because Eve was created with a rib from Adam. "Taking a rib from Adam obviously required a surgical operation," he said, "hence surgery must be the oldest profession."

The second person, a public health activist, was not very impressed with this explanation. She pointed out that long before Adam and Eve there was chaos. "It took someone highly skilled and committed to social change to bring order out of chaos," she said. "Obviously, this person was an activist who had great organizing skills. So, it was activism and organizing, not surgery, that is the world's first profession."

The third person was a politician. He sat and listened to the others' arguments, but was not impressed in the least. Finally, on behalf of politicians everywhere, he simply asked, "Who do you think created all that chaos to begin with?"

The task of public health is to bring order out of chaos, to make sense of the world from a health perspective. There is a little of the surgeon, activist, and politician in each of us working in public health and attempting to balance all three perspectives. Science and medicine, community organizing and activism, and the nuts and bolts of politics are the raw materials of public health—raw materials that are blended in the context of community life to generate appropriate solutions for health and social problems. The conflict and controversy involved in this iterative and developmental process reflect the competing values and divergent interests that form the foundation for how we, as a society, address health.

Public health is essentially political. As Rudolf Virchow, one of the founders of social medicine and a person who strongly influenced the development of public health, wrote more than a century ago, "medicine is a social science, and politics nothing but medicine on a grand scale." He reached this conclusion after visiting a German province that was suffering from a typhus epidemic. Poverty, hunger, poor housing, and general deprivation characterized the lives of the province's workers. Virchow reasoned that these material conditions were central to the epidemic, because they rendered the population susceptible to disease. If the origins of ill health were in social conditions, he argued, the most reasonable approach to epidemics was to change the conditions that allowed them to occur. He believed that health was the direct concern of the society, that social and economic conditions have an important impact on health, and that steps taken to combat disease must be social as well as medical.

Public health professionals rediscover Virchow's principles on a daily basis in communities all across the country. The major determinants of disease are factors now known to be external to the individual, factors located in the social and physical environment. As C. Arden Miller (1976) said in his presidential address to the American Public Health Association,

> For the vast majority of people in our society the life circumstances leading to poor health are not adopted as a matter of personal choice, but are thrust upon people by the social and economic circumstances into which they are born. (p. 56)

General social forces, to a great extent, determine people's exposure to risk (e.g., work-site hazards and air and water pollution) and to life-style habits (e.g., alcohol, tobacco, diet, exercise, and drug use) that result in differential effects on health. Lack of adequate employment, safe working environments, housing, education, and access to health care further render populations susceptible to risk factors, injury, and disease.

In blending the science and politics of public health at the community level to develop solutions to public health problems, the activist must change the dominant understanding and perception of those problems from personal or life-style issues to social policy issues. This means moving away from strategies that "glorify personal autonomy and self-realization" (Tesh, 1988) and in effect blame the victim while letting off the hook those who profit from the conditions that give rise to and sustain disease. For example, the tobacco, alcohol, and food industries do more to affect people's health than any doctor, hospital, or prevention program ever will. Yet these major industries share very little in the burden of prevention.

Contemporary public health is as much about facilitating a process whereby communities use their voice to define and make their health concerns known as it is about providing prevention and treatment services. The public debate, argument, and participation at the heart of a democratic society are fundamental to public health work as well.

Bringing order out of chaos is a challenging task. It requires broad-based participation to stimulate the political will necessary for social change. The Institute of Medicine (1988) report defined the mission of public health as "fulfilling society's interest in assuring conditions in which people can be healthy" (p. 7). It further notes that the primary mode of intervention is "organized community action." This definition stresses collective actions that address conditions and not just personal behaviors or habits. It shifts focus from disease conditions to the conditions that give rise to and sustain disease (Wallack, 1990a).

Advocacy is necessary to steer public attention away from disease as a personal problem to health as a social issue, and the mass media are an invaluable tool in this process. Advocacy is a strategy for blending science and politics with a social justice value orientation to make the system work better, particularly for those with the least resources. The effective use of media toward this end must be an integral part of social change efforts.

Who Runs Faster?

The second story involves two seasoned campers who meet while hiking and agree to set up a common camp for the night. In the middle of the night they are awakened by the unmistakable sound of a bear in the camp site. Outside of their tent they find a huge, hungry bear. One camper sees the other putting on boots and says, "What are you doing? You know you can't outrun a bear."

The other camper continues pulling on the boots and says, "I don't have to outrun the bear, I just have to outrun you!"

Competition provides many benefits and is a fundamental value in our society. There is, however, a downside to competition, which public health tries to address. The organization of society results in an uneven playing field. Some groups of people have a built-in advantage because of the position into which they are born. A physician once claimed that she could go into a hospital nursery and predict the general life expectancy of the babies by knowing just one critical fact—the ZIP code or neighborhood of the parents. As Hawley (1973) noted,

> Individuals may expound at length on the reasons for their having a given number of children, for migrating from one place to another, or for engaging in any other kind of activity, but only a few are perceptive enough to recognize that the degrees of freedom in their decision making are fixed in the structure of society. (p. 1199)

Market Justice

Today's most important public health issues reflect an undercurrent of profound social transformation. On the surface, the dialogue centers on access to health care and disease risk factors such as alcohol, tobacco, and nutrition, but the core reveals the tension among competing values to determine how benefits should be distributed in society—the issue of justice. A progressive perspective regards social justice as the foundation of public health (Beauchamp, 1976). The larger society, however, resonates more closely with principles of market justice. It is the dominance of the market justice ethic that Beauchamp (1976) argues is the "critical barrier to dramatic reductions in death and disability" (p. 3).

Market justice is based on key assumptions that largely determine the acceptable range of approaches to public health problems. For example, notions of rugged individualism, self-determination, strong individual control and responsibility, limited individual obligation to the collective good, and limited government involvement in social activity are corner-stones of the market justice ethic. The reason that we tend to think about problems in individual terms is in large part the result of the rigid individualism so ingrained into American life. Individualism lies at the base of how we think about health and disease, economics, and social policy. It is an invisible hand that guides societal thought and action. "Individualism," as Bellah, Masden, Sullivan, Swindler, and Tipton (1986, p. 142) note in their seminal work on American life, "lies at the very core of American culture." Concepts of individualism and self-determination carry an almost religious mystique and are central to the economic and social structure of American society. Individualism is a key part of America's classical liberal heritage (Ladd, 1981).

It comes as no surprise that the individual responsibility and personal choice that follow from individualism are invoked in discussions of health issues. Neubauer and Pratt (1981) suggest that the power of the concept is in the way it represents

> the ability of people to break the bonds of control over their lives and to use their independence, creativity and common sense to construct a good life. It has additional appeal because Americans have customarily believed that if each person independently applies his or her own talent to his or her own interest, the best possible, in this case the healthiest, society will result. (pp. 214-215)

Through wise, thoughtful, and prudent choices, individualism offers personal control over one's life and circumstances. It provides a strong moral and philosophical as well as practical basis for action. It focuses attention on what is most observable (the individual), where cause and effect seem most closely linked.

Market justice suggests that benefits such as health care, adequate housing, nutrition, and sustainable employment are rewards for individual effort (on a level playing field), rather than goods and services that society has an obligation to provide. Market justice depends on *enlightened self-interest* as a guarantor of the distribution of necessary goods and services to those in need.

On a broad social level, the market justice orientation can be seen in the punitive dimensions of welfare programs. For example, the horrible condition of welfare hotels in New York City was viewed as a motivational aspect of the system—the dirty and unsafe conditions apparently were tolerated by the government as a presumed deterrent to poverty (Kozel, 1988).

Market justice assumptions are played out when the alcohol industry claims the "abuser" who lacks self-discipline is the cause of alcohol problems and thus distances itself from its shared responsibility for the problem. The tobacco industry consistently emphasizes the value of individual choice as a basis for a fair society and as a justification for the widespread promotion and availability of its product. Market justice suggests that people act in their own best interest and assume risks knowingly and willingly. If the basic nature of behavior is volitional, then the consequences of behavior should be assumed by the individual.

The primary source of social and health problems, it is assumed, resides in individuals' personal behavior or biological makeup. In the case of personal behavior, blame is easily assigned; in the latter case, the individual is not culpable but bears the stigma of ill-health or disability. Both cases, however, deem social, political, or economic factors irrelevant; rather, health problems are a matter of individual choice or biological predisposition.

This idea of personal responsibility is embedded deeply in U.S. society. Galbraith (1973) argues that corporations have their own version of the divine-right-of-kings argument as a way of distancing themselves from responsibility for unsafe or harmful products. The corporate economy

> is not responsible—or is only minimally responsible—for what it does. . . .
> If the goods that it produces or the services that it renders are frivolous or lethal or do damage to air, water, landscape or the tranquillity of life, the firm is not to blame. *This reflects public choice. If people are abused, it is because they choose self abuse.* (Galbraith, 1973, pp. 5-6, emphasis added)

Another contemporary example of the placement of the locus of responsibility and blame for problems at the individual level is in the debate over the appropriateness of movies that have as their staple extreme aggression against and mutilation of women. In 1987, Tipper Gore, an organizer against slasher movies that depict extreme and graphic violence against women, argued on *Nightline* that these movies desensitize people to violence and that the content of such movies should be more tightly controlled. Frank Zappa, a 1960s rock star and currently a film distributor and critic of content warnings, countered that

> One of the reasons [slasher movies] do show aggression against women is because there is a market for films that show aggression against women.... Obviously, there is a sentiment in the American public that demands to see women being treated in this way. (ABC News, 1987, p. 6)

Zappa's logic promotes the idea that the consumer and not corporations control the marketplace. After all, consumers vote with their dollars, and if products and services fail to satisfy consumer needs, those products will not be competitive and will disappear. In the end, he believes the consumer provides the message and the producer responds. The illusion is that power and control reside with individuals who, through their decisions, define the marketplace.

This strong emphasis on individual behavior and responsibility as a way of understanding health issues has significant and adverse consequences for social change. The logical extension of the market justice metaphor is that organized social action to improve social conditions (i.e., advocacy) is not necessary. Because the problems we face as a society are characterized by flaws in the individual threads rather than tears in the social fabric, education and rehabilitation, not deliberate social change, are the primary strategies for health promotion and protection.

Blaming the Victim. Blaming the victim is an important consequence of the market justice metaphor. Ryan (1976) explains that victim blaming involves analyzing problems in terms of the deficiencies in the victim—the person with the problem. Two basic approaches to understanding social problems underlie the notion of victim blaming: exceptionalism and universalism. *Exceptionalism* means problems are a property of unusual events or circumstances, failures of individuals to adapt adequately to the system in which they live. Although the system may have gaps, remedies for those gaps are believed to be at the individual, not the structural, level. For example, unemployment would be attributable to lack of desire to work rather than lack of opportunity or lack of availability of jobs that provide a livable wage.

Victim blaming is so strongly ingrained in the way that many of us instinctively define and respond to problems that it becomes second nature and invisible. Consider the case of the woman who was raped in

Central Park, New York City, while jogging alone at night in one of the most dangerous cities in the United States. Many people admitted that their first thought on hearing details of the horrible crime was, "What was she doing jogging alone at night?" This response was immediate, involuntary, and intuitive. For many it was common sense. It is, however, not a neutral response. This response immediately focuses on the behavior of the victim and deflects attention away from the more basic question of safe and secure environments, personal freedom for women, institutionalized sexism, and broader societal protection.

The solution for those who might stick with their gut or "commonsense" response is for women to change their behavior—to stop jogging alone or at night. Root causes and broader issues are conveniently ignored. Now certainly jogging in safe, well-lit places is important, but to do this, such places must be easily available and maintained and individuals must be motivated to create and use them. Personal responsibility is obviously part of the solution, but it is sometimes mistaken for the *entire* solution. The more fundamental issue of toleration of victimization of women in society must also be addressed. In Ryan's (1976) terms, a "universalistic" view would have us question safety in public parks and violence against women rather than the singular behavior of this jogger.

The example of the Central Park jogger makes clear that how we define the problem determines its solution. This crucial act of definition relies on a particular analytical perspective, yet that perspective remains invisible. As we will see later, part of the media advocate's role is to make those underlying assumptions in problem definition visible.

One of the key elements in blaming the victim is that the victim is always seen as different from those defining the problem. The problem belongs only to those who have it. The "natural" next step is to blame those with the problem for the problem. We do this formally by labeling them deviants who somehow lack the capacity to adapt to an otherwise sound social system. They are the exception; those of us without the problem are the rule.

Exceptionalistic thinking is the norm for defining social problems. The victims are "other" in some way: They are poor, they are a different race, they do not know as much, or they do not have the same skills as the problem definers ("us"). If they were like us then we would be hard pressed to explain why ill fortune befell them but not us. Fate, of course, is one explanation, but when the numbers get too large (millions) or too personal (the person next door or on our block), this explanation breaks down, and explanations based on ascribed or acquired group characteristics become predominant. In contrast, a more truthful definition of social problems would require us "to admit that we mean they are a problem to those of us who are outside the boundaries of what we have defined as the problem" (Ryan, 1976, p. 13).

The *universalistic* position provides an alternative to blaming the victim. This position assumes that problems are rooted in the nature of social arrangements and are predictable rather than accidental events. Individuals are seen as subject to conditions that are outside their control. Remediation takes place on the broader societal level rather than the individual level with a focus on system failures rather than individual failures. The difference is, as Mills (1959) explains, between understanding problems as "individual troubles" caused by and occurring in the immediate milieu of the individual and as "public issues" that concern fundamental values of social structure. He points out that when, for example, relatively few people are unemployed in the midst of ample opportunities, the situation may well be defined in terms of "personal troubles," and the solutions would lie in the immediate environment of the person (e.g., skills and motivation). However, when relatively great numbers of people are without work, the situation must be looked at in terms of a public issue; solutions focused on the immediate environment of the person are unlikely to be adequate. In that case,

> The very structure of opportunities has collapsed. Both the correct statement of the problem and the range of possible solutions require us to consider the economic and political institutions of society, and not merely the personal situation and character of a scatter of individuals. (Mills, 1959, p. 9)

Problems from the universalistic perspective are defined as residing within the social system as opposed to under the skin of the individual. In the exceptionalism-universalism dichotomy the view that people act as individuals, differ from one another, and are motivated by internal factors is distinguished from the view that people and their actions need to be understood as part of a collectivity (the family, the group, the neighborhood, the community, the nation) and that behavior is best understood as a response to the social and environmental situations in which people live:

> Universalistic analysis will fasten on income distribution as the basic cause of poverty, on discrimination and segregation as the basic cause of racial inequality, on social stress as the major cause of the majority of emotional disturbances. It will focus, not on problem families, but on family problems; not on motivation, but on opportunity; not on symptoms, but on causes; not on deficiencies, but on resources; not on adjustment, but on change. (Ryan, 1976, p. 258)

Universalistic analyses of health problems avoid blaming the victim by refocusing attention on the social conditions that are determinants of disease. If the problem definition is universalistic, the problem's remedies are "public, legislated, promotive or preventive, general, national and inclusive" (Ryan, 1976, p. 18). For public health, the emphasis for prevention shifts to the physical and sociopolitical environment surrounding individuals.

The Environmental Perspective. In recent years, an environmental perspective has evolved that has directed attention to the role of policy and community-level factors in health promotion. This environmental perspective includes both a physical and a social element. For example, policies and practices that support product availability and marketing of alcohol and tobacco, both of which help cultivate positive social perceptions about these products, are primary targets for change. Thus tobacco-control advocates have shifted the focus from the behavior of the smoker to the behavior of the tobacco industry and to the policies that support advertising and general marketing activities contributing to premature mortality. Billboard advertising, tobacco vending machines, and industry sponsorship of community activities have become key targets for the tobacco-control movement.

This shift to an environmental perspective is now being seen increasingly in the alcohol field, particularly among communities of color. Advocacy and politics are emerging as fundamental tools for health promotion, while individual health behavior change remains an important, but secondary, focus. Prevention and health promotion, it has come to be understood, are processes of changing political behavior to make personal behavior change more possible; the overall quality of the social and physical environment can determine the likelihood of personal behavior change.

The focus on the immediate marketing or community-level environment is important, but still fails to address the most significant variable regarding health status. An extensive body of literature clearly indicates that social class is the single most important determinant of health (Haan, Kaplan, & Syme, 1989). Virtually every disease shows an association with measures of social class (Marmot, Koqevinas, & Elston, 1987). This is not the result of a simple rich-poor dichotomy but a graded response that can be seen even in the upper quadrant of society (Haan, Kaplan, & Camacho, 1987; Kitagawa & Hauser, 1973; Marmot, Koqevinas, & Elston, 1987; Smith & Egger, 1992). Recent work suggests that the most important factor within the social class construction may be level of education (Winkleby, Jatulis, Frank, & Fortmann, 1992). Also, in cross-cultural comparisons, it appears that a society's health status is not related solely to per capita income but to income variability and, therefore, to the extent of relative deprivation and discrepancy within a society (Wilkinson, 1992). The United States, for example, fares poorly on a number of key health indicators when compared with some countries that are less affluent but also show less variability in income across social strata. Thus successful health promotion relies less on our ability to disseminate health information and more on our efforts to establish a fairer, more just society.

There are two important reasons for emphasizing the environment. First, as the history of public heath amply demonstrates, prevention that is population based and focused on social conditions is more effective than efforts aimed primarily at treating individuals (Dubos, 1959; McKeown, 1978; McKinlay, McKinlay, & Beaglehole, 1989). The policies that define the environment in which people make choices about health appear to have the greatest potential to improve health. Second, universalistic analyses point to the importance of equality and social justice as the foundation for action. Universalistic- or environment-oriented solutions tend to confront the underlying conditions that give rise to and sustain disease and thus promise long-term change.

Social Justice

Social justice is concerned with whether conditions in society are fair and whether resources are distributed equitably. Too often they are not.

In health, for example, we know that virtually every disease occurs more frequently in poorer populations than in others. A social justice, universalistic perspective assumes that this is the result of the maldistribution of goods in society, not some inherent flaw in the makeup of poorer people. Ryan (1981) provides a graphic illustration of the maldistribution of resources by describing a symbolic dinner party at the nation's table:

> Imagine one hundred people at the banquet, seated at six tables. At the far right is a table set with English china and real silver, where five people sit comfortably. Next to them is another table nicely set but nowhere near as fancy, where fifteen people sit. At each of the four remaining tables twenty people sit—the one on the far left has a stained paper tablecloth and plastic knives and forks. This arrangement is analogous to the spread of income groups—from the richest 5 percent at the right to the poorest 20 percent at the left. Twenty waiters and waitresses come in, carrying 100 delicious-looking dinners, just enough, one would suppose, for each of the one hundred guests. But, amazingly, four of the waiters bring 20 dinners to the five people at the fancy table on the right. There's hardly room for all the food. (If you go over and look a little closer, you will notice that two of the waiters are obsequiously fussing and trying to arrange 10 dinners in front of just one of those five.) At the next-fanciest table, with the fifteen people, five waiters bring another 25 dinners. The twenty people at the third table get 25 dinners, 15 go to the fourth table, and 10 to the fifth. To the twenty people at the last table (the one with the paper tablecloth) a rude and clumsy waiter brings only five dinners. At the top table there are four dinners for each person; at the bottom table, four persons for each dinner. That's approximately the way income is distributed in America—fewer than half the people get even one dinner apiece. (p. 12)

Social justice requires resetting the table so that social goods in society are distributed more equitably, based not on one's success in the marketplace, as most benefits in our society are currently distributed, but on criteria that are consistent with the nature of the good itself (Walzer, 1983). For example, from a social justice perspective, one does not "deserve" adequate health care because one is successful in business, an accomplished entertainer, or an outstanding athlete. One deserves health care because one is a member of the community for which health is an important value (Beauchamp, 1988; Walzer, 1983). From a social justice perspective, minimal levels of income, affordable housing, employment, education, and health care are seen as basic rights rather than as privileges or rewards to be earned. The social good *health* is autonomous, that is, receiving it does not depend on having other social goods such as wealth or honor. Harking back to the story about the campers, protection from the bear should not be a question of which camper can run faster but what protection can be provided for both campers from the beginning.

Health is a fundamental good for individuals personally and for the working of a democratic society (Beauchamp, 1988). Therefore government involvement is necessary to ensure its equitable distribution. Social justice principles assume that as citizens, people share responsibility for the conditions in society as well as a strong obligation to the collective good. In practice, this means that we are obliged to hold ourselves as well as our social institutions responsible for ensuring the conditions in which all members of the community can be healthy. Social justice steers us away from a narrow concern over the health of individuals toward the health of the population at large. Individual well-being depends on community well-being.

This means that health is a political endeavor as much as, or at times even more than, a medical one. It means that how we operate as a society and who has a voice in decision making are public health concerns. A healthy republic, according to Beauchamp (1988), is "the result of a vigorous and expanded democratic discussion about the public's health" (p. 4). Social justice will flourish where community participation flourishes:

> Democracy is about having a stake because you are a real participant. It is about knowing whom to hold accountable, and it is about having the power to hold them accountable. Democracy is not about letting priorities be set by a bureaucratic or technocratic elite, or by the "blind forces" of the market (which always turn a blind eye toward human suffering); it is about constructing a social agenda, based on human need, through informed and active popular participation at every level. (Krieger, 1990, p. 414)

Contemporary public health labors under the hegemony of market justice. However, oppositional voices advocating the application of social justice principles as the primary organizing framework are increasingly being heard. Vigorous debate about underlying values of public health is crucial to the future of health promotion because the prevailing worldview will largely determine the form and content of strategies that are considered to be legitimate. While market justice perspectives legitimize and emphasize traditional (usually reductionistic) medical and technical approaches, social justice perspectives broaden the focus to include the social and political arena.

Complicating the issue of justice, public health and society face the challenge of confronting difficult issues in urban communities that have undergone dramatic ethnic and racial diversification and suburban and rural communities that have been shaken by economic problems. Along with this transformation has come a growing demand for recognition and acceptance of different cultural practices and patterns of varied groups. Public health advocates must address their personal and cultural "distorting lenses" (Duhl, 1990) and work to integrate the multiple models of interpretation that lie within the experience of diverse community groups. This requires the development of new and innovative conceptual frameworks for analysis and intervention that are sensitive to the particular characteristics, needs, interests, and values of the specific community.

The 1990s promise to be a time of great challenge for the public health community. Political pressures for change will undoubtedly increase and come from more and more diverse groups. At the same time, unstable economic conditions will likely result in less than necessary resources to meet current and still unknown future challenges. The more that democratic processes open up public debate to diverse expression, the greater the range of views that will prevail. Public health can play a central role in creating a unifying perspective to organize competing and conflicting viewpoints, if it can make its voice heard more clearly.

To respond to the new demands for participation in problem definition and planning, public health advocates will need to rethink their relationship with populations they seek to serve. The basic assumptions of doing well by doing *for* people, whether by providing a medical service, conducting research, or providing education, are being questioned by community members who want a greater share of the power to determine which problems should be addressed, how, and by whom. A major dimension of the "new public health" is a shift in power from bureaucracies to communities (Green & Raeburn, 1990). The realignment of major players in public health and, to some extent, the redefinition of expertise and knowledge are critical tasks, but they are without appropriate models. Filling the knowledge gap in this area must be a key focus for the 1990s. Rethinking the use of media as a strategy and linking media with community-level advocacy will play important roles in the new public health.

Who Can Swim?

The results of our efforts to promote health and prevent disease are really a measure of how well we are bringing order out of chaos. In thinking about what prevention entails, it is useful to reflect on one of the most fundamental public health stories involving three people (not necessarily the same three from the coffee shop discussion) who stood alongside a river on a brisk fall afternoon. All of a sudden they heard a cry for help from a person, caught in the river's fast-moving current, trying desperately to stay above water. One of the people along the riverbank started yelling at the drowning person, "What's wrong with you, why don't you know how to swim?" The second person offered the drowning person discount coupons for swimming lessons. Fortunately, one of the people on the bank was a public health worker who jumped in the water and pulled the drowning person out.

Over time more and more people came floating down the river in need of help, and this all created quite a commotion. This commotion attracted more people. Researchers showed up and counted how many people made it part of the way or all of the way out of the river and how many fell back in. They also collected other kinds of information about the risk-taking profiles of the people, family backgrounds, and educational levels. Survivors returned and started to talk with other survivors and their families. More community people grew interested and stopped by to cheer everybody on and occasionally castigated the poor swimmers and complained about how much all this cost. It got so busy at the river that fast-food restaurants started to appear. Nutrition advocacy groups came on the scene and started organizing, and there was talk of building a coalition.

It was difficult at the river because more and more people came floating down crying out for help, and it was not possible to pull them all out. Some floated by despite everyone's best efforts and were lost. Furthermore, it was very expensive to keep pulling people out of the river. Some of those who were pulled out ended up back in the river. The fact of the matter was people soon realized that pulling people out of the river was necessary but would never be sufficient to reduce the problem. Too many people kept falling in!

As time moved on more victims, more researchers, more community people, and more public health professionals were hanging around the river. All these people started sharing their perspectives, and as more different perspectives were discussed more insight developed. Finally, a critical mass developed and a group of people decided to get together and head upstream to see what was causing so many people to fall into the river.

Upstream, this group found signs that read, "Go for it," "Just do it," and "Come to River Country." There were signs that said the river "Won't slow you down" and that "It doesn't get any better than this." All around were cleverly constructed signs that associated friends, success, sex, self-esteem, and the good life with the edge of the river and the rushing water. As this small group of people looked around a bit more, it found that children were particularly transfixed by all these colorful signs showing sexy men and women, sports stars, sophisticated people, and charismatic role models. It found a few warning signs but generally the barriers to risky behaviors and the messages about caution were overwhelmed by the almost magical inducements promoting swimming in the potentially dangerous waters.

The upstream group decided to try to gain better control of the environment that contributed to so many people falling in the river. Its goal was to make the environment more conducive to keeping people out of the river. It was tough, however, and the group met a lot of resistance. The river marketers said that they were just trying to do their job and that the irresponsible behavior of a few people who did not know their own limitations when it comes to swimming should not be allowed to ruin the fun for everyone else. The real problem, they argued, was that people were just not responsible enough. After all, if each person would just be more careful, treat the river with more respect, and learn how to avoid the strong current or how not to fall in, there would be no problem. They argued that it was the responsibility of the family and the individual, not government or industry, to make sure the river was used wisely. Many community people nodded their heads in response to this argument. Wasn't individual responsibility really what it was all about? Shouldn't families begin instilling better values and teach their children how to navigate the currents in the river? Some of the people decided to leave the group and focus more on developing family values and swimming curricula for the local schools.

Others stayed to work upstream. There was a lot of conflict, but slowly victories were won. Some defied the law and painted over the billboards that were enticing people into the river. Others advocated for warning signs and counter-ads to be erected alongside the glamorous pictures. Still others brought attention to who was erecting the signs in the first place, claiming they must share responsibility for the adverse consequences of their promotions. The promoters enlisted the government, claiming that the protesters were infringing on their freedom of speech. The public health workers countered that it is government's role to protect those vulnerable to the messages, particularly children. Legal scholars debated whether commercial speech deserves the same protection as political speech. The heated battles began to get some media attention. The geography of prevention began to change as the boundaries of the discussion changed.

A small group of people realized that there was still more territory upstream to be explored. Certainly exploitive marketing practices, misleading advertising, and general lack of responsibility of various corporate interests were important, but there were more fundamental issues to be addressed.

This small group headed farther upstream and found conditions allowing huge parts of the population to slide in great masses into the river. It found high rates of unemployment, racism, lack of education and economic opportunity, and limited access to health care. These conditions meant high numbers of children were living in poverty; high rates of infant mortality existed; and a general sense of alienation, hopelessness, and despair prevailed.

Finally, the group decided that the problems it wanted to address existed across many levels of society. Individuals, families, communities, and the broader social and economic environment are all important parts of the larger environmental landscape. The members of the group agreed that they needed to try to work across these different levels, but that unless strategies to address the upstream source of the problems were developed, all other efforts would meet with limited success, if at all.

Ultimately, poverty, racism, lack of education, and hopelessness are the source of public health problems. One of the most significant findings in public health research is that the social and economic environment in which people live is the primary determinant of health. In simple terms, the level of economic and social resources people have is strongly correlated with their physical well-being. It is this upstream source of problems that ultimately must be remedied. The key point here is that it is important to begin to link what is observed downstream with upstream conditions. Doing this requires understanding the upstream-downstream connection and cultivating and using a voice to make these conditions visible and meaningful.

Make Every *Who* Holler!
Make Every *Who* Shout!

In the wonderful Dr. Seuss (1954) story *Horton Hears a Who!*, Horton, an elephant, hears a voice coming from a speck of dust. It ends up that the entire village of Whoville exists on this speck of dust. The problem is that none of the other animals believes there is a village with people living on a speck of dust. No one else hears what Horton hears. The other inhabitants of the jungle ridicule Horton and threaten to put him in a cage and put the dust speck "in a hot steaming kettle of Beezle-Nut oil!" Horton implores the mayor of Whoville to get every one in the town together to make noise so the other jungle creatures can hear them and thus believe they exist. The Whos make a terrible racket but still only Horton can hear. Horton then tells the mayor to make sure everyone is doing his or her best to contribute to the noise. Sure enough the mayor finds one person who has not been participating. When this additional voice is added to the clamor, the noise is loud enough for Horton's friends to hear and agree that the Whos do indeed exist.

The story of the Whos illustrates one of the key overall functions of media advocacy: to increase the capacity of communities to develop and use their voices to be heard and seen. The story of the Whos describes the process of claiming power in which the first step is using visibility to gain legitimacy. Not unlike the promotion for a local newscast that suggests to the audience that "it" really has not happened until it shows up on the news at 6:00 and 11:00, the Whos did not exist for the outside world until their amplified voice attracted attention.

The Train Is Behind You

Mark Twain once said that even if you are on the right track, if you are not moving fast enough, the train is going to run you over. The use of media to inform people about health risks has potential to improve health for some. However, risk factors linked to conditions outside of the individual also need to be addressed. In the end, trying to convince everyone to be moderate in his or her behavior is important but not sufficient for change. Providing people with the skills to identify and define the problem and better participate in developing educational and policy interventions is essential. The struggle to control problem definition and intervention design and implementation is a political as well as a scientific process. Media advocacy can provide the basis for enhanced community participation in this important area.

Social Marketing

Using the media as a political tool is not the typical way public health professionals have approached the media. More often they have used the media to market good health behavior. This widespread and commonly used approach, known as social marketing, attempts to apply advertising and marketing principles to the selling of positive health behaviors. Social marketing has become a key concept in addressing some of the shortcomings of previous public communication campaigns. In general, social marketing provides a framework to integrate marketing principles with sociopsychological theories to develop programs better able to accomplish behavior change goals. It takes the planning variables from marketing—product, price, promotion, and place—and reinterprets them for health issues. Ideally, social marketing also involves the mobilization of local organizations and interpersonal networks as vital forces in the behavior change process. A key principle of social marketing is that it seeks to reduce the psychological, social, economic, and practical distance between the consumer and the behavior.

Social marketing has gained high visibility from the careful application of its principles by community heart disease prevention programs in the United States (Farquhar, Maccoby, & Solomon, 1984) and Finland (Puska, McAlister, & Maccoby, 1985). Social marketers also have claimed success in promoting contraceptive use and oral rehydration therapy in developing countries (Kotler & Roberto, 1989). The positive health effects of these efforts, however, have yet to be convincingly demonstrated (Wallack, 1990a). Evidence also suggests that public service advertisements, a very limited application of social marketing, have limited effects and may serve to reinforce an individualistic understanding of health and social problems, thus serving as a hindrance to advocates (Salmon, 1989; Wallack, 1981, 1990a, 1990b, 1990c). These campaigns may reinforce a politically safe, but practically ineffective, approach to using media. On the other hand, many have found cause for optimism in such campaigns (Flay, 1987; Freimuth, 1985; Rice & Atkin, 1990).

Social marketing attempts to make it as easy and attractive as possible for the consumer to act in compliance with a health message by creating the ideal marketing mix of the right product, price, promotion, and place. *Product* refers to something the consumer must accept: an item, a behavior, or an idea. In some cases, the product is an item such as a condom, and in other cases, it is a behavior such as not drinking and driving. *Price* refers to psychological, social, economic, or convenience costs associated with message compliance. For example, the act of not drinking in a group can have psychological costs of anxiety and social costs of loss of status. *Promotion* pertains to how the behavior is packaged to compensate for costs—what are the benefits of adopting this behavior and what is the best way to communicate the message promoting it. This could include better health, increased status, higher self-esteem, or freedom from inconvenience. Finally, *place* refers to the availability of the product or behavior. If the intervention is promoting condom use, it is essential that condoms be widely available. Equally important to physical availability, however, is social availability. Condoms are more likely to be used when such use is supported and reinforced by peer groups and the community at large.

Careful definition of the problem and clear objective setting are important aspects of social-marketing approaches. However, the most significant contribution of social marketing has been the strong focus on consumer needs. Consumer orientation means identifying and responding to the needs of the target audience. This is a departure from many past public health campaigns (and many current ones) in which the target audiences had little input into message development.

Social marketing rests on the assumption that people will be willing to exchange some resource (time or money) for a benefit (product or positive attribute). The marketing process attempts to facilitate a voluntary exchange that provides the consumer with tangible benefits at a minimal monetary, physical, or emotional cost. If, in the end, the intervention is not able to facilitate this voluntary exchange then the likelihood of effectiveness will be slight (Lefebvre & Flora, 1988).

The primary tool to tailor public communication efforts to specific audiences is formative research. Although this concept of research predates social marketing, social marketing has popularized it. Applicable at all stages of intervention design and implementation, formative research provides important feedback to planners. For example, planners might convene small groups that represent the target audience to provide ideas about program strategy and reactions to specific messages. Planners can then make modifications to strategy and content based on the results of these focus groups.

Other kinds of formative research might include analysis of the audience to segment it into homogeneous groups, analysis of media habits of the target population so that messages can be placed in the proper media at the proper time, and an assessment of preexisting knowledge and attitudes in the target population. Formative research, when done correctly, serves to reduce some of the uncertainty associated with launching a campaign. Testing out possible campaign slogans, for example, can ensure that such slogans are culturally sensitive and likely to be interpreted in a way that furthers campaign goals.

Social marketing has a number of limitations that inhibit its usefulness and application. Some public health experts have criticized it as being manipulative and ethically suspect. For example, as one Kenyan physician explained, "Social marketing makes people mostly consumers, not protagonists and promoters. . . . It follows the basic principles of commercial marketing and can become an important inroad for the latter" (Schuftan, 1989, p. 198). These criticisms are not surprising given social marketing's close correspondence to more general advertising and marketing practices. Social marketing tends to reduce serious health problems to individual risk factors and ignore the proven importance of the social and economic environment as major determinants of health. In the long run, this risk factor approach that forms the basis for social marketing may contribute relatively little to reducing the incidence of disease in a population.

Motivating the voluntary exchange process with the consumer, which is crucial to social marketing's effectiveness, is a difficult task. The limited success of typical health promotion programs that seek to exchange increased health status, positive image, or presumed peer approval for delayed gratification (e.g., smoking cessation and dieting), increased physical effort (e.g., exercise), social rejection (e.g., abstinence from drugs), or physical discomfort (e.g., withdrawal from cigarettes) does not provide much basis for optimism.

Other critics claim that social marketing promotes single solutions to complex health problems and ignores the conditions that give rise to and sustain disease. For example, in developing countries, social marketing has focused on changing individual health habits rather than on improving environmental conditions such as ensuring a clean water supply.

Social marketing can help get the right message to the right people in the right way at the right time. For some people who have adequate resources and support, the messages alone might be enough; for others, however, the messages alone will not be enough. For many communities, individual change is linked to social change and social change means addressing the power inequity that contributes to the problem. If power is defined as fundamental to improving health status, getting a message will not be a sufficient intervention. In this case, getting a voice will be the strategy. Unfortunately, many of the populations that have the least power, the greatest health problems, and the least resources for change are also the least visible to those who have the power to have an impact on disease-generating social conditions. In contrast to social marketing, media advocacy can help communities gain access to the media to enhance the visibility, legitimacy, and power of their stories. Communities can use the media creatively to speak to those in power and mobilize pressure so they have to pay attention.

Social marketing assumes that power over health status evolves from gaining greater control over individual health behaviors. It provides people with accurate information so they can better participate in improving their own health. Media advocacy assumes that improved health status evolves from gaining greater control over the social and political environment in which decisions that affect health are made. It provides people with skills and information to participate better in changing the environment that creates the context for individual health decisions. Both approaches, used in proper balance, have an important role to play in making the mass media more responsive to health issues.

Social marketing is a seductive concept. It serves as common ground for media outlets, community groups, government agencies, and advertisers to work together. Unfortunately, the condition for this cooperation is too often the avoidance of controversial issues and the definition of health in narrow disease-oriented terms. It tends to be noncontroversial because it focuses on individual behaviors as the cause of disease (and presumably the cause of health) and deflects attention away from harmful products and the environment through which these products are made available. Social-marketing campaigns may well offer new opportunities to those motivated to change their health habits. On the other hand, such campaigns may do little for those most in need of change but who have the fewest social, economic, and personal resources to facilitate that change.

Conclusion

The central argument of this book is that because research and historical experience have established that the major determinants of health are in the social and physical environment, the power of media should be used to make that environment healthier. Media advocacy is a part of a strategy to exert pressure on those whose decisions influence that environment, a strategy that uses the mass media appropriately, aggressively, and effectively to support the development of healthy public policies.

Subsequent chapters will explore the theoretical and practical aspects of media advocacy. Chapter 2 describes advocacy as prevention and emphasizes that the power of media advocacy is rooted in community advocacy. Chapter 3 explores the workings of the media and gives a brief overview of the forces that shape the way media cover social issues. That chapter concentrates on the agenda-setting and framing functions of the news media. In Chapter 4, the basic concepts and practices of media advocacy are detailed, and examples illustrating key elements of the approach are provided. Chapter 5 describes how media advocacy unfolds in the real world and emphasizes planning for media advocacy initiatives. Chapter 6 presents eight case studies that illustrate various aspects of media advocacy. These cases range from a small group of teenagers in New Mexico that used media to remove alcohol billboards near its school to an AIDS coalition that used media to promote national legislation. Chapter 7 provides a brief summary and places media advocacy strategies in the context of classic protest movements.

2

THE ADVOCACY
CONNECTION

There is an old folk tale about a man who sat in a deep, dark pit. Neighbors would yell down to the man and warn him to get out of the pit saying, "The worms will get you!" or "You will go blind down there!" After some time, the neighbors stopped talking to the man, convinced that he was crazy and beyond help. One day a little boy was playing near the pit and fell in. To his astonishment, he discovered that the man had lost the use of his voice and the use of his legs. Over time, this man had built quite a home in the pit using just his hands and had learned to feed off of the creatures that lived there. The boy showed the man how he could use that same strength to lift himself out of the pit. When the man reached the top, his first act was to fill the pit so that others would not suffer as he did. The gods smiled on him and restored his voice but the gods also took the voices of the village people because they would not go beyond warning the man and come to his aid.

In some ways, we face the same outcome as the neighbors in this story. If we rely solely on a strategy of providing information, we not only abandon our communities by not providing real support for change but lose our voice in shaping the social, political, and economic contexts in which the information is given. Public health advocates and all concerned people can ill afford not to be involved in influencing these forces that fundamentally shape the public's health. Advocacy is our most important tool in this process as it is key in the promotion of healthy policies as well as in increasing community resources for building healthier communities. If media advocacy is the use of media to amplify our voices and be heard in our efforts for change, then advocacy means using all of our faculties, our voices included, to make a difference. In this chapter, we will describe more fully what we mean by "advocacy as health promotion" and why media advocacy is only one tactic for use as part of a comprehensive advocacy plan. Most important, we will explore why advocacy is a crucial strategy for public health to adopt.

Defining Advocacy

There is no magic bullet that can singularly solve public health problems. This effort requires a diverse and complementary set of approaches, and media advocacy can play an important role. However, media advocacy is only a tool to support public health policy initiatives. The reality is that mass media, whether public information campaigns, social marketing approaches, or media advocacy initiatives, are simply not sufficient to stimulate significant and lasting change on public health issues. The power for change comes from a broader advocacy that has widespread community support. Coalition building, leadership development, and extensive public participation form the foundation from which successful advocacy and media initiatives can make a difference. To succeed, these initiatives require a host of skills, including grassroots organizing, lobbying, fund-raising, and substantial media savvy.

Advocacy is a catch-all word for the set of skills used to create a shift in public opinion and mobilize the necessary resources and forces to support an issue, policy, or constituency. Advocacy involves much more than lobbying in support of a certain piece of legislation. Health professionals routinely engage in a wide array of advocacy activities, including patient advocacy, client advocacy, and policy advocacy, all designed to make the system function better to meet health and safety goals. This can range from representing the interests of staff and clients in hospitals and social service agencies to providing tours of a facility to educate policymakers, to circulating petitions urging legislators to increase program funding and to enact stronger laws in the interest of public health and safety. Whatever you do, it is important to remember that advocacy can be integrated into your daily work, helping you to maximize resources for community service.

There are many different ways to think about and define advocacy. The key point is that advocacy seeks to increase the power of people and groups and to make institutions more responsive to human needs. It attempts to enlarge the range of choices that people can have by increasing their power to define problems and solutions and participate in the broader social and policy arena. Amidei (1991) emphasizes several characteristics of advocacy:

- Advocacy assumes that people have rights, and those rights are enforceable. For example, the rights to adequate health care, pollution-free environments, employment, and housing are being addressed by various groups. Activities attempt to ensure that these rights are exercised.
- Advocacy works best when focused on something specific. Often diverse groups come together in advocacy, and it is important that the task at hand be clearly defined. A clear objective will help keep groups with different interests focused on common ground.
- Advocacy is primarily concerned with rights and benefits to which someone or some community is already entitled. For example, gay and lesbian groups and other disenfranchised populations are consistently advocating for equal protection of rights that are generally protected in the mainstream population.
- Policy advocacy is concerned with ensuring that institutions work the way they should. For example, nutrition advocates were instrumental in pressuring the Food and Drug Administration (FDA) to change food labels substantially. The new labels reflect the interests of consumers to have useful, clear nutritional information and better fulfill the ethical and legal responsibility of the FDA.

Act Locally, Link Globally

Advocacy does not always mean a national or huge regional project. Advocacy can help change attitudes generally and policy specifically. Policy exists at many levels: institutional, local, state, national, and international. Institutions and sites in the community—such as schools, manufacturing plants, labor unions, churches, temples, synagogues, workplaces, public libraries, airports, bus stations, restaurants, small businesses, large corporations, supermarkets, small shops, and so on—create their own policies and are subject to policies that have consequences for health. The advocate's goal is to increase the capacity of the community to participate more fully in determining its own issues and developing and implementing strategies that best address these issues.

The environmental justice movement, for example, involves hundreds of groups across the country, organizing to counter environmental health threats to communities of color. These groups, rooted in the civil rights movement, emphasize social justice, advocacy strategies, freedom from pollution, and community empowerment in trying to control toxic dumping and environmental threats (Suro, 1993). The movement is essentially local; "With little coordination and with no well-known national leaders, the environmental justice movement has developed out of many individual local protests, usually focused on a single nearby problem" (Suro, 1993, p. A12).

The tobacco control movement has had tremendous success enacting local nonsmoking ordinances in more than 541 places across the country (Americans for Non-Smokers' Rights [ANSR], 1993). Working on the local level provided the nonsmokers' rights activists with many advantages. At the state level, the tobacco industry is strong and has the resources to influence the media and politicians; the antitobacco forces cannot compete with them financially. However, local politicians may be less susceptible to large donations of money, primarily because they do not often need them to win local elections. In addition, accepting money and its resulting influence would be more visible at the local level, where politicians and their actions are more likely to be well known to their constituents. In the mid-1980s when the nonsmokers' rights movement was gaining speed, Walker Merryman, spokesperson for the Tobacco Institute, said of that movement, "It's like being pecked to death by ducks" (quoted in ANSR, 1987). The power of the movement, in this case, lies in its local focus. Although the different groups nationwide enjoyed the leadership of figures like surgeons general Koop and Novello and assistance from national groups like Americans for Non-Smokers' Rights, the policy success was local.

These local efforts provided a base of support for regional and national efforts. As environmental tobacco smoke (ETS) became more of a health issue, public health advocates sought policies to protect nonsmokers on the state and federal level. These efforts resulted in, among other things, a national smoking ban on domestic airline flights in 1989. In an interview on Congressional passage of the ban, Meyers, staff director of the Coalition on Smoking or Health said, "This time around, there were very few issues on which there were broader public support . . . that public support led to absolutely burgeoning interest in a stronger ban in Congress" (quoted in Pytte, 1989).

The Fight to Stop "Killer" Marketing

During the 1960s, health workers and pediatricians working in developing countries found a disturbing trend: a steady decline in the incidence of breast feeding, particularly in urban areas. Studies had found a correlation between declining breast feeding and increased malnutrition in children as result of the rise in bottle feeding, which caused infection from improper or unclean feeding practices and the absence of the immunological protection that breast feeding provides. In fact, Dr. Derrick Jelliffe, director of the Caribbean Food and Nutrition Institute in Jamaica (and a leader in this area) had estimated that 10 million cases of infectious disease and infant malnutrition were directly attributable to improper bottle feeding every year.

Health professionals joined forces with religious and consumer advocacy groups to identify policies that would address this problem. In 1974, Consumers Union published a book that drew strong connections between the problem of infant malnutrition and the promotional practices of infant formula producers, most notably Nestlé. After 3 years of effort to try to pressure Nestlé to change its marketing practices, Infant Formula Coalition Action (INFACT) organized an international boycott of Nestlé's products. A star-studded cast of celebrities joined the effort, which included Benjamin Spock and Cesar Chavez. CBS aired a 30-minute documentary (hosted by Bill Moyers), investigating infant formula-related health problems in the Dominican Republic. This program, which focused on industry marketing practices, attracted 9 million viewers (Baudot, 1989).

Nestlé fought hard to reframe the boycott. A spokesman for the company said in 1978 that Nestlé "has advised me that their research indicates this is actually an indirect attack on the world's free economic system" (Hilts, 1984, p. A1). Nestlé went further and formed the International Council of Infant Food Industries and adopted their own voluntary code of ethics for formula promotion. However, with a strong international coalition and public opinion now firmly on their side, advocates were in a prime position to push their policy goal: to establish an international code that strictly regulated the marketing of infant formula. The World Health Organization (WHO) adopted the International Code of Marketing Breast Milk Substitutes in 1981, but Nestlé remained opposed to it in spite of the fact that the code passed 118 to 1 (the United States cast the sole negative vote).

Advocates kept the heat on with the boycott as well as media advocacy efforts that continued to shame the company publicly for its infant formula marketing practices. It was not until January 1984 that Nestlé finally agreed to comply fully with the WHO code. In addition to this victory, advocates won additional concessions from Nestlé, including an agreement to promote breast feeding explicitly in the company's educational literature as the superior method of feeding and to strengthen its label warning against misuse of formula (Hilts, 1984). Thanks to these efforts it is no longer common to see misleading ads exaggerating the benefits of infant formula here or abroad.

When public health initiatives affect corporate profits, advocacy efforts are critical. Implementation of virtually every major public health policy—from getting lead out of paint and pencils to banning tobacco advertising on electronic media—has depended on concerted advocacy efforts. These efforts are necessary because they shift the balance of power from corporate-directed health policies to more public health-centered policies. The process required to accomplish this shift is not without struggle. In fact, any strategy to develop healthy public policies must take into account how these policies affect corporate interests and plan accordingly.

Mastering the System

In some cases, advocacy seeks not to change policy but to shift the public perception of power and interest so that public agencies are free to enforce existing laws. Since 1935, the Bureau of Alcohol, Tobacco and Firearms (BATF) has had the power to regulate alcohol advertisements under the Federal Alcohol Administration Act. Although this act prohibits beer advertising that promotes product strength, malt liquor advertisers in particular had flouted this law in their advertising targeted at inner city (and mostly African-American and Latino) communities. Slogans like Pabst Olde English 800's "It's the Power" and Schlitz Red Bull's "It's the Real Power" were commonplace violations of the potency rule. Many of these advertising campaigns had gone on for more than a decade.

When G. Heileman Brewing Co. announced plans in June 1991 to market yet another high-powered malt liquor (to be called PowerMaster) to African-American communities, a nationwide coalition of African-American public health activists said enough is enough. The National

Association of African Americans for Positive Imagery (NAAAPI), fresh from a victory banning the introduction of Uptown, a new cigarette targeting African-Americans (see Chapter 6), believed it had a good chance of banning the apparently illegally labeled product before it went on the market.

Initial activity, at the grassroots level, targeted five major cities (New York, Chicago, Philadelphia, Detroit, and Los Angeles), encouraging merchants not to stock the product in their stores. Media interest in racial and ethnic targeting was high as a result of the Uptown campaign, giving advocates unprecedented access as reporters contacted them for comment on PowerMaster. In the 2 weeks after *The Wall Street Journal* announced PowerMaster, more than 30 articles and several television and radio stories, including ABC's *Nightline*, focused on the product and the controversy.

In media interviews, public health advocates struggled to counter the alcohol industry's contention that marketing and promotion had little impact on alcohol problems and that protesting PowerMaster was a violation of Heileman's right to free enterprise and the individual drinkers' freedom of choice. NAAAPI and others believed that Heileman's marketing strategy not only preyed immorally on communities at risk but also violated the Federal Alcohol Administration Act's prohibition of beer advertising that promotes potency. In addition, they asserted that beer companies committed these violations in poorer, inner city communities because BATF did not enforce the law in these communities.

On July 1, 1991, BATF announced that it was revoking label approval for PowerMaster based on the potency rule. Said NAAAPI Chairman the Reverend Jesse Brown, "I think we were able to effectively partner media and mass activity and that made the difference in this effort. Heileman and BATF expected PowerMaster to roll out to business as usual. Thanks to grassroots activity nationwide, we were able to put an end to that."

In the year after the PowerMaster decision, BATF extended the ruling to require changes in seven advertising campaigns by other malt liquor brands found to be in violation of the potency rule. The shift in enforcement behavior by BATF on malt liquor, fortified wines like Cisco, and other similar products combined with the groundswell of support for increased regulation of alcohol sales and marketing significantly changed the playing field for alcohol policy advocates and, in turn, reformed alcohol regulatory policy on the federal level.

Policy Efforts
Challenge Business as Usual

> *So this ... woman calls up and said she has a 9-month-old baby with*
> *diarrhea and the doctor on call gave her the right advice, said go to the*
> *pharmacy and buy Pedialyte. She had Medicaid, the doctor called the*
> *pharmacy, but when she got there, they said they couldn't give it to her for*
> *free without a written prescription. So she takes the kid home, and over the*
> *next 36 hours the baby gets worse. She doesn't call back—she should have*
> *called back. The kid appears in the emergency room 36 hours later,*
> *moribund, and dies three days later. . . . My wife and I drove up there to that*
> *neighborhood, we went to every pharmacy. The rehydration solution cost up*
> *to $6.30 a liter. It's obscene charging this much for a product that ought to*
> *be cheaper than Coca-Cola—it has less in it.*
> —Meyers (quoted in Klass, 1992, p. 55)[1]

Even if education did work perfectly 100% of the time, it would not be
enough. Communities cannot combat health problems with information
alone, they need power to enact better health policies so they can build
safer, healthier communities. As noted in Chapter 1, prevention requires
that we move upstream to the root of health problems. As public health
advocates, we must be cognizant of the ways in which existing policies
present barriers to healthy communities and be prepared to advocate on
behalf of changing those policies in the interest of public health. Changing policy can make a difference.

- Dramatic declines in the numbers of children injured or killed by sleepwear-related burns can be traced directly to the "promulgation of strict
  federal and state standards for flammability of children's clothing" (Mc-
  Loughlin & Clarke, 1977).
- Changes in minimum drinking age laws have had a significant impact on
  fatal traffic crashes among youth under 21. One study found a 15.4%
  decrease in fatal crashes involving drivers under 21 compared with a
  decline of 5.4% involving drivers 21 and older (O'Malley & Wagenaar,
  1991).
- California's successful initiative to raise the state excise tax on tobacco
  resulted in a 14% decrease in tobacco consumption compared with a 3.5%
  to 4% decrease nationwide (McGuire, 1992).

These dramatic results are the fundamental reasons why advocacy
groups focus on policy change rather than individual change. Instead of

placing all of the burden for change on individuals, public health's strong focus on social justice encourages shared responsibility that is proportional to one's ability to shoulder the burden of prevention. That means

> all persons are equally responsible for sharing the burdens—as well as the benefits—of protection against death and disability, except where unequal burdens result in greater protection for every person and especially potential victims of death and disability. In practice this means that policies to control the hazards of a given substance, service or commodity fall unequally (but still fairly) on those involved in the production, provision, or consumption of the service, commodity, or substance. (Beauchamp, 1976, p. 8)

Corporate interests advocate policies that place the primary responsibility for change on the individual, and thereby distance corporate actions from the problem and minimize their own responsibility. This focus on changing individual behavior and defining public health problems from an individual perspective shifts blame and accountability away from corporate action (or inaction). Given the relative resources, responsibility, and social and political agency of corporations versus individuals, policies that focus on individual behavior alone will not bring about the fundamental changes required to address the prevention of disease and disability.

Expanding the
Definition of Prevention

The PowerMaster campaign is the kind of grassroots effort that is breathing new life into a proven prevention strategy: community empowerment. Voluntary participation in local community institutions and organizations has long been considered vital for effective crime and drug abuse prevention (Curtis, 1987; Florin, 1989; Mayer, 1984). Efforts that engage community residents and give them a sense of their own power can make a substantial difference in a community's ability to solve problems as well as strengthen individual members' sense of community (McMillian & Chavis, 1986). Lack of a sense of community, or neighborhood disorganization, is considered a critical risk factor for alcohol and other drug problems (Hawkins, Catalano, & Miller, 1992). The act of advocacy addresses public health problems not only through the policy changes it may achieve but also in the way it aids communities in addressing the factors that put them at risk in the first place.

A coalition in South Central Los Angeles provides another example of far-reaching advocacy as an integral part of prevention efforts. In April 1992, the nation watched the Los Angeles area go up in flames, from Bellflower to Beverly Hills, a response, in some measure, to the acquittal of three white police officers charged with the videotaped beating of African-American Rodney King. Before the uprising, a small but dedicated group of public health activists from South Central Los Angeles's Community Coalition for Substance Abuse Prevention and Treatment (CCSAPT) had been diligently working to convince California state and city officials that the area's high concentration of liquor stores posed a serious health hazard to South Central residents. A recent study by the University of Southern California School of Medicine (Scribner, 1992) showed most South Central census tracts had more than twice the one outlet per 2,500 persons prescribed by California law and that there was a positive correlation between the high density of alcohol outlets and an increase in violent crime in the area. In fact, the University of Southern California study showed that "the threat to public safety associated with a 10% increase in a Los Angeles County community with 50,000 residents or more and with 100 existing outlets was 25 additional violent crimes annually" (Scribner, 1992). South Central Los Angeles before the uprising had 728 alcohol outlets (Johnson, 1992).

Apparently, many residents agreed with CCSAPT, judging by the number of liquor stores that were targets of destruction. More than 250 liquor stores were damaged over the 3-day insurgence (Barrett, 1992). CCSAPT was deluged with calls from the media and residents who wanted to participate in the campaign to reduce the area's alcohol outlets. They planned a careful strategy that assessed their allies, their opponents and policy changes that would significantly affect the root problems of slow economic development and poverty. It was their belief that the prevalence of liquor stores was creating crime and other problems that influenced the community's ability to attract other businesses. While other retail establishments and businesses did not want to locate in the high-outlet-density/high-crime areas, the number of alcohol outlets was increasing, profiting off of what residents referred to as "the misery market" of poor, unemployed drinkers, many of whom were reported by residents to be underage.

The idea of closing down profitable businesses did not sit well with the retailers and wholesalers who had come to depend on South Central Los Angeles for their living. Many of the retailers, drawn by cheaper store rents, were working-class first-generation Korean-American families. There had been years of cultural and political conflict between Korean-American store owners and the mostly African-American residents who patronize the stores. The uprising, its resultant destruction, and the subsequent efforts to cut down the number of outlets, only exacerbated these tensions.

The CCSAPT worked to shift the media's definition of *us* and *them*, changing *them* from the working-class Korean-American store owners to local and state government, who neglected to bring regulatory order to the situation. In addition, the coalition gathered nearly 30,000 signatures in less than 2 weeks in support of an initiative to further regulate liquor stores. This kind of grassroots support enabled CCSAPT to face a powerful liquor lobby and affect policy in their area.

"The response was amazing," Castillo (1993), an organizer, said. "People would say, 'Can we do this?' It gave people a way to express their concerns. It gave direction to the frustration." By the end of 1992, the CCSAPT had been responsible for passing two pieces of local legislation to regulate alcohol.

Improving health status for populations is more a consequence of political will than personal change. CCSAPT demonstrates that developing broad-based support through community organization and coalition building is a fundamental mechanism for developing the political will necessary for policy change. Media advocacy is most powerful when rooted in broad-based community support. This support signals to media gatekeepers that a particular issue is important. It is fundamental to the capacity-building process that media advocacy promotes. If a basic principle of media advocacy is to develop skills for people to make their voices heard, then there cannot be any media advocacy without attention to developing community support. Advocacy skills that contribute to system change are the foundation of media advocacy.

Doing Advocacy

Advocacy is an integral part of any prevention strategy and public health professionals and community activists must invest time and resources in learning how to do it. It requires the same kind of attention to details, resources, and capabilities that any other organizational effort requires—perhaps more so. There is no precise road map to effective advocacy. However, there are some basic steps that can provide guidance and help you avoid common pitfalls.

Data Are Important

Advocacy always needs to be based on a strong and credible data base. While it is true that policy often seems to develop from no rational foundation, data remain an important basis for presenting an argument. Usually there are solid data that can be brought to bear on any number of public heath issues.

Data on the extent of the problem and how it is distributed across the population are important for at least two reasons. First, they indicate the size of the problem and justify concerns and social action. Second, by showing that some populations are disproportionately affected by the problem, the data establish that the problem is not randomly distributed but is demonstrably linked to specific social and environmental variables.

What this means practically is that you should have a clear analysis of the issues you wish to address. In the area of alcohol studies, for example, there is extensive research that examines the effects of advertising on youth (e.g., Atkin, 1989, 1992), explores public opinions about policy options (e.g., Lipman, 1991), and establishes the role of excise taxes as a significant prevention strategy (e.g., Moore & Gerstein, 1981; Saffer & Grossman, 1987; Wagenaar & Farrell, 1989). It is one thing to say, "We have a problem with youth drinking." It is quite another to say, "We have alcohol-related problems because local youth are purchasing alcohol at outlets at West Beach" and connect those problems with local policies concerned with the availability of alcoholic beverages. The difference is research. Gather reports, surveys, personal observations, and other resources that accurately describe the problem so you can pinpoint effective policy options. In this scenario at West Beach it would be helpful to know, among other things, the number of youth alcohol-related arrests, injuries, and other incidents; the source of the alcohol; the preferred beverage type and brand; and specifically where the youth are drinking.

Research can shed light on existing policy initiatives and suggest new ones. When community groups in Oakland, California, formed a coalition to fight youth access to alcohol and tobacco they expected to propose policy initiatives concerning billboard regulation. However, research conducted on possible policy options and their effectiveness in other communities indicated that their efforts might be better rewarded if they focused on alcohol outlet licensing issues. The group adjusted strategies accordingly and approached their city council with specific licensing recommendations soon after. In less than a year, they had convinced their council to pass what is currently one of the strongest ordinances regulating alcohol outlets in California—one that included the passage of a moratorium on new outlets in certain high-density areas.

Another reason to have detailed information to substantiate policy recommendations is that all legislation must be based on findings or a set of facts that provide the rationale for enacting the law. If you are interested in seeing your policy recommendations codified, then be prepared with the facts. Above all, have information that clearly describes the problem in ways that help your community, coalition, and the media grasp how serious it is.

Goal Setting Is Critical

Advocacy efforts need clear and specific goals and objectives. People are sometimes reluctant to sit down and discuss goals and objectives, because these can often be a source of disagreement and the process can be time-consuming. On the other hand, being clear about goals provides a specific sense of direction, a unifying theme, and a specific end point for a particular effort. Goals also establish a standard to help groups evaluate progress and gain the feedback necessary for the maintenance and operation of the group.

The goal is the overall outcome you want to achieve, such as a policy banning cigarette sales through vending machines. Objectives focus on what must happen to accomplish the overall goal. Media objectives (see Chapter 3) address what must happen to develop a media strategy to gain access, frame the issue, and advance the policy. Advocacy objectives address coalition building, community capacity building, and expanding the base of support.

All advocacy must operate within the framework of an organization's purpose and long-range goals. It is important to compare the organization's goals with the goal for the issue. In the assessment, you should ask yourself, What constitutes victory? How will this policy address the problem and/or have an impact on the quality of life of the clients, members, and community?

Take time to assess each of the objectives that must be achieved to meet the advocacy goal, and determine the activities that must be undertaken to meet the objectives. These activities should be geared to gaining the support of local politicians, other gatekeepers, or regulatory agencies and accessing the media to stimulate changes in local, state, or institutional policy. This assessment requires developing a extensive list of all the steps necessary to accomplish each short-term objective.

In *The People Rising*, Pertschuk and Schaetzel (1989) provide a wonderfully clear analysis of how different groups came together around a common goal: defeating the nomination of Robert Bork to the U.S. Supreme Court. To attain this goal, a series of objectives needed to be accomplished. In this example, political lobbying was necessary, as was coalition building and maintenance. Media advocacy played a key role but only in the context of the larger goal and the specific objectives that needed to be addressed. Media advocacy was an activity used to achieve specific objectives that in turn increased the likelihood of the overall goal being met. In this case, it was successful.

A final advantage of establishing a goal is that core group members are encouraged to think long term. This means moving further and further back from obvious cause-and-effect relationships to look at the general way that the policy-shaped environment influences behavior and social relationships.

Advocacy Can Be Threatening

If there is no struggle, there is no progress. Those who profess to favor freedom, and yet deprecate agitation, are men who want crops without plowing up the ground. They want rain without thunder and lightning. They want the ocean without the awful roar of its many waters. This struggle may be a moral one; or it may be a physical one; or it may be both moral and physical; but it must be a struggle. Power concedes nothing without a demand.

—Frederick Douglass (1857)

Public health professionals are most comfortable with management models that rely on consensus building. However, advocacy efforts often call on us to deal with opposition and dissent because, when it is done right, advocacy can be threatening. It challenges staid notions about the role of public health at the same time that it challenges vested interests in the status quo. Implementing policy change can adversely affect powerful corporate interests.

When we move our efforts upstream, beyond individual treatment to prevention initiatives that address environmental factors, we often find ourselves at odds with powerful institutions in both the public and private sectors. Therefore, gaining community support is essential and using the media is a crucial strategy in this endeavor. "A successful advocacy campaign doesn't make friends. It makes enemies. It points a finger, names names, and starts a fight. It tells us who's responsible and how to fight back. It tells us which side we're on" (Public Media Center, n.d.).

Advocacy Efforts
Require a Thorough Assessment

Advocacy is not just threatening for powerful interests, it often creates conflict that can threaten your organizational health. Before taking on any policy initiative, you should thoroughly assess what resources you have to support it. Ask yourself, Can I win? Or perhaps more important, Can my organization afford to lose? Advocacy campaigns can strengthen organizations by building a sense of team spirit, expanding the leadership base, deepening the leadership's level of experience, and broadening an organization's membership and contact base. Of course, the organization must bring something to the campaign in the first place (i.e., membership, staff, money, reputation, facilities, media contacts, allies). Make a careful assessment of your assets and liabilities and plan strategies that make the best use of your resources.

The best kind of advocacy campaigns not only meet short-term policy goals but also build a sense of community and community power. Building broad, cohesive coalitions is critical to these efforts—particularly if they are to have an impact on more powerful, corporate interests. One way to think about coalition building is to develop a list of groups and individuals who share part of the problem the organization would like to address, and then assess what each party would gain from supporting the effort. Of course, these issues are not black and white. Assess each party's depth of support, what it—and you—risk by coming together, what it brings to the effort, and how much effort is required to reach the party and maintain its presence in the coalition.

Coalition Ethics and the
Changing Definition of Expertise

The community environment is constructed around the recognition of fallibility rather than the ideal. Most institutions, on the other hand, are designed with a vision of imagining a structure where things can be done right, a kind of orderly perfection achieved, and the ablest dominate.
—John McKnight (1987)

In academic terms it is those with the most formal education that are considered expert ("ablest"), while those with more experiential training are considered significantly less so. The dichotomy created in these distinctions implies that experience and training in community organizing and institution building are somehow less valuable than the experience and training one receives in academic institutions, regardless of their relevance to project goals. Given the enormity of advocacy, there are obvious shortcomings to these distinctions as illustrated by the following example.

A well-respected social worker in private practice was interested in developing a local AIDS hot line. After a plea for support of the effort at one gathering of health professionals, she was approached by a participant who suggested she contact a local, grassroots organization doing AIDS prevention work among high-risk populations. Her reaction was intense. Even though she had not met the organization's leaders, she did not feel cooperative work was possible because the people who ran the project were "uneducated" (i.e., not classically trained in public health) former sex industry workers. The truth was that this organization played a key role in AIDS prevention in the community in which she wanted to establish the hot line. Her narrow view of what constituted expertise effectively blocked her from reaching a significant part of the population she wished to help.

Recent federal initiatives, such as the Center for Substance Abuse Prevention's Community Partnership Program, focus on community-based organizations as the loci for developing prevention strategies and programs. Individuals who are able to bring community members together and conduct other advocacy play key roles in these partnerships for prevention. In doing so, they find themselves abandoning the old, institutionally bound definition of expertise for a new, more flexible one. Advocates committed to policy-driven prevention efforts must also abide by a more pragmatic definition of expertise, one that gauges diversity of experience and cultural competency as well as academic training in the context of the tasks to be accomplished.

The Importance and the Dilemma of the Authentic Voice

As will be discussed in Chapter 4, the media are often interested in putting an "authentic voice" or face on a story they cover to give it human interest. Part of a new, flexible definition of expertise requires a thorough examination of who can speak with that authentic voice. It is important to provide those who are most affected by a policy or problem with opportunities to speak out on their own behalf. In fact, the act of speaking out on one's own issue (which is the highest goal of using an authentic voice) is an act of claiming power in and of itself. This may require leadership development, mentoring, and support of spokespeople who have not traditionally played such roles. Mothers Against Drunk Driving is a good example of individuals using their authentic voices to make themselves heard on policy issues and gathering personal strength in the face of tragedy.

Of course, advocates must exercise caution in how they employ "victims" in their coalition building. Problems can arise when authentic voices are simply used for photo opportunities without any effort to integrate them into coalition efforts. Again, advocates must be vigilant in their endeavors to forge a broad, inclusive definition of expertise that allows for the greatest range of human expression and creativity.

Race and Diversity

Studies by the Urban League and others show that racism is still a significant factor in the quality of life in racial and ethnic communities. A recent study by Massey (1992) supports these findings. Massey (1992) concluded that "racial segregation shapes, and to a large extent determines, the socioeconomic environment experienced by poor minority families" (p. 1). As advocates, we have little choice but to confront policies that reinforce racism if we are ever to make fundamental improvements in social conditions and public health.

Unfortunately, confronting racism not only affects macrosocial and economic relations but also has an impact on human relations. Perhaps the hardest lesson any advocate learns is that coalition work among diverse groups requires acknowledging the racism within himself or herself. When you conjure up a mental picture of an expert, whom do you see? What race is that person? What gender? Now, what is your picture of a grassroots activist? Oftentimes, we assume certain characteristics about each of these people that are stereotypical and limiting. For example, one participant at a community planning meeting described "community people" as "operating without any theoretical framework." This comment revealed that the speaker had clearly defined an "other" and feels separate and distinct from, perhaps even superior to, community people.

Aside from the issue of advocates' personal attitudes about race, class, and notions of expertise, there is also the issue of the ethics of "inorganic" organizing. Inorganic organizing is community organizing done by individuals or groups who are not members of the community being organized. This is an issue of great controversy among community organizers and health educators, with strong opinions on both sides. Regardless of where you stand on this issue, oftentimes it is communities with little resources and communities of color that are targeted for advocacy efforts by outside groups. Minkler (1978) explores the ethical dilemma inherent in organizing the disenfranchised, calling it "an unfair distribution of the burden of change in society." Minkler (1978) argues that organizing those with few resources may really be part of the problem rather than part of the solution:

> To focus the great bulk of our organizing efforts on the powerless and disenfranchised is to unwittingly perpetrate the view that such groups need to take full responsibility for changing the system which has placed them in disadvantageous positions since they are, after all, the ones who stand to gain the most from change. (p. 203)

Part of the intent of organizing in less powerful communities is to ascertain what policies or solutions are needed and wanted in these communities. However, one-sided efforts that completely place the onus for change on communities already overtaxed may not only be ethically suspect but create tensions between groups as well.

One African-American advocate was very concerned about a local, predominantly white San Francisco Bay Area effort to address racism that focused its efforts on a poor African-American community. The advocate's concern was that it was another example of how "they make racism our problem" when the real source of the problem—the racism outside of the African-American community—was not being addressed. She said to one organizer, "How can you come to my community and talk to my grandmother about something you can't talk to your grandmother about?" Her statement makes an eloquent point: Organizing that focuses exclusively on the disenfranchised can serve to create tensions that portray the organizer (accurately or not) as arrogant and patronizing.

The Principled Use of Power

Who organizes whom or who "helps" whom does create a certain power dynamic in a coalition. Those who do the organizing assume they have an answer or, at the very least, that they should join forces with someone else. Those being organized are assumed to be available to support the effort in some way if they can be convinced of its value. Often, when groups do not respond to a call to join an effort, they are labeled apathetic, cementing this uneven power arrangement that enables the organizing group not only to define what issues are important and what groups (based on their response) are valuable and viable but also to label them for others in the field.

It may be that part of the attraction of organizing disenfranchised groups is that it is often easier than communities with more resources. More affluent communities have more corporate actors within them and, therefore, are less open to being organized against their own interests. In coalitions, organizers must balance these power issues so that those with the least resources are not always called on to change. Members of society at all levels have responsibility.

In considering the pitfalls of inorganic organizing, one must look at the assumptions that form the foundation of his or her view of community versus that of expert. Who are media advocates and public health activists anyway? How do we begin to break down these outmoded notions of who are the activists and who are experts? We might start with our own personal lexicon, our professional jargon, our words.

At first, naming things may not seem important and to some may even seem silly or trivial. However, consider the importance of the term *person with a disability* versus *disabled person* or *handicapped person*. The former term emphasizes the person, whereas the latter terms emphasize the disability. The same is true for *AIDS victim,* a term that suggests powerlessness and is defined by the disease, versus *person with AIDS.* The latter term puts the person first; he or she is not defined by the problem.

There is power in the act of naming things, and in our advocacy efforts, we should use this power to support and not detract from our efforts. For example, when we gather groups together for technology *transfer,* it connotes that only one side of the interaction has something to offer. To organize a technology *exchange,* on the other hand, assumes that both sides have something to offer and both will benefit. The term *empowerment,* too, assumes that someone is conferring power on another, that the empowerer is giving something that the empoweree did not already possess. Instead of saying that a group was empowered by a project one might more accurately say that the project facilitated the claiming of power by the group. There are certainly other cases in which our language could be more sensitive to—and consistent with—our real objectives. The key is to practice being conscious of these issues and to incorporate them into your advocacy work from conceptualization to execution. Thinking about the impact of language is challenging but necessary if we are to ensure adequate sensitivity and appropriateness.

Assess Who Has Power

The primary barrier to enacting policy initiatives is not the media but the policymakers and other institutionalized interests that oppose the advocate's efforts. A successful advocacy strategy must take into account who and what institutions must be targeted to achieve the goal. Once one has decided what institutions or individuals have power or influence to enact the policy, then the advocate must research the ways to gain access to them and influence the process of policy enactment (i.e., through personal contacts, media, as a voter or taxpayer, etc.).

From January 1991 to June 1992, tobacco political action committees spent nearly $1.5 million in congressional political contributions (Wolfe,

Wilbur, & Douglas, 1992). With this kind of financial clout on the federal level, not to mention industry contributions to state and local officials, advocates seeking policies that affect these interests may do well to factor in the likelihood of significant opposition from these companies. Study the opposition carefully. Learn their arguments, develop counterarguments, and carefully analyze their interests. As the coalition is put together, keep the opponents' strengths and weaknesses in mind to ensure the coalition's effectiveness.

Money Won't Buy You Love

One problem many public health advocates face is the yawning gap in resources advocates and corporations have access to when advancing their individual causes. Strong coalition building and media advocacy are important tools to bridge that gap as shown by one grassroots effort in Milwaukee, Wisconsin.

The Milwaukee Coalition Against Drug and Alcohol Abuse is a broad-based coalition in the heart of brewer country. The coalition was based in Milwaukee's predominantly African-American inner city and started by a small grant that supports one full-time staff person. Members knew that they could not raise enough money to compete with the alcohol industry for financial influence so they set high goals for the number of people they needed to organize to influence alcohol policy in their community.

The coalition, through a series of campaigns, was able to expand its membership so that it could mobilize more than 200 people at any given time. They built this impressive coalition with an almost militaristic attention to detail. Coalition leadership would first brainstorm about who might be interested in joining them, who had an interest in the problems they sought to address, and what it would take to bring them in. This was a long process that involved personal follow-up on each nominee to invite him or her in. They did not attempt to organize "by flyers," according to former coalition chair Terrence Herron, because they knew they had to ascertain each organization's and individual's commitment to the project to know that they could be counted on to raise the convincing crowd they needed to hold their policymakers accountable.

The trade-offs were significant. High-quality participation by a diverse set of groups meant that the coalition leadership had to share power. This often meant giving the spokesperson roles to civic leaders who were not as studied in the various issues as some of the more veteran members. One presentation before the city council ended in defeat as spokespeople were convinced of industry arguments and folded in the middle of a fight to regulate billboards.

The coalition decided to continue to have these spokespeople but invested more time in leadership training. The investment paid off. It was able to maintain a broad, effective coalition organized and led by groups organic to the community. Although opposition to its policy proposals was often tough, it was able to affect a number of policy changes due to its grassroots organizing efforts, including billboard reform and regulations concerning alcohol outlets.

Herron said of their efforts,

We knew that we would face a lot of barriers when we undertook this effort. But we also knew that there were a lot of people out there who wanted to see things change. People power is much more powerful than money power. It's the purest form of power. It's a power that lasts a lot longer and changes the relationship between a community and its leadership. (personal communication)

Thinking About Tactics

Once you've assessed your organizational and community capacity, your allies and opponents, and the gatekeepers who have the power to enact your policy, you are ready to develop an action plan for your campaign. The actions you take should be flexible and engage the community. It is important that the policy recommendations you are advancing are specific, can be articulated in a way that is easily understood, and are realistically attainable. The individual (e.g., mayor) or organization (e.g., State Department of Alcoholic Beverage Control) should have the power to institute the change you are requesting. It would make little sense to focus your efforts on a city council when the power to implement your recommendation resides at the state level.

Set time limits for certain tactics and develop an alternate plan if your original tactics are not yielding results. South Central Los Angeles groups fighting alcohol outlet concentration developed the petition drive described earlier in this chapter after other tactics proved ineffective. Their commitment to constant evaluation provided the group with the information they needed to initiate an alternate and more effective strategy. It is also important to include a plan for monitoring your target institutions as well as the policies once they are implemented. Above all, be tenacious and remember that changing policy means changing minds—and that takes time.

Tactics include boycotts, informational pickets, public shaming, and letter-writing campaigns. African-American advocates in Chicago, led by activist Mandrake and a local alcohol treatment facility, took a busload of youth, recovering adults, and civic leaders to G. Heileman Brewing Co.'s corporate headquarters in Rosemont, Illinois. Their mission: to shame Heileman publicly for its role in the production of St. Ides malt liquor. Advocates set up a picket line and blocked access to the building's elevators to make the point that Heileman's product was disrupting life in the African-American community. Youth held up handmade signs chiding the company for its lack of corporate ethics, and adults who blocked the elevators passed out educational materials to Heileman employees. A prominent article about the demonstration appeared the next day in the *Chicago Tribune* and featured a photo of advocates holding a sign criticizing the brew. In addition to the photo, the newspaper printed this quote by Dr. Paul Kelly, director of Alcohol and Drug Prevention at the renowned Bobby Wright Comprehensive Community Mental Health Center: "The [St. Ides] advertising, it's tied to gangs and sexual promiscuity. If gangs and promiscuity are not major agendas in the African American community, there are none. They are talking dollars. We are talking lives" (Thomas, 1991).

The story gave Heileman three paragraphs at the end to deny responsibility, saying that Heileman was the brewer of the product but McKenzie River Corp. in San Francisco marketed it. Advocates successfully shamed Heileman in the media and also prevented the company from hiding behind the complicated contractual relationship between Heileman and McKenzie River. This tactic helped the coalition meet its objective.

However, it is also important to note that civil disobedience or, as the Reverend Dr. Butts of Abyssinian Baptist Church calls it, "civil obedience," has its consequences. Advocacy that breaks the law, no matter how unjust that law may seem, can result in arrest and conviction. For some organizations, having their members arrested, regardless of the reason, may not be acceptable. One must always carefully weigh these risks against the anticipated rewards.

Evaluating Success

Evaluation, if done well, informs your work on an ongoing basis. An advocacy group should periodically review each step of its action plan to assess if it is working. Here are some questions to ask:

- Did we do what we said we would do?
- What have we gained (people, resources, exposure—related and not related to our goals)?
- What have we changed (policy, community, or media relations, etc.)?
- How might resources be better allocated to tasks?
- Is there something that should be dropped because it is not working?

Use your evaluation information and make any necessary changes to your action plan. Also, make sure that you just do not focus on your shortcomings. Advocacy is hard work so take time to celebrate your achievements no matter how small they may seem.

Conclusion

A small group in Washington State working on low-income issues provides a wonderful example of how the different elements of advocacy can come together to create change. As reported by Amidei (1991), the group had only one full-time and one part-time staff member and a volunteer board when it set out to find out what its low-income constituents needed from the legislature. After surveying people in shelters, welfare offices, and food lines the group was surprised to find that dental care was the need most often cited. Although there seemed to be access to medical care through emergency rooms, there was no such outlet for dental care.

Advocates researched available policy options and found that the most effective approach to the problem was to expand Medicaid to cover dental care. The group faced significant odds as this initiative required substantial funding with little chance of support in a state legislature already grappling with a budget crunch. However, the group, which included low-income people, ignored experts' counsel characterizing its efforts as doomed to fail and continued forward. Its perseverance paid off as it was successful in getting the state legislature to extend the

Medicaid coverage. There was, however, one problem: No money was allocated to pay for the added coverage. It was clear that more had to be done.

After declaring victory on phase one of the campaign, the group announced phase two: the formation of the "Molar Majority," a concerted advocacy effort to convince the legislature to provide additional Medicaid funding for dental problems. The group began by forming a coalition with religious groups, civic organizations, dental professionals, and others. Over the next year the coalition waged a campaign through the media and by lobbying to build support for the program. After 18 months, the legislature voted to appropriate money and a dental care program was shortly under way. What was thought to be impossible was accomplished with grassroots organizing, broad coalition building, and legislative lobbying. At every step in the process the low-income population, for whom the policy change was intended, participated in strategic planning, decision making, education, and lobbying.

One interesting aspect of this story is that the group was not successful in attracting media attention. In the end, the media appeared to play no role in the success of this advocacy initiative. Considering the basic elements of this advocacy initiative, there were many ways that media might have been used to enhance the promotion of the policy goal. A media strategy might have served coalition goals, to recruit new members, or policy goals, to heighten visibility of the issue to pressure policymakers to act. However, what was central to the success of this initiative was a broad coalition and a strong lobbying effort. Although media advocacy could have supported these objectives, it was not necessary to achieve policy success.

This story illustrates the importance of research, coalition building, specific policy change, and identification of policymakers who have the power to make the change. It also emphasizes the importance of using advocacy initiatives to help people claim the power to which they are entitled. Left to "the experts," advocates would have decided that change was not possible, and would have quit before they had begun. Fortunately for those directly affected by the problem and living with its consequences, they did not give up. Through concerted advocacy focused on a specific policy goal, a big change was created by a relatively small, but determined and well-organized group.

Advocacy is a creative, effective, and necessary way of "doing" public health. Education is necessary but not sufficient to stimulate the kind of policy change required to improve or eliminate the conditions that contribute to social inequality, disease, and premature death. For many public health professionals and community groups, advocacy requires developing new skills and new ways of looking at community, health, and illness. Advocacy is an intervention that addresses the root causes of disease and injury: poverty, racism, and lack of economic development. We must develop flexible, inclusive approaches to public health problems that include forming community-based coalitions and grass-roots organizing to build power for policy change. Public health advocacy often demands that we take on the nation's or community's most powerful corporate interests on behalf of its least powerful citizens. This is difficult work but the rewards can be considerable.

Successful advocacy requires a respectful approach to building communities, an approach that views the community as a powerful partner with a leadership role in advocating on its own behalf. Our efforts should, as McKnight (1989) has said, "build capacity" in communities and not focus on deficiencies. Building capacity means allowing for and standing out of the way of the development of power, participation, and self-determination in a community.

This book focuses primarily on the role media advocacy can play in these efforts. Remember, however, that the goal of advocacy is not media coverage but policy change. Media advocacy is a wonderful tool, but still only a tool. You would not build a house with just a hammer, nor would you build an advocacy effort with just media exposure. The foundation on which to build an advocacy effort must always be diverse and widespread community support.

Note

1. Quote from Klass is copyright © 1992 by The New York Times Company. Reprinted by permission.

3

THE MEDIA
CONNECTION

*In our "mass-mediated" democracy, public health battles are fought
not only in the clinics and the courts, but also on the 10 PM news,
the front pages, financial section, and even on 24 hour all talk radio.*
—Jeffrey Chester, Center for Media Education

E very decade has been punctuated by media events that
captured national attention. In the early 1990s it was
the Persian Gulf war (Operations Desert Storm and Desert Shield), the
Clarence Thomas-Anita Hill hearings, the Kennedy-Smith rape trial, and
Magic Johnson's announcement of his HIV status.

Consider the last example. By 6:00 p.m. Thursday, November 7, 1991,
whether or not you were a basketball fan, you knew Johnson was
infected with HIV. Johnson's disclosure was at the top of the nightly news
broadcasts and on the front page of every major daily the next morning.
For the next few days, everywhere you went, in public and privately,
people were talking about Johnson and AIDS. For health educators, Rock
Hudson's and Magic Johnson's announcements of AIDS and HIV status
have been important milestones. People still refer to education about the
AIDS epidemic before and after Hudson. For a new generation of educators, it may become before and after Magic. In just one county in
California, for example, the weekly average number of HIV antibody
tests increased from 62 to 152 after Johnson's announcement (Contra
Costa AIDS Program, 1991). Nationally, the Centers for Disease Control
and Prevention's (CDC) AIDS hot line received millions of calls, more
than ever before, far more than it could handle. This single news event

inspired more response than had all the CDC's prior public service advertisements on AIDS (Jorgensen, Nunnally, & Dunmire, 1992).

The speed with which the electronic media can inform the public sometimes has dramatic consequences. But in far more subtle and mundane ways, the mass media, and especially the news, set our national agenda every day. The topics journalists choose to report, and the ways in which they report them, influence public discussion and private conversation. The news media in 1990 may not have given us our private opinions about the Gulf War, sexual harassment, rape, or AIDS, but the coverage did mean that many of us were forming and discussing our opinions on those topics. The corollary is that when the media ceased its coverage of those issues, many of our conversations also turned to other topics.

What Is News?

The media bring attention to specific issues and thereby can set the agenda for policymakers and the public. Agenda setting is an important concept for media advocates and will be discussed in some detail below. First we will examine the specific institutional practices, traditions, and constraints of mass media that affect whose agenda is set and how.

The Media Mean Business

The media provide the forum in which the major discussions of our society take place. This forum is extremely important in a democracy, where citizens need access to information to be involved in the political process and make good decisions. The media have a legal and ethical responsibility to contribute to the democratic process by communicating useful information to the citizenry. In addition, it is important to remember that the public owns the airwaves. Radio and television stations lease the airwaves from the public and their activities are licensed, monitored, and regulated by the Federal Communications Commission (FCC). Although many of those regulations were weakened during the Reagan administration in the 1980s, broadcast stations still have an obligation to be responsive to their communities. However, the media do not remain responsive to community interests simply because they strive to maintain democratic ideals, though certainly some do. It is more likely that the media are responsive to their communities because to do so is good business practice. Above all, mass media are businesses.

Media effects on social practices, democracy, and health need to be considered from a business perspective. The media operate under marketplace constraints that restrict the range of actions and attitudes they communicate. The first concern of a broadcaster or publisher is attracting the largest audience possible (Barnouw, 1978; Gitlin, 1980; Lazarsfeld & Merton, 1948/1975). Mass media's primary customers are the advertisers "whose business is to rent the eyeballs of the audience" (Gitlin, 1983, p. 3). Television is the most popular—and most extreme—example. Keeping audiences tuned in is the television news broadcasters first priority, and journalists who desire to deliver "objective" information must work within this constraint. As journalist Bill Moyers notes,

> You can tell a lot about a producer of television if you know whether or not he looks out and sees a nation of consumers or a nation of citizens. If he sees them as consumers, then the truth becomes that which sells, nothing more. If he sees them as citizens, he sees them as yearning to know, to matter, to signify. (quoted in Burns, 1989)[1]

The information delivered in the news is constrained by its commercial form. The ever-quickening pace of television news, its fast cuts, and entertainment look—always subject to being zapped away—demonstrate how the form of television is conforming to its business imperative. To get on the air, news must be visual, lively, short, and compelling, regardless of whether those qualities apply to the story at hand. In print media, publishers attempt to attract a larger audience for their newspapers by using graphics, color pictures, and larger headlines. It may not always be obvious that news choices are simultaneously business decisions, but news departments package the events of the day to attract large audiences for advertisers and sponsors.

Producing the News

There are three ways to think about producing the news: from the perspective of journalism and journalists, from the perspective of the organization or company that employs the journalists and producers, and in terms of events that happen outside the newsroom. Each of these ways of thinking about the news media will be useful for media advocates, because each provides different possibilities for approaching and gaining access to the news. For example, many of the stories in Chapter 6 describe how groups created events that captured news attention, and later in this chapter, we describe in detail how AIDS was not covered until journalists were personally interested in the story.

By and large, news appears to be shaped by the professional judgment of journalists. According to journalists, news serves the public interest when it follows journalism's own rules about the process of gathering the news. For example, balance and objectivity are important guiding concepts for journalists. Balance is a professional constraint, requiring that two sides of an issue be routinely presented (e.g., pro-choice and pro-life). Balance is one technique journalists use to ensure their objectivity. In fact, they may determine whether or not a story was done objectively by whether both sides were presented. However, this news routine arbitrarily imposes a dichotomy when, in fact, there may be three, four, perhaps even five sides to the story (Tuchman, 1978).

Journalists maintain that the news serves the public interest when it remains insulated from extrinsic considerations such as political pressure, publisher pressure, news executives, advertisers, or other interest groups. Furthermore, news is what journalists say news is. They trust their instincts, which have been shaped by their training, to tell them when a story is newsworthy. Kinsella's (1989) study of AIDS coverage is a critique of the news from a journalist-centered perspective. Kinsella asserts that AIDS was not adequately or properly covered until or unless reporters had a personal interest in and commitment to the issue. He calls it the "personal threat rule": "The closer the threat of the disease seemed to move toward those setting the agenda, the bigger the story became" (Kinsella, 1989, p. 252).

Others maintain that the structure of news organizations, which are sensitive to commercial pressures, has the largest effect on story choices. Publishers must sell papers, and publishers and broadcasters both must sell advertising and attract large audiences to view those ads. Hence stories that are deemed attractive become regular choices, ingrained in routine journalism as journalists internalize their employers' expectations. For example, one television producer, choosing between two stories to feature during the evening broadcast, chose a story about how video games can trigger epilepsy in children over a story about a new treatment for sickle-cell anemia. The producer made this choice because she believed that the video game story would attract more viewers, even though she considered the sickle cell story to be important. The sickle cell story was complicated; the video game/epilepsy story, more interesting. The producer would be able to use images of children playing the games as well as shots of the games themselves. On the other hand, it would have been much more difficult to craft a visually interesting story about the complex new treatment for sickle cell disease. The producer in the newsroom chose the video game/epilepsy story because she believed more people would want to watch it.

The video game/epilepsy choice illustrates another important influence on the content of the news, that is, the demands of the medium itself. Television is a visual medium; it wraps every story in pictures. Sometimes this means if there are not any pictures, the story will not be told or will not be told to the extent it warrants. The video game story was chosen in part because the images were attractive and readily available in the station's archives. Both radio and television stories are short, which means that they may not include the complexities explored in print. The sickle cell story, which was explored in detail in a newspaper article, was deemed too complicated even for a 2-minute television news story.

Some who study the media see it as a mirror of real life, as in Walter Cronkite's "and that's the way it is" sign-off line. This idea assumes that news stories reflect a neutral reality outside the journalists' or organizations' making. Big events naturally capture the attention of journalists and are reported as the news; stories are covered not because they will attract an audience but because they contain an inherent value that makes them newsworthy. However, "news is never 'the facts' pure and simple, it necessarily involves a selection, an analysis and, crucially, an evaluation of reality. This is the work journalists do when they 'present the news' to their audience" (Glasgow Media Group, 1982, p. 115).

Newsworthy events happen every day. There is a lot more potential news than television, radio, or newspapers have the time or space to cover. This means that there is a great deal of discretion in what kind of events are covered and how they are covered. Fortunately for health advocates, news organizations know that there is a great public interest in health issues. Because health coverage can attract viewers and readers, it can be good business for the media to focus on health-related stories. Unfortunately, media attention on health tends to be framed in terms of personal, individual issues that revolve around life-style, disease, and medical breakthroughs (Wallack & Dorfman, 1992). As discussed below, the media advocate's task is to influence this focus.

"Subtlety Is Not Our Middle Name"

60 Minutes, the most popular prime-time news program, provides an ideal example of how the media's commercial interests influence the structure of news stories and so the content of the news. According to its legendary producer, Don Hewitt, there are two rules at *60 Minutes*:

1. *60 Minutes* does not cover issues, it tells stories; and
2. Every story must feature a captivating central character or two, and he or she must speak clear English. (quoted in Hertsgaard, 1991)[2]

It is in the act of telling stories that news programs displace attention away from social conditions and highlight the motivation of actors in the stories. The story form favors an exclusive rather than inclusive interpretation of social problems. That is, stories usually have individual characters that seem to operate independently of social institutions. As one television executive said, "The networks are always mistaking real social issues for little human condition stories" (quoted in Gitlin, 1983, p. 179). Therefore, news programs, of which *60 Minutes* provides the most indepth example, focus on the personal. When the role of the character in the story is elevated, who that character is and what they say becomes very important.

Ultimately, characters must serve the needs of the story or they will not appear. As with all features of a news story, who the characters are—or at least who speaks—is a choice producers make. As one former *60 Minutes* producer noted, "They don't like stories about Central America or people who speak other languages. Don [Hewitt] also doesn't like stories about American Indians. Not because he doesn't like American Indians, but because Indians tend to be very stoical people, and on camera that doesn't make for so-called good TV" (quoted in Hertsgaard, 1991).

Information is subject to the constraints of storytelling on *60 Minutes* as in other news shows. This can be particularly frustrating for those in public health not used to thinking of issues in terms of stories. "Acid rain isn't a story," says Hewitt, "it's a subject. Tell me a story about somebody whose life was ruined by acid rain, or about a community trying to do something about acid rain, but don't tell me about acid rain" (quoted in Hertsgaard, 1991).

Balance, objectivity, and other journalistic ideals are enacted, or restricted, through the structures of the institution, through the daily work
of gathering the news, and through storytelling. News work transfers
occurrences into news events. It draws on aspects of everyday life to tell
stories, and it presents us to ourselves (Tuchman, 1978, p. 12). Thus in
Lippmann's (1922/1965) now classic notion of "pictures in our heads"
through which we make sense of the world outside our experience, the
pictures are not neutral. The pictures come from the media, either
verbally, or more often these days, visually. Each picture is a choice made
under a variety of constraints, including the commercial interests of the
corporations that own the media.

The influence of commercial interests does not mean that certain
stories are quashed because they would bode poorly for the company on
the stock exchange, although that could happen. More often, in fact
routinely, commercial interests mean stories are chosen and their format
is designed to attract an audience. Commercial interests displace democratic ideals as the media pursue the largest audience possible. This
means the news tells simple dramas about personal foibles. As Mike
Wallace notes, "Complex stories do get short shrift here—it's hard to do
a complex economic or geopolitical story like the factional fighting in
Lebanon" (quoted in Hertsgaard, 1991). So even an hour-long, in-depth,
extremely popular prime-time news show cannot offer anything but the
most simplistic analyses that easily fall into the good guy versus bad guy
mold, complete with action-packed plot and appealing characters. This
is how television news, by adhering to the narrative form of the story,
systematically limits what is presented, including the range of analysis,
conception, and the construction of reality. The drama must be clear and
distinct. Thus Morely Safer says of his medium, "Subtlety is not our
middle name" (quoted in Hertsgaard, 1991).

Conferring Status and Legitimacy

By telling stories from within its institutional context, the media confer
status on ideas, issues, people, and groups that capture their attention
(Lazarsfeld & Merton, 1948/1975). It seems that simply being selected
for attention by the media lends a story a certain legitimacy in the eyes
of the audience, which can lead to prestige or, conversely, notoriousness.
For example, Olien, Tichenor, and Donahue (1989) illustrate how media
provided initial legitimacy for a Minnesota group protesting the place-

ment of a high-voltage power line. On the other hand, Gamson (1989) points out that media coverage of a nuclear power protest demonstration in Seabrook, New Hampshire, focused on counterculture types "in search of a cause" and compromised the legitimacy of the demonstration and the credibility of the issue.

One of the positive consequences of legitimacy and status conferral on social problems is the increased likelihood that people feel comfortable discussing an issue. In a simple sense, because something is in the media it becomes more acceptable to talk about it. Hence, the media stimulate public discussion. Recent health concerns like alcoholism and unsafe sexual behavior are good examples of how the media contribute to legitimizing topics, which stimulate broader discussion and lessen the stigma associated with some problems by bringing them into popular conversation.

Reinforcing Existing Arrangements

Mass media ownership is growing increasingly concentrated. Bagdikian (1987) estimates that fewer than 29 corporations control more than 50% of all media output. This level of control, guided by commercial interests, results in a relatively narrow range of ideas, generally supportive of the existing sociopolitical relationships in society. The potential for diversity in the large number of media outlets is deceptive, because the content tends to be uniform across the various forms and channels of mass media.

The mass media, because of their commercial nature, are extensions of the most powerful groups in society and thus are, at best, reluctant to provide credibility to interests that diverge from their own. The interests of a broader corporate community receive primary attention, whereas the concerns of the general population are more lightly addressed. Because corporations have the greatest stake in the social and economic institutions that buttress their power, the media, over which they have significant influence, will be hesitant to challenge existing arrangements (Lazarsfeld & Merton, 1948/1975).

It may be the case that various media outlets and specific stories sometimes might challenge existing structures and contribute to social change. However, as Schiller (1973) notes, "these exceptions cannot conceal the main point: that the aim of television and radio programming and films in a commercial society is not to arouse concern but to lessen concern about social and economic realities" (p. 31).

Although most people would disagree that the mass media really "keep us in line," Rogers and Dearing (1988) note that "the mass media softly but firmly present the perspective of the ruling class to their audience. The result is consent and support." This happens because the media are "structurally dependent upon dominant power institutions both for definitions of the problem and for information" (Olien et al., 1989, p. 149). In this way they reinforce "established bureaucratic authority structures" (Olien et al., 1989, p. 149). For example, the media have been quick to support the designated driver concept to help decrease alcohol-impaired driving fatalities (DeJong & Winsten, 1990). However, the ease with which the designated driver was accorded legitimacy can be explained by the uncritical way the concept fits into the way advertisers, the National Association of Broadcasters, the alcohol industry, and the government define alcohol problems (DeJong & Wallack, 1992).

Selection and framing of individuals and groups by the mass media can highlight deviant behaviors or situations and lead to a loss of legitimacy or credibility, thereby reinforcing existing arrangements (Gitlin, 1980). The media thus serve as agents of social control not only by delegitimizing and marginalizing oppositional voices but also by constantly reminding the audience about what constitutes acceptable behavior.

The media are an important factor, reinforcing the exceptionalist thinking that keeps mainstream America separate from other groups, facilitating the kind of thinking that blames the victim for social problems. In 1992, for example, reporters covering the civil unrest in Los Angeles routinely referred to the situation as a *riot*. Some social critics, on the other hand, called the situation a *rebellion*. The definition and presentation of the situation as a riot suggest lawlessness, a lack of social or political basis for action, and blatant greed and opportunism. Defining the situation as a rebellion suggests a sociopolitical response to injustice and oppression and questions the legitimacy of the larger system. As the media defined it, the rioters were the primary problem, but the broader analysis, which received only limited attention, described the disturbance as a predictable outcome of a fundamentally flawed system.

Because of their dependence on bureaucratic sources, the media function to reinforce established norms and authorities and to delegitimate or marginalize detractors (Olien et al., 1989). Successful media advocacy challenges existing arrangements and usual problem definitions. Media advocates study the form and content of the news with close attention to how the media frame their particular issue. The object is to understand the needs of journalists to be able to help them prepare stories that will confer status and legitimacy on upstream definitions of health problems. Media advocates use the media to set the health policy agenda.

Agenda Setting

Mass media are like the beam of a searchlight that moves restlessly about, bringing one episode and then another out of darkness into vision.
                                                    —Walter Lippmann (1922/1965)

This classic image is as relevant today as it was when first put forth in 1922. The image suggests the mass media have a brief attention span on any particular issue. The breaking news of today disappears to make room for a different story tomorrow. But certainly, for today, the media provide illumination and a focus of attention that is enormously powerful, particularly when the spotlight can be held in place. Through the agenda-setting process, the mass media can provide the first step to public awareness and change, or by withholding attention, they can leave issues in the dark reaches. From a policy and prevention perspective, agenda setting is one of the most important aspects of the mass media.

A primary task of media advocacy is to focus the spotlight on a particular issue and hold it there. In other words, the media advocate wants to extend the attention span of the media to increase the saliency of the topic for a given audience.

Agenda setting has been one of the principal themes of mass communication research, "the process by which problems become salient as political issues meriting the attention of the polity" (Cook et al., 1983, p. 17). Using the searchlight image, agenda setting means an issue is illuminated, its importance is acknowledged by the general public, and subsequently, action is taken on the issue. The agenda-setting process involves setting the media agenda (what is covered), the public agenda (what people think about), and the policy agenda (regulatory or legislative actions on issues).

In 1963, Cohen put forth the specific idea of agenda setting in his book *The Press and Foreign Policy.* He provided the basis for the agenda-setting concept when he explained that the press

> may not be successful much of the time in telling people what to think, but it is stunningly successful much of the time in telling people what to think *about.* And it follows from this that the world looks different to different people, depending not only on their personal interests but also on the map that is drawn for them by the writers, editors, and publishers of the papers they read. (Cohen, 1963, p. 13, emphasis in the original)

Using Cohen's general concept, McCombs and Shaw (1972) analyzed the agenda-setting role of mass media in the 1968 presidential election. They compared what the voters said were the key issues with the actual content of the media. They confirmed the agenda-setting function when they found that the media influenced voters' judgments of what were considered to be the main campaign issues.

Since the McCombs and Shaw (1972) study there has been a great deal of research on the agenda-setting process (see Rogers & Dearing, 1988, for a review). This research established a positive association between amount of mass media content and placement on the public agenda (Rogers & Dearing, 1988). In addition, the public agenda seems to follow and not lead the media agenda (Iyengar & Kinder, 1987). The agenda-setting process may be complicated for any given issue because people have their own opinions and "do a fair amount of their own filtering, amplifying, and interpreting of the flow of political information" (Neuman, 1990, p. 162). The agenda-setting process is context dependent in that it reacts to what is going on in the world (larger events such as foreign policy) as well as to what goes on in one's more immediate environment (personal experience such as being victimized by a crime or paying more for gasoline) (Neuman, 1990). Some issues are far removed either personally or geographically from the person. In this case, the only way an individual experiences the issue is through the media. Other issues, such as paying higher prices at the grocery store, are experienced and known without the aid of mass media. The agenda-setting function is likely to be greater with more immediate issues. That is, if your personal experience is consistent with what the media describes, this will reinforce the media's effect. This working assumption was confirmed by Iyengar and Kinder (1987) in a series of experiments that showed that agenda-setting effects are stronger among those with direct experience with the problem.

There is some evidence for a strong media effect despite contrary personal experience. In its study of union and management portrayals on British television, the Glasgow Media Group found that the news stories blamed the UK's rising inflation on union demands for higher wages, despite the fact that real wages had not increased. When the Glasgow Media Group brought its findings to trade union schools and conferences and asked the union members what they thought caused inflation, the members overwhelmingly agreed with the television reports that it was rising wages. This was so even though they believed "their *own* wages had fallen in real terms. This apparent contradiction was resolved time and time again by each individual group of trade unionists saying that while *their* wages had fallen *other* people's must have gone up" (Glasgow Media Group, 1982, p. 2, emphasis in original). This is evidence of a strong media effect. The union members in this case discounted their actual experience in favor of what the news told them.

Entertainment programs and advertising also can be agenda setters. Situation comedies and dramatic series use social issues for plot lines so they can be interesting and contemporary. They both follow and stimulate the public's attention to specific issues. In addition to writers and producers drawing on their own interests in current affairs, various advocacy groups try to influence program content (Montgomery, 1989; Stevenson, 1990). Battles over controversial social issues (including abortion, race relations and civil rights, gay rights, violence, sexual abuse, AIDS and other diseases, contraception, and alcohol and other drug issues) have taken prominent and often contentious places in entertainment television. In 1990, advocacy groups such as the Environmental Media Association, the Harvard Alcohol Project, and Prime Time to End Hunger worked to place agenda-setting prosocial messages in a variety of programs, including *My Two Dads, A Different World, The Cosby Show, Growing Pains, Dallas, Cheers, Golden Girls,* and *Head of the Class* (Stevenson, 1990). These portrayals and others like them helped focus public attention on social issues. However, most agenda setting is done via the news.

Agenda setting works on basic principles of mass communication having to do with source credibility, resonance with one's own experience, consistency with other communication, and individual judgments about saliency of the issue. Although the amount of media coverage of a topic is clearly associated with placement on the public agenda, it appears that the various contingencies influence how quickly an issue is embraced and how long attention lasts and what, if anything, happens to the issue over time. Media coverage of AIDS provides a good illustration of how mass media can set an agenda or keep a topic from getting on the public agenda.

The Media Agenda

Rogers, Dearing, and Chang (1991) followed the agenda-setting process for AIDS from June 1981 through December 1988. Rather than just looking at the amount of media coverage (the media agenda) and how it related to public attributions of the importance or seriousness of the problem (the public agenda), they examined how the media agenda actually evolved over time.

The research team found a number of personal and political factors that slowed the emergence of AIDS on the national media agenda and then identified how, once on the media agenda, AIDS continues to have high visibility. Surprisingly, several factors that did not seem to be important for media agenda setting in this case were the actual number of cases of AIDS and the reporting of important scientific findings such as HIV in the blood supply, heterosexual contact as a means of transmission, and the identification of the HIV virus as the cause of AIDS—all pre-1985 events.

The number of cases, the high fatality rates, and the march of science in tracking down the cause (and presumably cure) of the disease would seem to be well suited to gaining media attention. This did occur in the San Francisco media; however, Rogers et al. (1991) found that for the three major television networks and *The New York Times*, the *Los Angeles Times*, and the *Washington Post* coverage was slight. The reasons for this lack of attention and the factors that eventually led to increased coverage are very informative.

The New York Times is considered the newspaper of record; this means that other newspapers and television networks take their cues from *The Times*. In other words, *The Times* sets the agenda for other media. According to Rogers et al. (1991), personal and organizational variables at *The Times* limited coverage of this critical public health issue. An editor thought that news stories about gays were not appropriate for the paper. This resulted in a clear message to reporters that the story had a low priority. The Rock Hudson and Ryan White stories in late 1985 and the retirement of Abe Rosenthal as editor in 1986 resulted in vastly expanded coverage of AIDS issues in *The Times*. This illustrates how, even at a newspaper almost universally respected, personal fears and prejudices can drive the definition of what is news.

Because AIDS was not covered there, it was simply not considered an important issue. Kinsella (1989) noted that many editors responded to story pitches from their correspondents and reporters by asking, "Has *The New York Times* done it yet?" A negative response to this question can kill a potential story (Kinsella, 1989, p. 89).

In addition to *The New York Times*, the president of the United States also sets the media agenda. By including a topic in a speech or mentioning an issue at a news conference, the president has the ability to set the news agenda for media outlets. For example, in 1989 President Bush announced he would give a major speech on drugs. This announcement was followed by a 2-week spurt of intensive news coverage (*Tyndall Report*, 1991) and a prime-time speech announcing the war on drugs. Subsequently, 64% of the population volunteered the response that "drugs is the most important problem facing this country today" as part of a national survey. This was more than twice as high a response than for any other problem from January 1985 to January 1991 (Kagay, 1991). Here is a clear example of the president setting the media agenda, which in turn sets the public agenda. In the case of AIDS, however, President Reagan did not talk about AIDS until the epidemic was already 6 years old. In addition, "until mid-1987, news people did not ask any questions about AIDS at White House press conferences" (Rogers et al., 1991, p. 14).

At the national level, AIDS faced two formidable barriers that kept it off the media agenda: The disease had no familiar human face and it had not been acknowledged by the president. This was to change with the reporting of two significant stories: the announcement that Rock Hudson was seriously ill with AIDS and the controversy over whether 13-year-old Ryan White, who had AIDS, could attend school. Rogers et al. (1991) noted, "Hudson's familiarity to the American people, combined with the 'boy next door' image of White, were enough to personalize and humanize the issues of AIDS, something that prior media reports based on the CDC statistics about the number of AIDS cases per month had not done" (p. 13). Kinsella (1989) explained that as a result of Hudson, AIDS now became everyone's problem: "The simple fact is, newsmakers, from the executive producer at the major network to the assignment editor on the metropolitan daily in Des Moines, were for the first time touched in a direct, personal way by the epidemic" (pp. 144-145).

The Hudson story changed the way that newspeople saw the problem. AIDS now had a human face that mainstream America could identify: The epidemic had come home. In addition, when President Reagan called Hudson to wish him well, he created an entrée to the White House for the press corps on this issue. This same general scenario would be repeated many times in what would become a key category of the media agenda on AIDS—public figures with AIDS. In 1991 Magic Johnson was in the spotlight, and in 1992 Arthur Ashe told newspeople that he had contracted the disease. Each new public figure raised new aspects of the epidemic. Johnson's case highlighted the issues of heterosexual trans-mission from females to males and young African-American males as a risk group. With Ashe, the issue was the right to privacy and the role of the media. Thus both stories generated a great deal of primary and secondary spin-offs and stories on related topics.

AIDS has been able to remain on the media agenda as subcategories of new AIDS issues generate new stories. As one issue fades, another takes its place. Every new issue starts from a base of AIDS stories that was higher than the previous one. Rogers et al. (1991) identified four distinct eras of AIDS coverage from 1981 through 1988 in six major media outlets: the "initial era," with little media attention (average of only 4 stories per month); the "science era," focusing on reports of transmission by casual contact (average of 24 stories); the "human era," focusing on Hudson and White (average of 112 stories); and the "political era," focusing on testing and privacy issues (average of 168 stories).

The lessons from the AIDS research on agenda setting are important. First, in some cases there are institutional and personal variables that can limit access to the media. This is by no means limited to AIDS and attitudes about current higher-risk groups such as intravenous drug users, gays, and the poor. For example, the controversial nature of alcohol issues, tobacco issues, and family planning can also lead to limited or slanted coverage.

Second, some events are too big, or fit too closely with the definition of what is newsworthy, not to be covered. It would be impossible not to cover the war in Iraq or Johnson's announcement of his HIV status. These significant events provide opportunities for unlimited spin-off stories that help expand the media agenda both in terms of quantity and topics.

Third, just as personal experience and prejudice can make a story unattractive, the same variables can make it attractive. For example, a newsperson with an alcohol problem may be reluctant to go with a story on alcohol availability. On the other hand, a newsperson with a friend or family member with an alcohol problem might have an enthusiastic interest in the story. Kinsella points out that a *Newsweek* journalist did not begin aggressively reporting on the epidemic until his brother was diagnosed with AIDS.

Fourth, although numbers are important, it may be more important to have a human face on the problem. Contrary to popular belief, White's situation generated more news coverage than did Hudson's disclosure that he had AIDS (Rogers et al., 1991). The face-of-the-victim approach, however, can have significant risks. The "victim" may be portrayed unsympathetically (e.g., an injection drug user), or the problem may be reinforced (e.g., as a personal rather than social issue).

Framing

News is not just factual information. It is an act of creative construction, influenced and guided by professional standards.
—Shaw and McCombs (1989)

The mass media have a two-step function. First, they select certain people and events for attention and thus contribute to setting the public agenda. Second, they frame the issue, telling the audience what is important to know about the story. The oft-cited classic agenda-setting quote by Cohen (1963) that the media may not tell people what to think, but may well tell people what to think about, might be wrong. By presenting a problem in a specific way, the media may indeed tell people not only *what* issue to think about but *how* to think about that issue. The Glasgow Media Group (1982) found in its study of television news in the UK that "it very largely decides what people will think *with*: television controls the crucial information with which we make up our minds about the world" (p. 1, emphasis in the original). Despite ideals of objectivity, in practice the reporting, shaping, and presentation of news and information are subjective. Everything cannot be said about every issue in every story in the short space of a newspaper article or television broadcast. Certain things are included in the package, while other aspects are left out. The selection process, what is left in and what is left out, is called *framing*.

Frames Create Meaning

Framing is the process by which someone packages a group of facts to create a story. When a photographer or a painter composes a picture, some things are left in the frame because they contribute to the composition and other things are left out because they are seen as unimportant or distracting. The same is true of a journalist. The decision about what is and what is not important to a story is based on professional training and personal experience. The meaning of facts is shaped by the context in which they are presented.

Nelkin (1987) explains that the framing of a story helps to create the basis by which public policy decisions are made. Indeed, Iyengar (1991) shows that framing is essential to the attribution of responsibility for addressing public issues. Who the audience deems responsible for fixing the problem depends on how the story is framed.

There are several journalistic conventions through which framing processes can be seen, including the presentation of images and symbols, the use of selected spokespersons, the use of selected words, and the emphasis on individual levels of problem definition. For example, news stories on television routinely portray people in white coats to symbolize science or show stock footage of test tubes as background for medical stories. Government representatives appear at news conferences surrounded by flags and official insignias to lend authority to their story. Language also is extremely important. During the 1970s, activists in the women's movement thought that their cause was demeaned when the press dubbed it "women's lib" (Tuchman, 1978, p. 137).

Framing social and health problems in the mass media occurs in a predictable way, based in American individualism. As a result, the audience sees problems as individual in nature and disassociated from broader social and political factors. Iyengar (1991, p. 142) explains that the primarily individual frame used by television news has the effect of obscuring the connection between social problems and the actions of political leaders—social and political change become secondary to personal and behavioral change.

In health stories that focus on life-style, news coverage usually emphasizes the need to exercise, have a nutritious diet, quit smoking, and be moderate in the use of alcohol. These stories take on the form of warnings and tips that link personal behavior to health status. Disease stories tend to focus on illnesses that are new (Lyme disease), obscure (rare outbreaks of exotic diseases), unusual (environmental sensitivity), or near hopeless (certain cancers). These stories are typically personalized in that they focus on the "struggle" or "battle" against disease. Oftentimes there is also a focus on advanced technology, as with transplant surgery. Although many stories focus on the deadliness of disease and suggest that there is no hope, there is often another set of stories that suggest new hope (Cohn, 1983). These are the medical-breakthrough stories that talk about new cures and new technologies. For example, it is common to see reports of new drugs that might be effective in treating Alzheimer's disease, although such a drug might only be in the early stage of testing and may still be 10 or more years from the market.

Because the media reflect mainstream views of American society, they will usually frame issues to portray the overall social system as fundamentally sound and attribute problems to corrupt, irresponsible, or simply unfortunate individuals. These media frames reflect the prevailing exceptionalist view that the flaw is not in the fabric of the society but in the loose thread of the individual. For example, Nelkin (1987) explains how "accidents, whether of space vehicles or in industrial plants, are blamed on aberrant individuals, sloppy corporate practices, or unfortunate decisions—and then euphemistically labeled 'human error.' " By defining problems in terms of human error the media and their audience end up ignoring basic structural problems regarding how society is organized.

Nelkin's quote inadvertently provides another example of a dominant frame that has implications for how audiences attribute responsibility for a problem. The use of the term *accidents* suggests that these events are unavoidable, unpredictable, almost acts of God with inevitable consequences. Research indicates, quite to the contrary, that many events from playground injuries to car crashes to childhood poisonings to nuclear meltdowns are far from inevitable events and, in many cases, are preventable. The use of the term *accident* rather than *injury* or *event*, however, not only is subjective and inaccurate but conveys a key point that is misleading—that because it is an accident it is an unpreventable product of individual carelessness.

The view that social and health problems are individual problems pervades the society and is reinforced through framing in the mass media. For example, Johnson (1989a) explains that the media portray child abuse as a strictly individualistic problem: "Society and its institutions are not seen as causal agents in producing child abuse and neglect; rather, the press takes the view that society and its institutions represents functional responses to the problem tending to control it" (p. 15). The media treat drinking and driving, smoking, illicit drug use, and HIV infection primarily as problems of individual life-styles. This reinforces the element of personal choice and with it personal responsibility and blame. An ideal world would maximize personal choice and responsibility, but the sine qua non for this is an informed public. This is hardly the case when alcohol and tobacco companies saturate the message environment with sophisticated and misleading product claims and the federal agency charged with informing the public about HIV and AIDS can spend millions on research but not mention the word *condom* in any of their mass media materials. People make personal choices within boundaries largely set by groups and institutions outside of the immediate environment or control of the individual.

Contested Frames

Framing is also potent in defining people, positions, and solutions. Ryan (1991) notes that "every frame defines the issue, explains who is responsible, and suggests potential solutions" (p. 59). Facts are presented and interpreted via cultural symbols that convey meaning in a concentrated way. For example, Archbishop Helder Camara of Brazil said, "When I feed the hungry, they call me a saint. When I ask why they have no food, they call me a Communist" (quoted in Quinn, 1991). This shows how two symbols, evocative of strong emotions, can be used to describe the same activity, yet one frame conveys a supportive, positive image and the other a negative, hostile image.

Groups are in a constant struggle to define themselves and create an image that conveys their issue and mission. Levine (1981) notes that the American temperance movement was successful in reframing alcohol in the 19th century from being viewed as "the good creature of God," an image deeply rooted in history and society, to being seen as "Demon Rum." One image conveyed health and the other poison, one image freedom and the other slavery, one image success and the other failure, and one image home and family and the other saloon and liquor

(Levine, 1981). Perhaps the most popular instance of reframing comes from Mark Twain's tale of how Tom Sawyer passed on the burden of whitewashing the fence to his friends by reframing the task as fun rather than drudgery.

More recently, the battle for framing is evident in how the tobacco industry uses symbols and images to promote itself as a good corporate citizen, defender of the First Amendment, protector of free choice, and friend of the family farmer. The industry paints antitobacco people, on the other hand, as zealots, health fascists, paternalists, and government interventionists. One of the great successes of the antitobacco movement has been to win the framing battle with the tobacco companies and erode the credibility and legitimacy of the tobacco interests. As a result of the movement's efforts, the general public increasingly views the tobacco industry as "merchants of death."

The framing battle can also be seen in public arguments about nuclear energy. The industry has used a health frame stressing safety, an economic frame stressing low cost, a nationalism or patriotic frame stressing independence from foreign oil interests, and even an environmental frame stressing nonpolluting qualities (Salmon, 1990). Of course, the antinuclear activists have countered with alternative frames drawing on conservation and safety in their efforts to discredit the industry frames.

The abortion issue also provides a contemporary example of contested frames. When the U.S. Supreme Court was considering the *Webster* case in 1989, thousands of demonstrators converged on Washington and used symbols to get their point across through media coverage. The challenge was to have the best symbol. Wearing white, kneeling in prayer, erecting white crosses, and displaying coat hangers were all efforts to convey in a dramatic way, through evocative symbols, a pro-life or pro-choice position (Johnson, 1989b).

Emphasizing the positive is a common tactic in framing contests. In 1990, a conservative Republican group put out a list of 133 words that political candidates should use to promote themselves and attack their opponents. This list included the following terms that were to be applied to the opponent and his or her record, proposals, and party: *decay, sick, unionized bureaucracy, greed, corruption, radical, permissive,* and *bizarre.* On the other hand, the terms that the conservative Republicans were told to apply to themselves included *opportunity, challenge, courage, pristine, principled, caring, common sense, peace,* and *pioneer* (Oreskes, 1990).

Episodic and Thematic Frames

The way that the news frames issues is critically important, because it affects public perceptions of who is responsible for the solution. Iyengar (1991) has demonstrated the considerable power of framing in his studies of television and the public policy process. Iyengar examined perceptions of causal and treatment responsibility. Causal responsibility refers to who is responsible for causing the problem. Treatment responsibility refers to who has the power to fix it. Iyengar (1991) concluded that "there is substantial evidence, primarily in nonpolitical domains, to suggest that attributions of causal and treatment responsibility for national issues will dictate the opinions people hold on these issues" (p. 10). The main source of these opinions, the main environmental cue that people are exposed to, is television news.

Iyengar (1991) explored the way that the news framed issues such as poverty, crime, and unemployment and the effect that this framing had on whom audiences held responsible for the problem. He found that television news frames stories as either "episodic" or "thematic." Episodic frames tend to be event oriented, specific, and concrete. They use compelling pictures to tell a short, simple, and personal story. A standard episodic frame will use the victim of a drunk driver or someone struggling to recover from drug addiction to dramatize the issue and tell the story. Although the episodic frame does illustrate social problems, it does so by using individual-level illustrations.

Thematic frames, on the other hand, are issue oriented, general, and abstract. They tend to rely on data, reports, and talking heads to tell a longer, more complicated social story. A standard thematic frame is the government official or news anchor talking about unemployment with charts and graphs cut into the story. Thematic frames present the collective case of an issue rather than the individual or personal one. Many television news stories contain elements of both types of framing, but within stories and across the news in general, episodic framing dominates, appearing more than 80% of the time (Iyengar, 1991).

By and large, episodic framing results in an emphasis on individual responsibility for social problems such as poverty. Audiences hold the individuals portrayed responsible for the problem. As a result, politicians and public institutions are insulated from responsibility to address the problem. Iyengar (1991) noted that President Reagan criticized journalists during the 1982 recession because they were always interviewing someone who had just lost a job—an example of episodic framing. The president was obviously feeling uncomfortable, because the image of unemployed workers was a powerful one and, he believed, one that would lead people to attribute responsibility for the problem to him. However, according to Iyengar's (1991) evidence, it was far more likely that viewers held the unemployed worker responsible rather than the president and his policies: "Instead of raising questions about presidential responsibility, these stories have precisely the opposite effect" (p. 138).

Thematic framing, on the other hand, leads to attributions of societal responsibility for problems such as poverty. Consequently, in stories with thematic frames, audiences hold politicians and public institutions responsible for addressing the problem. However, because episodic rather than thematic frames dominate television news, the overall effect of news stories is to reinforce an exceptionalist, individualistic frame for social problems.

One of the key barriers that media advocates need to overcome is the predominant episodic frame. According to Iyengar (1991), "In the long run, episodic framing contributes to the trivialization of public discourse and the erosion of electoral accountability. . . . Television news may well prove to be the opiate of American society, propagating a false sense of national well-being" (p. 143). A central struggle for media advocates, which we shall return to later, is balancing journalistic and general media needs for the characteristics of episodic framing with advocate needs to focus on the major thematic causes of the problem.

Understanding Media Advocacy

The mass media constitute an important part of the environment in which the selection, presentation, definition, and discussion of public issues occur. Media advocacy seeks to influence the selection of topics by the mass media and shape the debate about these topics. Media advocacy's purpose is to contribute to the development and implementation of social and policy initiatives that promote health and well-being and are based on principles of social justice. This is what media advocacy is all about.

Successful media advocacy ensures that the story is told from a public health perspective. This means maintaining a focus on the public policy dimensions of prevention; emphasizing the social, cultural, economic, and political context of health problems; and stressing participation and empowerment as primary approaches to prevention. Media advocacy uses a range of media and advocacy strategies to define and stimulate broad-based coverage of a health or social issue to reframe and shape public discussion to increase support for and advance healthy public policies. The success of media advocacy, however, may depend on how well the advocacy is rooted in the community (see Chapter 2).

Local media outlets feel a legal and civic responsibility to the community. They want to be good community citizens and contribute to the quality of life. They also are concerned about what the community wants as viewers, and local viewers tend to like local stories. The more support and participation at the local level for a media initiative the more likely that journalists will define the issue as relevant and newsworthy. As Tuchman (1978) notes, "the more members, the more legitimate their spokesperson" (p. 92). Media advocacy, then, combines the separate functions of mass communication with community advocacy.

How Media Advocacy Differs From Traditional Approaches

Media advocacy differs from traditional uses of mass media in public health in a number of ways. First, as primarily an advocacy strategy it relies on coalition building and community organization for its base of support. Traditional strategies tend to focus on putting the health message out from a centralized point. Media advocacy, on the other hand, seeks to provide community groups with skills to communicate their own story in their own words.

Second, agenda setting and framing are the key theoretical perspectives that media advocates use. These theories are rooted in political and social sciences, as opposed to traditional campaigns, which have tried to change individual health behavior by relying on theories from the behavioral sciences.

Third, traditional strategies tend to see individuals and groups as parts of the audience to be addressed in a one-way communication. Usually, if the audience is included in the planning at all, it is after major parameters of the issue have been set. Media advocacy treats the individual or group members as potential advocates who can use their energy, skills, and other resources to promote social change.

Fourth, media advocacy develops healthy public policies rather than health messages. The policy focus reflects a long-term planning perspective on social change in contrast to the short-term problem-solving approach, which places attention on immediate concerns. Media advocacy typically addresses short-term, pressing issues (e.g., a specific advertising campaign for a new youth-oriented alcoholic beverage) only in the broader context of overall policy development and change.

Fifth, media advocacy shifts the focus from changing the individual to changing the environment in which the individual acts. This emphasis on environmental change reflects a great body of research in public health, generally, and prevention, specifically, which strongly indicates that environmental factors are key determinants of health. Attitudes and norms reinforcing individual rather than collective approaches to public health issues can be considered part of the social and political environment that can be targeted by media advocacy.

Finally, media advocacy moves the focus for media access from the public affairs desk to the news desk. One of the fundamental tenets of media advocacy is that health activists confront issues that are newsworthy because of high levels of public interest and direct links to community well-being. Rather than being supplicants for limited public service time, media advocates present themselves as partners in the news-making and -gathering processes.

Another element of this is the careful use of paid media placements to put a specific message out to a clearly defined group of people. This is not possible through public service time where the message is controlled by gatekeepers (e.g., controversial messages are not allowable) and placement is not guaranteed to reach the people you want to talk to most. The struggle for access to tell a story is fundamental to media advocacy and creating news or guaranteeing placement through purchase are basic tactics for the practitioner.

The Information Gap
Versus the Power Gap

Traditional forms of mass media interventions emphasize the information gap, which suggests health problems are caused by a lack of information by individuals with the problem or at risk for the problem. Health educators then attempt to provide information to fill that gap. When people have the information and know the facts, it is assumed that they will then act accordingly and the problem will be solved. The role of the media is to deliver the solution (knowledge) to the millions of individuals who need it. Media advocacy, on the other hand, focuses on the power gap, viewing health problems as arising from a lack of power to create social change. Media advocacy's target is the power gap. It attempts to motivate social and political involvement rather than changes in personal health behavior.

A classic example of using the media to fill the information gap is the Partnership for a Drug Free America. This program produces public service ads based on the idea that "if only people really knew how bad and uncool drugs were they wouldn't use them." Many of these ads are memorable, but their strong statements generally do not take a public health approach. Instead, they focus almost exclusively on individual behavior and personal responsibility. The Partnership ads insist that

> the drug problem is *your* problem, not the government's. The ads never question budget allocations or the administration's emphasis of [law] en-forcement over treatment. . . . If there are mitigating reasons for drug use— poverty, family turmoil, self-medication, curiosity—you'd never know it from the Partnership ads. (Blow, 1991, pp. 31-34)

The Partnership ads laud volunteerism, self-discipline, and individual-ism (Miller, 1988, p. 34), precisely the values that resonate with the American people. The Partnership strategies meet with little political resistance because they reinforce an exceptionalistic or victim-blaming view of public health.

The Partnership campaigns assume that information is the magic bullet that inoculates people against drugs. The campaigns ignore social conditions such as alienation, poor housing, lack of education, and lack of economic opportunity that form the context of the problem. Because the context of the problem is part of the problem, any solution that does not take the context into account inevitably will be inadequate. In fact, the Partnership's public service advertisements, despite their intent to improve the public's health, ultimately may do more harm than good by undermining support for more effective health promotion efforts that focus upstream on power relationships and social conditions. The ads occupy valuable media time with compelling messages that reinforce a downstream, victim-blaming approach. This is typical of public service campaigns that routinely omit social causal factors of problems (Paletz, Pearson, & Willis, 1977).

Media advocacy's focus on policy addresses determinants of health that are external to the individual. These determinants include variables such as basic housing, employment, education, health care, and personal security and might be considered under the general rubric of social justice issues. A second set of determinants focuses more closely on immediate marketing variables associated with health-compromising products such as alcohol, tobacco, and high-fat foods. These marketing variables include advertising and promotion, pricing, product development, and product availability. For example, alcohol activists are concerned about advertising and promotion of alcohol at events or in media that attract large youth audiences. In addition, the pricing of alcohol so that it is competitive with soft drinks, coupled with its easy availability, contributes to an environment that is conducive to problematic use of the product. Store owners who indiscriminately sell malt liquor to children or companies that develop new products such as wine coolers that target youth further contribute to the seductive environment. These are all potential focal points for media advocates.

Media advocacy, by embracing the policy side of public health, puts health problems into their *political* context. For instance, legislators commonly accept political contributions from the tobacco and alcohol industries and sometimes have other financial connections as well. Nevertheless, they are expected to be objective when legislation is introduced to address the health-compromising outcomes of these industries. Highlighting these contradictions is a media advocacy function that pressures legislators to act in the public interest rather than their own economic interests. For example, in California in 1992 Governor Wilson and the state legislature found time in the midst of the greatest budget crisis since the 1930s to pass special-interest legislation for Anheuser-Busch, allowing the company to sell beer at Sea World, a marine park frequented by schoolchildren. Advocates pointed out in an opinion piece on the op-ed (opposite the editorial) page that Governor Wilson owned $100,000 worth of Anheuser-Busch stock and that the company spends an average of $125,000 a year to lobby the state legislature (Alexander, 1992). In Chapter 6, we present the details of how local media advocates used these events to focus attention on alcohol policy issues in their community.

Similar to the news, the primary strategy of media advocacy is story-telling. But unlike the news, media advocacy attempts to tell a story in a particular way to promote specific outcomes. As Michael Pertschuk, one of the architects of this approach explains, "Media advocacy is the strategic use of mass media for advancing a social or policy initiative." There are many steps in the definition of media advocacy that Pertschuk provides. Initially, the goal of the media advocacy must be determined. Then a story needs to be developed based on facts and values and made meaningful to a clearly defined target audience so that it can attract attention. It is safe to say that the general population is always a target, but usually secondary rather than primary. The primary audience will likely be a more clearly defined group of decision makers, legislators, community leaders, or community groups: "Media advocacy isn't about a mass audience. It's not about reaching everybody. It's about targeting the two or three per hundred who'll get involved and make a difference. It's about starting a chain reaction. And reaching critical mass" (Public Media Center, n.d.). In some cases, the target of media advocacy can be just one person as in the "narrowcasting" approach of Schwartz (see Chapter 4). Generally, decision makers who affect the lives of others through their influence on the public policy process are the target audience. Secondary audiences are used to increase pressure on these groups.

Having a coherent story with a clear audience in mind is essential but will have little value if there is no forum for getting the story out. Mass media are society's primary forums for storytelling and access to these resources is the lifeblood of media advocacy. Access means having an outlet to reach the audience. These outlets might include the editorial page, news coverage, public affairs, or talk radio. As we shall see later, there are many potential points of access at which the advocate can have the opportunity to present and define an issue. However, access is closely guarded by the media, creating an underlying tension that permeates media advocacy—the struggle to control the terms of access. Media gatekeepers might see access routes for a community agency through public affairs time or space. They may not see the activities of the agency as interesting or newsworthy. The community agency may unwittingly reinforce this belief because lack of skill or experience in dealing with the media. Hence, the activities of the agency are effectively minimized, its story limited, and its access restricted. On the other hand, an agency or community group might view its activities as newsworthy and of vital community interest. By learning how to frame issues to attract media attention and not being reticent about the importance of their mission and relevance to the community, local groups can gain access to the media.

Gaining access is essential, but only part of media advocacy. Influencing how and where the story is reported is the other half. For example, during the 1970s the women's movement began to get media attention. However, stories on the early activities of the women's movement were relegated to the women's pages of the paper, despite movement leaders' beliefs that their activities were hard news. The trade-off was that their stories got more column inches, but the audience they reached was not the principal one they sought to influence. "Placement of news on the women's movement on the segregated women's page classifies those stories among food, fashions, and furnishings, not among the pressing affairs of the day" (Tuchman, 1978, pp. 153-154).

Key Elements of Media Advocacy

Media advocacy includes three concrete, fundamental steps: setting the agenda (framing for access), shaping the debate (framing for content), and advancing the policy. Media advocates organize all other activities around these three steps. Framing for access means shaping the story to get the attention of journalists to gain access to the media. Often it means being able to create an event that will be interpreted as news. Framing for content means telling the story the way you want it told, emphasizing root causes and upstream conditions. The story should be framed so that its conclusion is the policy you seek to advance. There is a delicate balance between framing for access and framing for content. Sometimes, the aspect of the story likely to draw media attention is not what you want to emphasize. Nevertheless, both gaining access to set the agenda and shaping the debate are necessary to achieve the ultimate goal of advancing the policy.

Setting the Agenda:
Framing for Access

A local news program in the San Francisco Bay area used billboards and television commercials to tell people, "If it goes on here, it goes on [channel] 4 at 10." The implication was that if you do not see it on the news, then for all intents and purposes, an event has not happened.

When AIDS was not covered by *The New York Times*, it did not make it on the nation's policy agenda either. If the press does not cover your demonstration to highlight a contradiction in health policy, it might as well have not taken place as far as the broader community is concerned. Daniel Schorr, a National Public Radio commentator and longtime journalist, says, "If you don't exist in the media, for all practical purposes, you don't exist" (quoted in Communications Consortium Media Center, 1991, p. 7). Gaining access to the media is the first step for media advocates who want to set the agenda.

Gaining access is important for two reasons. First, the public agenda-setting process is linked to the level of media coverage, and thus the broad visibility, of an issue. Second, media are a vehicle for gaining access to specific opinion leaders. Politicians, government regulators, community leaders, and corporate executives are people you might want to reach specifically. In successful media advocacy both objectives will be met. For example, as we discussed briefly in Chapter 2, recent efforts to remove PowerMaster malt liquor from the market were able to get the problem out in the media, which helped to make it a public issue. At the same time, specific politicians and government regulators at the Bureau of Alcohol, Tobacco, and Firearms were exposed to media reports that gave them a greater sensitivity to the issue and a greater expectancy that others around them would be aware of the issue. Journalists themselves put pressure on bureaucrats just by doing the story, apart from what happened with public opinion after the story was broadcast. With tape rolling, officials had to answer for their actions.

Newsworthiness

None of us is the president of the United States or an editor for *The New York Times*, so how can we get access to the media? Media advocates gain access by interpreting their issue in terms of newsworthiness. In a variety of ways, media advocates take advantage of what is known about how news is constructed and what its objectives are. An issue will be covered only to the extent that it is timely, relevant, defined as in the public's interest, and/or meets a number of other news criteria. Shoemaker and Mayfield (1987) present an extensive list of factors that go into determining newsworthiness. Criteria for selecting news "include sensation, conflict, mystery, celebrity, deviance, tragedy, and proximity" (p. 4). To that list Dearing and Rogers (1992) add "the 'breaking quality' of a news issue, how new information can be molded to recast old issues in a new way, and the degree to which new information can be fit into existing constructs" (p. 174). Unusual human interest stories of people doing something new, overcoming difficult odds, or helping others are also newsworthy.

Very few social problems are new. Alcohol problems, teen pregnancy, drugs, and poverty have been around for a long time and are periodically rediscovered. Gaining access for a particular issue may depend on where it falls in a cyclic media attention span. Downs (1972) has identified a well-ordered "issue-attention cycle" for many domestic problems. His first stage is the preproblem stage. At this stage the problem fully exists and can be quite bad, but it is yet to be discovered and seen as a problem by the broad public. The April 1992 civil unrest in Los Angeles brought to light basic problems of racism, poverty, and alienation that have long existed but were below the threshold of mainstream public attention. The uprising provided the basis for the second stage of the cycle: "alarmed discovery and euphoric enthusiasm" by the media and the mainstream public. Many thought that racism was no longer a problem in our society; the uprising brought home the fact that conditions remained, in fact, quite bad. Fundamental to the American character is a basic optimism that even the most intractable problems can be solved. Soon the media enthusiasm moved from the horrors of the violent disturbances to the road to recovery, highlighting how volunteers from many different areas were pitching in to clean up the devastation. The media pictures and descriptions of people joining together to clean up reinforced the idea that by joining together the problem can be solved.

Downs's third stage involves a realization of the cost of making significant progress. Most important here is the awareness that change will require sacrifice and that groups with better or more resources may have to bear a larger burden than those who are less well off. However, from this stage it is a short trip to a decline in public interest and to pessimism about whether change can take place at all. Next is the postproblem stage, which is a kind of twilight in which the problem continues to exist but gets little public or media attention. The trail in Los Angeles from Watts of 1965 to South Central of 1992 illustrates two complete cycles of the attention process.

When the media spotlight fades, attention recedes, and often we return to prior arrangements and prior levels of attention. The shift of the media away from a problem is a curious form of both cause and effect of public perceptions. Lack of the media spotlight causes issues gradually to fall out of public discussion and to lose a sense of legitimacy and urgency. On the other hand, the media shift because they sense that people are bored with the issue or because some new, more pressing problem has emerged. The media, after all, are in the business of attracting large audiences, and if they bore or threaten people (because the solutions are complex or call for personal sacrifice) they will lose their audience and their economic base.

Shaping the Debate: Framing for Content

Gaining access to the media is an important first step, but only a first step, in influencing the public and policy agenda. After access, the next barrier that media advocacy seeks to overcome is the definition of health issues in the media as primarily individual problems. As Blum (1980), a well-known health planner notes, "there is little doubt that how a society views major problems . . . will be critical in how it acts on the problems" (p. 49). If we alter the definition of problems, then the response also changes (Powles, 1979; Watzlavick, Weakland, & Fisch, 1974). Problem definition is a battle to determine which group and which perspective will gain primary ownership of the solution to the problem.

The tendency in the United States is to attempt to develop clear and concise definitions of problems to facilitate concrete, commonsense type solutions. This is a very pragmatic approach with strong appeal. Often, however, problems of health and social well-being are difficult to define, much less solve, and increasing levels of problem complexity are highly correlated with rising degrees of disagreement in definition. The tendency is to simplify the problem by breaking it down into basic elements that are easier to manage. In most cases, health problems are broken down into either a biological unit, and the solution is medical, or an information unit, the solution for which lies in education. This misguided pragmatism reduces society's drug problem, an enormously complex issue that involves every level of society, to an inability of the individual to "just say no" and resist the temptation to take drugs. Generally, diseases are reduced to cognitive, behavioral, or genetic elements. Public and private institutions end up allocating significant resources to identifying the gene for alcoholism while leaving the activities of the alcoholic beverage industry largely unexamined. Even though 30% of all cancer deaths and 87% of lung cancer deaths are attributed to tobacco use, the main focus of cancer research is not on the behavior of the tobacco industry, but on the biochemical and genetic interactions of cells.

The alternative is to see problems as part of a larger context. Tobacco use, for example, rather than being seen as a bad habit or a stupid thing to do, can be seen as a function of a corporate enterprise that actively promotes the use of a health-compromising product. Decisions at the individual level about whether to smoke could be seen as inextricably linked to decisions at the corporate level regarding production, marketing, and widespread promotion. Smoking, in this larger context, is seen as a property of a larger system in which a smoker or potential smoker is one part, rather than simply as a property of individual decisions. The same could be applied to automobile safety, nutrition, alcohol, and other issues. This type of analysis takes the problem definition upstream. The key for media advocates is to frame their issue in terms of upstream problem definitions.

Conclusion:
Advancing the Policy

Mass media can be used to put pressure on policymakers. But the pressure is not automatic. The media coverage must be carefully crafted and strongly supported. Otherwise, it is just another story.

Consider a typical, and tragic, example from a major city in California. Early in the evening, on her way home from work, a woman was kidnapped while walking to her car from public transportation. Her abductors put her in the trunk of her own car, and later robbed, raped, and murdered her.

The tragedy received tremendous coverage on television and in the local papers. Community members were horrified, frightened, and desperate to do something about public safety. A local church held a candlelight vigil for the woman, and more than 500 community members attended her funeral.

Several community-based organizations were involved in organizing the vigil, which they anticipated would attract significant media attention. It did. Nevertheless, members of the community-based organizations were frustrated with the type of coverage the woman's death and the vigil received. They blamed the reporters for focusing too much attention on the drama of the event, rather than on the issues of importance for safety and well-being in the community.

Indeed, news reports that discussed safety emphasized what individuals should do to protect themselves. Articles quoted mass transit officials giving advice such as:

- Observe all posted parking regulations and park in designated areas.
- Before leaving, check your headlights, lock your car, and do not leave valuables or packages where they can be seen.
- Carry your keys in your hands.
- When at stations at night, be aware of your surroundings and stand in the center of the platform. If you need help, call the station police.
- If you do not feel safe walking to your parked car, go back to the station.

While all of this is good advice, it places almost total responsibility for safety on the rider. This is important. However, no one asked this question: "What would it take to make the environment safe, regardless of what various individual passengers do?" Thus stories did not focus on environmental factors such as lighting in the station area, cutbacks in station security personnel, or the much larger issue of violence against women.

The problem with news coverage does not rest solely with journalists. While members of the community-based organizations were unsatisfied with the coverage, they also had not clearly articulated the solutions they desired in terms the media could easily use. Access, in this case, was abundant. From the media advocacy perspective, work needed to be done to frame for content to articulate the solution and move a policy forward.

One of the key goals of media advocacy is to advance a policy or approach to address the problem. Getting the media's attention and having your story air or appear in print is often the easy part of the job. The difficult part occurs when you have to frame your issue and solution in the media for the people you want to reach.

The important work of media advocacy is really done in the planning stage before you call the media. You need to know how you will advance your approach, what symbols you will use, what issues you will link it with, what voices you will provide, and what messages you will communicate. Your issue can be reexplored in terms of media opportunities. Strategies can then be developed to frame for access and frame for content. Framing for access and framing for content force us to think in terms of the media and its needs.

In reality, most community-based organizations do not have the resources or training to use mass media effectively. In this example, the community-based organizations were in a reactive position. Community groups can anticipate similar situations, prepare their policy solutions, and determine how they want them framed in media coverage. Articulating this vision is the hard work of media advocacy. It is then that media advocacy can effectively be used to help communities claim the power and confidence they need to tell their story better.

Notes

1. Quote from Burns is copyright © 1989 by The New York Times Company. Reprinted by permission.

2. Quotes by Mark Hertsgaard from *Rolling Stone*, May 30, 1991, by Straight Arrow Publishers, Inc. 1991. All rights reserved. Reprinted by permission.

4

THINKING MEDIA ADVOCACY

For advocates, the press is a grand piano waiting for a player. Strike the chords through a news story, a guest column, or an editorial and thousands will hear. Working in concert, unbiased reporters and smart advocates can make music together.
—Susan Wilson, New Jersey Network for Family Life

This chapter defines and illustrates the basic tactics for gaining access to the media and framing the issue to tell the story from a progressive public health perspective. As we cover the different elements of media advocacy, do not lose sight of your overall strategy. For example, some people worry a lot about being able to get the media to show up to an event or cover a story, but give little attention to the problem of what to say, or how to say it, when journalists do show up. Planning, flexibility, and the ability to assess continually the connection between media needs and your policy goals is essential.

Access Points

We live in a media-rich environment with constantly expanding outlets. Common outlets for access include newspapers, radio, television, billboards, newsletters—anything that can get your message out. Within each medium there are several possibilities for gaining access, depending on how you frame your story.

Table 4.1 Media Outlets

Medium	Access Points
Television	News, public affairs, entertainment, paid advertising, editorials, public service advertising
Newspapers	Front page, sports, life-style, paid advertising, arts, comics, financial, letters to the editor, editorial, op-ed page
Radio	News, paid advertising, talk shows, editorials, public service advertising
Billboards	Paid placement

The first step is to become a student of the media—find out what your local resources are. It is a good idea to monitor your local media to see what kinds of coverage your issue is being given, where the coverage is, and who is providing the coverage. For example, you might find a story about beer industry sponsorship of local cultural events on the life-style page, the business page, the music page, sports page, or anywhere in the newspaper. Recently, tobacco policy issues have even shown up on the comics page as the "Doonesbury" strip has focused sharp attention on how tobacco companies target youth. Television has regular news programs, magazine news shows, public affairs programming, and free speech or editorial announcements. Each media outlet contains within it several possibilities for coverage. Knowing your issue and knowing your media are fundamental to taking full advantage of available resources. Table 4.1 provides a summary of major media outlets and their related access points.

Strategies

Although there are many access points, there are essentially three strategies to gain access: paying for it, earning it, and asking for it. Asking involves going the public service advertising route and will not be discussed here except to note that this is the format in which advocates are least able to control placement of their story or frame it in an appropriate way. Media advocacy strategies use paid placements and earned media.

Paid Placements

Paid placements are the surest way to see that your message reaches the people you target. There are several advantages to using paid media in your mix of strategies. When you pay for placement you can control the content of your message and the audience that it reaches. Television stations are unlikely to accept public service advertisements (PSAs) that are even potentially controversial (Hammond, Freimuth, & Morrison, 1987). This means that PSAs that get on the air are conservative messages that emphasize the dos and don'ts of personal health behavior. For example, messages that say don't drink and drive are acceptable, but a PSA encouraging popular involvement in local alcohol availability issues is not likely to be seen. Newspapers do not generally donate space for public service messages so paid placement may be the only way to make your voice heard through that outlet. (The Partnership for a Drug-Free America has been successful in getting newspapers to donate space. For example, *The New York Times* commonly runs full-page Partnership advertisements; see also Chapter 3.)

Controlling content and placement are two important reasons for buying time. A third reason is timing. Often it is important to take advantage of unfolding events to maximize the impact of your message. Tony Schwartz, a guerrilla media guru, created radio spots keying off the crash of a 747 jumbo jet to emphasize that the number of people dying from tobacco-related diseases was the equivalent of 920 fully loaded jumbo jets crashing every year.

Gar Mahood of Canadians for Non-Smokers' Rights has used full-page print advertisements to speak directly to legislators at critical points in the development of public policy. For example, at a critical stage in the legislative process of the Tobacco Products Control Act, the Canadian Non-Smokers' Rights Association took out a full-page ad in the *Toronto Globe and Mail* to reach a House of Commons committee working on the legislation (Mintz, 1990). The advertisement included a picture of the prime minister, whose party controlled the committee, and his close friend, who had just been appointed president of the Canadian Tobacco Manufacturers Council. The headline above the pictures of these two men stated: "How Many Thousands of Canadians Will Die From Tobacco Industry Products May Be in the Hands of These Two Men." The text of the ad explained the importance of the legislation and highlighted the relationship between the two key players. It ended with an appeal to the prime minister to act in the interests of future generations with the statement that the lobbyist would understand. Mintz (1990) explains, "The ad devastated [the lobbyists'] influence by personalizing the tobacco lobby and making whatever success it might have politically damaging to [the prime minister]" (p. 31). The legislation passed and the ad certainly was a significant contribution. It was timed, it was finely targeted, it shed light on the specific issue of conflict of interest so that it could not be ignored, and it attracted notice and controversy by suggesting the prime minister might be influenced more by the tobacco industry than by concern for the public's health. There was no alternative to the use of paid media in the Canadian case. The investment paid big dividends for the advancement of antitobacco forces and the health of Canadians.

The cost of paid placements is often thought to be prohibitive. While sometimes this may be the case, local radio and television time can be relatively inexpensive, as can local newspaper space. Strategic billboard buys can also help you place your message where you want it. Remember, however, that in addition to buying time or space, you must consider the costs of production. Production costs for local radio spots or newspaper ads can be reasonable. Television production, on the other hand, can be quite costly. It is also important to note that media outlets can and have rejected more controversial ads. This still provides opportunities for advocacy that we discuss later in this chapter.

Paid placements can generate a great deal of additional free media coverage. For example, the Advocacy Institute purchased a full-page ad in the *Washington Times* making a "drug-free challenge" to William Bennett, who was President Bush's two-pack-a-day nominee to be the nation's drug czar. The purpose of the advertisement was to raise the issue of nicotine as an addictive drug and smoking as a drug problem. Advocates also created a 60-second radio spot, reinforcing the basic message of the print ad for the local Washington, DC, market. They hoped that senators would question Bennett about tobacco issues during his confirmation hearings—and that happened and more.

Compared with the almost $40,000 a similar ad would cost in the *Washington Post*, the *Washington Times* ad cost only $3,800. The ads themselves were newsworthy, and several news organizations ran stories about them (e.g., the *New York Post, USA Today*, and the *Washington Post*). Thus a relatively small amount of money bought not only the readership of the *Washington Times* (just under 100,000) but readers, listeners, and viewers of other major outlets, reaching a population estimated in excess of 7.5 million people. One notable reference to the Bennett issue occurred in a *New York Times* editorial on the confirmation of President Bush's cabinet nominations: "For William Bennett, what's relevant is smoking, period. He cannot plausibly lead the national drive against drug addiction while himself addicted, two packs a day, to nicotine" ("In Defense," 1989, p. A26).

Paid placements are a strategic weapon in the media advocacy arsenal to be used sparingly, if only because of the cost. And, too, there is a downside to paid placements. You can make the opposition extremely angry, rendering future cooperation on related issues impossible. As with all media strategies it is important to keep the long-term goal in mind and continually ask whether the immediate activity contributes to overall goal attainment.

Earned Media

Getting your message on the news is the core of media advocacy. Some people think of this as free coverage because you do not have to pay for it. The reality is that you need to work hard to get your message on the news. All the time and effort that goes into this is far from free. Thus it is more appropriately called *earned* media.

News coverage can be reactive or proactive. Journalists often call on people who work in public health or social service agencies to comment on a story. For example, a health-care provider might receive a phone call and be asked to make a comment regarding the effects of a budget cut on provision of services. This kind of call makes many people feel uncomfortable, as fears of going public and being visible on the media combine with the pressure of little or no notice to organize your thoughts and consider what you might say. Reacting to a story often means that the story already has been framed and you are being called on to provide a necessary, but predetermined perspective—it is likely that the reporter already knows what he or she would like you to say to fill in the picture. In a story told on the *CBS Morning News* about designated drivers, Lawrence Wallack was the designated skeptic. CBS edited Wallack's interview and placed it at the very end of a 3-minute story to show the other side of the issue. By responding to an overall positive analysis of designated drivers, Wallack was positioned on the fringe, even though his position reflected that of major prevention groups in the alcohol field.

When you are the marginal voice squeezed into the final few seconds, the value of the piece may be limited.

Another story on the designated driver concept, which aired as part of the "American Agenda" series on the *ABC Evening News*, came out differently. While the story reportedly started out to highlight the designated driver strategy, the reporter's background interviews with alcohol control advocates repeatedly questioned the appropriateness of the strategy. Consequently, she reframed the story. For the first time, a strategy that previously had received almost universally uncritical coverage in the media had serious questions raised about it, and viewers were exposed to alternative perspectives.

Media advocates emphasize working proactively by seeking opportunities to frame the story and force opponents to respond to points or defend their position. When Surgeon General Koop released his recommendations to prevent drunk driving in 1989, groups in several cities mobilized to promote the story. One of the most striking aspects of the television coverage generated by the group working in the San Francisco area was the degree to which the alcohol policy advocates were able to define the coverage and put the alcohol industry in the marginal opposition role. In some stories, the industry did not appear on air but only had their position described by the reporter.

There are a number of general ways to achieve news coverage proactively. First, it is important to cultivate relationships with members of the local media. You can start by reviewing your newspapers and watching the various newscasts to assess which journalists are interested in which issues. Package some material and send it to them with a note about your interests. For example, if you are involved with a coalition to reduce infant mortality you might put together some fact sheets on rates in your community compared with rates in other places. You could provide a brief description of the principal determinants of infant mortality and illustrate how these play out in your community. When providing materials to journalists the cardinal rule is that accuracy is the highest value. All data should be referenced so that it is clear where they came from.

Journalists need information and ideas for stories that have importance for the local community. Advocates need to think of themselves as resources who can make it easier for journalists to do a good job. Useful accurate data, examples of local activities, a summary of key issues, and names of potential sources can serve this purpose.

A second way to draw news coverage to your topic is to create news. This is somewhat easier than it sounds. You have to remember that your group's activities may be more newsworthy than you think, and you may have to redefine your idea of what constitutes news. Opportunities to create news exist everyday. For example, the release of a report can be newsworthy, as can a community demonstration to highlight some problem. The Center for Science in the Public Interest (CSPI), a Washington, DC, advocacy group, conducted a small study in a few classrooms in a Washington, DC, area school. Students in a fourth-grade classes were asked to name U.S. presidents and brands of beer. The children were able to name more beer brands than presidents and were more likely to spell the brand names correctly than the names of the presidents. CSPI designed the study to gain access, and there was a great deal of news coverage because the story dealt with issues about which people are very concerned—education, youth, and alcohol.

A more scientifically sophisticated research project found that young children were as likely to identify Joe Camel (spokesanimal for Camel cigarettes) as they were Mickey Mouse (Fischer, Schwartz, Richards, Goldstein, & Rojas, 1991). These findings along with related research (DiFranza et al., 1991; Pierce et al., 1991) were published in the *Journal of the American Medical Association* and generated widespread media coverage. The coverage highlighted the health and ethical issues inherent in companies marketing tobacco to youth.

A group in Illinois, trying to draw attention to the problem of hungry children in their town, used a different approach (Amidei, 1991). To get their point across they started a letter-writing campaign on paper plates. They made their point, recruited new participants, and learned a couple of interesting lessons. First, people who had never written letters to a legislator felt comfortable writing letters on paper plates. The paper plate seemed to take the edge off of a serious issue and allowed more people to feel all right about participating. Second, the paper plate campaign attracted the attention of journalists. This generated good local coverage, and afterward people contacted the program to volunteer. A story in the *Washington Post* inspired a letter from the White House (Amidei, 1991, p. 47).

A final example involves the "Erase and Replace" initiative of the Milwaukee Coalition Against Drug and Alcohol Abuse. This initiative sought to reduce outdoor alcohol advertising in Milwaukee's African-American community. The group combined a picnic in a city park with a road rally, which involved an assessment of billboard content across the city. As each car team returned, volunteers placed its data on a billboard constructed in the park to record the results. Extensive media coverage meant heightened visibility and legitimacy for the project, provided positive and immediate feedback for participants, and commanded the attention of the billboard companies in a way that other strategies had not.

A third way to attract news coverage is to piggyback onto breaking news. Linking your issue to an existing story or finding a news peg can get your story into the media. As an illustration one can look at high school graduation, a story routinely covered by local news media, as an opportunity to highlight drinking and driving issues among teenagers. A story on the lack of enforcement of alcohol sales to minors can be pegged to the graduation story and thereby be more newsworthy than at another time of year. In planning media strategy, it is good to keep in mind natural news pegs (Ryan, 1991) such as graduation, holidays, the first day of summer, or any other local event or time that might be used as a meaningful context for your story.

Every day news occurs that has implications for health and social welfare. Media advocates can use these opportunities to contribute to coverage of a policy issue. To test out this idea, pick up a copy of your local newspaper. Carefully look through each section and assess the opportunities for localizing one of the national stories or building on one of the local stories. Tobacco advocates have been remarkably successful using this strategy. For example, when the federal government ordered a halt to all imports of Chilean fruit because of the discovery of cyanide on two grapes, tobacco control advocates converted this to a local story. Various communities held news conferences emphasizing that the amount of cyanide in one cigarette exceeded that found in more than a bushel of grapes. This presentation raised the policy issue of why the government would act so quickly and restrictively on one product, while ignoring another common but more lethal product (Wallack & Sciandra, 1990-1991).

Other coverage in news media that can be extremely important includes editorial pieces, letters to the editor, op-ed pieces, and talk show appearances. Meetings with editorial boards can result in supportive editorials. All newspapers have an editorial board even if it consists of just one person. This board decides the position that the newspaper takes on particular issues. During a campaign for a ballot initiative in California to increase the excise tax on alcohol, both sides targeted the editorial boards of newspapers. Both groups met with boards (at different times) and stated their position, provided background material, and responded to questions.

When meeting with an editorial board it is important to have no more than three people and prepare background documents to leave with the board. Practically, it is a good idea to read the local paper and have a good sense of the editorial bent of the paper before you visit. Make sure you anticipate possible objections to your position that are particular to the community served by the paper. In emphasizing the value of your position make sure you link it to potential local benefits. For example, when advocates met with the editorial board of a newspaper in California's wine country they knew that the board would be concerned about the economic effects and would be supportive of economic arguments from the groups that opposed the alcohol tax increase. Although you cannot always convince the editorial board to support your position (only two newspapers in the entire state supported the alcohol tax) your presentation could influence the board in moderating their position against you. Also, whether or not you succeed with a particular presentation, by establishing contact and presenting yourself as a knowledgeable professional and willing source for future stories and editorials on the topic, you can contribute to your long-term goals.

Op-ed pieces are an opportunity to get your story out to opinion leaders and policymakers. These pieces should deal with a specific issue, highlight contradictions, emphasize local importance, and present some specific policy to be considered or action to be taken. Letters to the editor can be used to support or criticize news stories, editorials, or op-ed pieces.

A final point for getting your story out is news-talk radio. Talk radio is an opportunity to get your issue on people's personal agendas. The audience may not necessarily be the opinion leaders that you might most want to reach, but they are potential supporters. Americans listen to a lot of talk radio. Approximately 95% of those aged 12 or older listen to the radio, and depending on the time of day, 10% to 15% of them are tuned in to talk radio. On average, people spend almost 8 hours per week with news-talk radio (Arbitron Company, 1991), and this time will increase as the population ages. Generally, talk radio is easy to access and can provide an opportunity for extended discussion, in addition to allowing you to reach a broad and sometimes motivated audience. Talk radio can have considerable impact, as was the case when the public interest group Congress Watch served as a catalyst to block congressional pay raises—radio stations all over the country picked up on this issue. Mandrake, an African-American activist in Chicago, used talk radio shows to gain exposure and support for a campaign to remove alcohol and tobacco billboards in the black community (Smikle, 1991). Other groups have successfully used talk radio to mobilize political action, make people aware of health issues and services, and recruit new members (Aufderheide & Chester, 1990).

Talk radio provides some useful opportunities for advocacy but like other outlets needs to be thought of in a proactive way so that it fits in with an overall media strategy. As with other media outlets it is important to know the different talk radio formats and who the audience is for particular broadcasts. Reacting to talk show requests without knowledge about the style of the program can be a problem. For example, while speaking at a conference in New Zealand, Wallack was asked to do a telephone interview with a well-known talk show host. He agreed but found out little about the person or show. He was taken aback when the interview immediately became hostile. Local friends later told him that hostility was part of this very conservative person's on-air style. But Wallack's lack of advance knowledge about the host's style limited his ability to get his point across.

Talk shows want to cover topics that are of interest to their audience. This can mean any number of things. Pocketbook issues are important as are other media factors such as timeliness, controversy, conflict, personal impact, and local relevance. Getting on talk shows involves the same principles as getting news coverage. You need to develop a relationship with your local station so that you are seen as trustworthy, rooted in the community, and credible. Sending a brief summary of your issue with possible guests and following up with a phone call is a good way to start the process. As Aufderheide and Chester (1990) explain, "The basic method is simple: get a list of the talk shows you need for your issue, and call and write them" (p. 14). For example, if your organization puts out a newsletter with interesting local information you should send a copy to radio stations with a cover letter. Be sure to name a contact person. You can also use this opportunity to offer some ideas about topics for future shows.

It is very important to understand the style of the talk show so that you can be prepared. Some groups avoid talk radio because they feel that they are used as a lightning rod for audience anger or as a target of abuse by the host. Talk shows can also be particularly frustrating because of the constant barrage of commercials and breaks for news, weather, and sports. The actual air time you have might be very limited. Nevertheless, talk radio presents a forum in which you can discuss issues in depth while reaching a specific and relatively large audience.

Framing Tactics

The tightly interrelated principles of access and framing are the dynamic duo of media advocacy. The degree to which these principles are integrated and practiced will largely determine if your message says what you want it to say and whether it is communicated through the mass media.

Framing stories is a difficult task because the public health version of the story will usually run counter to the accepted commonsense view of the world. For example, the advocate sees advertising by the alcoholic beverage industry as a contributing cause to alcohol-impaired driving problems and tries to frame the story to highlight the responsibility of the alcohol industry. Corporate irresponsibility might be the frame in contrast to the usual frame of individual responsibility and personal choice evidenced in "Don't drink and drive" messages. The narrower focus on individual responsibility resonates well with our commonsense view that individual autonomy is our primary value; it needs little justification. On the other hand, the focus on advertising is physically far removed from the driver and the car and conceptually far removed from ideas of immediate and direct causation. It fits less neatly with a simple, commonsense understanding of the world. Hence, the oppositional view requires some degree of explanation to make the point. The challenge of framing is to take a more complex (and realistically more complete) understanding of a problem and make it resonate succinctly with the values of the intended audience.

It bears remembering that because the media advocate usually challenges the everyday understanding of what constitutes health problems and the best way to address these problems, the message is in opposition to, rather than in accordance with, what most people believe. This means that the advocates' message tends to be complicated rather than simple, longer rather than shorter, and contrary to rather than consistent with popular understanding. Even more problematic is that the public often perceives the public health message as negative in that the policies being advocated are perceived as placing limits on rather than extending individual choice and opportunity.

For the most part this means that we have to explain, our opponents just have to state; we need to change people's minds, they just need to reinforce what people already think; we need to emphasize shared responsibility, they just need to highlight personal choice. All this adds up to a difficult and complex task for the media advocate. It means constantly swimming against the current of popular belief and questioning the legitimacy of those who have considerable power. Nonetheless, creative, committed media advocates around the country have shown it can be done and that success is possible.

Episodic Versus Thematic: The Framing Dilemma

An essential task of the advocate is to frame social and health issues in a social and political context to highlight public policy approaches rather than personal-behavioral solutions. However, the journalist looks to the individual or episodic frame as a way of organizing the facts of a story to draw the attention of the viewer. This contributes to the very thing that the advocate wants to move away from—reinforcing an individual-level definition of cause and solution. To accommodate journalists' needs, the advocate will often have to use an individualistic frame to gain initial access and later try to reframe the issue using a broader social perspective. Framing for access then will often involve presenting personal stories that highlight the face of the victim for a particular problem rather than going right to the policy focus. Focusing on the policy aspect or framing for content addresses the challenge of shaping the story to reflect the policy dimensions and will be covered in more detail below.

Framing for Access

To gain access to journalists, media advocates have to structure stories so they meet the criteria of what constitutes news. Table 4.2 lists some common features of newsworthy stories. Structuring a story around these conventions of newsworthiness can enhance the prospects for

Table 4.2 Framing for Access: Elements of Newsworthy Stories

Anniversary peg	Can this story be associated with a local, national, or topical historical event?
Breakthrough	What is new or different about this story?
Celebrity	Is there a celebrity already involved with or willing to lend his or her name to the issue?
Controversy	Are there adversaries or other tensions in this story?
Injustice	Are there basic inequalities or unfair circumstances?
Irony	What is ironic, unusual, or inconsistent about this story?
Local peg	Why is this story important or meaningful to local residents?
Milestone	Is this story an important historical marker?
Personal angle	Who is the face of the victim in this story? Who has the authentic voice on this issue?
Seasonal peg	Can this story be attached to a holiday or seasonal event?

obtaining access to the media. In many stories several of these factors come together. The more newsworthy elements your story contains and the broader the audience it can interest, the more likely it will show up on the evening news.

Controversy

Media outlets tend to assume that if an issue is controversial, audiences and readers will want to know about it, and will tune in or buy newspapers to find out about it. Recently, tobacco and alcohol control advocates have been able to capitalize on the controversy concerning marketing to youth and racial-ethnic populations. When the surgeon general's recommendations on drunk driving (described in detail in Chapter 5) were being pitched to journalists, one of the key themes was the controversy generated by the alcohol industry's efforts to stop the meeting at which the recommendations were developed. The pitch that helped get the interest of the media was "These are the recommendations that the alcohol industry did not want people to see."

Lately, commercial advertisers have developed a new approach to the creative use of controversy. The goal is to use a little bit of paid media to gain substantial free time through electronic and print news coverage (Rothenberg, 1990). For example, in late 1989 a manufacturer of cold remedies used images of then-presidents Bush and Gorbachev to illustrate this slogan: "In the new year, may the only cold war in the world be the one being fought by us" (Rothenberg, 1990, p. D1). When two networks rejected the ad, it became controversial and newsworthy, and aired many times as part of news broadcasts.

In another case, when three New York City television stations refused to air an advertisement for an aerosol drug-detection device to help parents determine if their children were using drugs, the manufacturer took out a full-page ad in *The New York Times*. This ad showed a photo board of the television ad and led to news coverage of the controversy (Levin, 1990). When Neighbor to Neighbor, an advocacy group concerned with Central American issues, tried to place a television ad urging a boycott of Proctor and Gamble's Folgers brand coffee, several stations rejected the ad. One station did accept the ad, only to have Proctor and Gamble withdraw all their advertising. This controversy generated national attention. Coverage in *Time, Business Week, The New York Times*, and major television networks brought the advocacy groups' issue into the spotlight. The media director of Neighbor to Neighbor told *Advertising Age* that the ad "probably got thousands and thousands of dollars of free publicity for an ad that cost us less than $5,000 to make and get on the air. . . . The publicity that was generated around it was publicity we could never have bought" (Levin, 1990, p. 76).

This planned approach to controversy has special relevance to advocacy groups whose political positions sometimes result in their paid advertisements or public service announcements not being aired. When the response to your effort becomes the issue, your issue still gains coverage.

Milestone

Framing an event as a milestone from which future progress will be marked is a good way of emphasizing the importance of an event. For example, groups publicizing the surgeon general's recommendations on drunk driving described the report as equivalent to the 1964 surgeon general's report on smoking and health. This clearly framed it as a milestone that would serve as an important historical mark. It was helpful that Dr. Koop had made a similar analogy in his comments published in the report.

Anniversary

Anniversaries present a good news peg for journalists. Many stories revisit an issue after some period of time has elapsed. The anniversary of an event provides opportunities to develop related stories. For example, the anniversary of a tragic shooting such as the one that occurred in a Stockton, California, schoolyard in 1989 presents a vehicle for approaching a journalist with a story updating the number of firearm deaths and reviewing legislative progress in this area. In the same way, when the 25th anniversary report of the surgeon general's report on smoking came out, many communities used this event to highlight current smoking and health issues. In Vallejo, California, a front-page story on a sting operation in which underage youth easily were able to purchase tobacco products began with the following lead: "In an event marking the 25th anniversary of a landmark health report that linked cigarettes with cancer and heart disease, local health organizations . . ." (de la Torre, 1989, p. A1). You can anticipate anniversaries particular to your field or region and craft news stories around them. In the San Francisco Bay Area, anniversaries of the Golden Gate bridge generate news stories. Other regions will have similar routines.

Seasonality

Seasonal events are built into the calendar and are potential news pegs. High school graduation, the first day of summer, the opening of spring training for baseball players, major holidays, and the first day of school all present opportunities for stories. If a group is concerned about skin cancer, the start of summer vacation presents an excellent opportunity for access. For stories on youth and drunk driving, one of the prime opportunities for access is the high school prom season. New Year's is the natural season for general drunk driving stories. Surgeon General Koop's recommendations on drunk driving were deliberately released within a week of the Memorial Day holiday to capitalize on media interest in what is often a tragic weekend for alcohol-impaired driving fatalities.

Tobacco-control activists know that the "Great American Smoke-Out" held annually in November is a good time to be ready with fresh angles on what many journalists think is an old story but one that their editors insist they cover. Other health issues may have their own natural holidays. For example, nutrition activists might focus on Valentine's Day to highlight policy issues around diet and heart disease. Similarly, those working on infant mortality might use Mother's Day as a theme.

Ethnic and religious holidays also provide special opportunities for approaching news outlets with health issues. Cinco de Mayo, Juneteenth, Kwanzaa, and the Chinese New Year each provide opportunities for shaping health stories regarding the particular community involved.

Irony

Reversing a conventional situation or framing stories as out of the ordinary can enhance access. Journalists call this *a man bites dog story.* According to Romano (1987), this is the type of story that freezes the reader's cup of coffee—or at least the arm holding it—in midair (pp. 44-45). His example is a headline from the *Philadelphia Inquirer:* "Guest Drowns at Party for 100 Lifeguards." The story involves a man who drowned in a New Orleans city pool at a party attended by 100 lifeguards that was held to celebrate the first summer in memory without a drowning (Romano, 1987, p. 44). Although this is an unusual example, it provides a good sense of how journalists use irony.

Many child abuse stories use irony, emphasizing that someone who had the social role of protector ended up to be an abuser. When a father of the year, a clergy person, or a teacher is charged with child abuse, the news value of the story, for better or worse, is enhanced by the contradiction between the position and the behavior. For example, a physician in Arizona who was a leading expert on child abuse and had won many awards was charged with child abuse and sexual molestation. The contrast between his expertise and his reported behavior provided the ironic contrast that made this story more newsworthy than other child abuse stories (Johnson, 1989a).

The media advocacy initiative to focus attention on the confirmation hearings of William Bennett (presented earlier) made good use of irony. Advocates in this case emphasized the fact that President Bush had appointed an active tobacco addict to fill the post of drug czar. Irony, in this case, was successfully used to contrast the addictive quality of a legal substance (tobacco) with illegal, but less lethal, substances.

In 1991, community activists were surprised to find out that popular singer Gloria Estefan received $18 million from Bacardi rum to sponsor a musical tour. Estefan had worked with the federal Office for Substance Abuse Prevention on a campaign to urge children not to start using alcohol or other drugs. The activists used the irony in Estefan's contrasting positions of urging children not to drink and then being associated with the promotion of a youth-oriented alcoholic product to get media attention. The all-important first two paragraphs of a story in the *San Diego Tribune* read as follows:

> As a former spokesperson for the federal government's Office of [sic] Substance Abuse Prevention, Gloria Estefan used to warn kids: "Get [sic] Smart, Don't Start."
>
> Now, Estefan appears to be encouraging people to start drinking alcohol . . . providing they drink the proper brand. (Godfrey, 1991, p. E4)

An example from the tobacco field is the finding that very young children are more likely to recognize cigarette-pushing Joe Camel than the well-loved children's friend Mickey Mouse. The irony lies in both the contrast between the two characters and the claims of advertisers that their ads do not appeal to youth.

Celebrity

One of the surest ways to gain access to the media is to enlist a celebrity to be involved in your issue. Celebrities attract audiences and ensure media attention. During the controversy about alar on apples, Mothers and Others for Pesticide Limits made good use of celebrities. After a Washington news conference in which actress Meryl Streep announced the formation of this new group, it was covered on the *Today* show, on *Phil Donahue*, on the front page of *USA Today* and numerous other newspapers, in magazines, and on electronic outlets ("How PR Firm," 1989). Each interview and each news report served as a building block in setting the agenda of the American people. However, there is a downside to working with celebrities. The Gloria Estefan story discussed above illustrates the danger of relying on celebrities. In so doing, you are harnessing your issue to their personal decisions, which may backfire.

The federal government has been embarrassed several times by celebrities who participated in antidrug efforts and then attracted attention because of their drug-related behavior.

Most advocacy groups try to include a celebrity in the witness list when legislative hearings are held on policy issues. The presence of a celebrity can almost guarantee the media attention. In 1990, when AIDS groups were trying to obtain more funding for AIDS care as opposed to AIDS research, a leading AIDS lobbyist with more than 10 years' experience in Washington arrived at the Capitol at 7:00 a.m. one morning to make sure that all arrangements were in place for an 11:00 a.m. news conference on the bill. Much to his surprise, at that early hour, the line of television crews and reporters waiting to enter the hearing room where the news conference was to take place extended far down the hallway. In all his years in Washington he had never seen such an advance on a news conference. What brought out the media? Elizabeth Taylor was to speak at the news conference.

Breakthrough

Many of those who have worked with the media know that journalists often ask, "What is new or different about this?" The concept of breakthrough can be constructed to include not only some sort of technological or medical change but also some kind of social or political one. For example, the breakthrough aspect of a story can focus on bringing together diverse groups that have not cooperated before, such as efforts to find common ground between proabortion and antiabortion groups. Related to the concept of milestone, a breakthrough can be any sign that basic assumptions about an issue have fundamentally changed. Advocates mobilizing against malt liquor marketing in the early 1990s framed the response of the BATF, the primary regulatory agency on alcohol policy, as a breakthrough: It was the first time that BATF had taken action in clear response to public outcry from the alcohol control movement. Advocates predicted that this would herald a change in how BATF would operate from that time forward.

Localize and Personalize

Jacqueline Teare, a correspondent for Newhouse News Service, explains, "Localize the information. Give the editor a reason for getting their paper involved in the story. Give the editor a reason why their readers would care about the issue" (quoted in Duncan, Rivlin, Williams, & Orgata, 1990). Media outlets know that they have a responsibility to be responsive to local issues and that everyone is interested in how events will affect him or her as an individual and as a family member. Localizing a story enhances the probability that a media outlet will pick it up. Many breaking stories on the national level have implications for communities all across the country. Changes in policy mean that local people may have more or less risk of a problem or will have to pay more or less in taxes, insurance, medical, or social welfare costs. When you localize and personalize a story, you focus on the meaning it has for the average community member of a significant group in the community. For example, early in 1993 when the U.S. Environmental Protection Agency (EPA) released a report establishing environmental tobacco smoke as a carcinogen comparable to radon and other well-known risks, local media outlets wanted to know what might happen locally as a result of the report. How high was the risk in terms of disease and lives lost? Would local employers who allowed smoking face liability lawsuits for workers who became ill? Would all restaurants be forced to go smoke free?

Injustice

Injustice is a powerful hook on which to frame a story. Fairness and equity are basic values for most American people, and individuals respond strongly when these are violated. For example, the media typically use an injustice frame when an insurance company cancels someone's coverage after the person has paid premiums for years or when a worker is fired after a lifetime of service. Injustice involves the system not working the way it should for people, the powerful mistreating the powerless, or other fundamental violations of American values and rights. Discrimination, limited opportunity, and lack of due process are potential injustice hooks.

AIDS activists used an injustice frame to build support for more federal resources for the care of persons with AIDS to supplement research funds already allocated to this issue. They named the legislation for Ryan White, a child with AIDS. His mother served as a key lobbyist and spokeswoman for the bill. The use of Ryan White as a symbol highlighted two aspects central to this particular injustice frame: (a) the basic unfairness of someone so young dying and (b) that no matter how one feels about AIDS, it is unjust to punish people with AIDS by denying them access to medical care.

A successful access frame draws the attention of the journalist and convinces him or her that the topic is newsworthy. Telling a simple, short story with a human face is often a good way to start. Integrating the factors discussed above and highlighting the importance of the story to the local community will further enhance your chances. The danger of this kind of framing is that it may not move the issue beyond an individual's experience of it and so may act to reinforce the very perception you are trying to change—that this is a personal problem rather than a social issue.

Most stories have elements of both episodic and thematic framing. In developing your story, it is important to keep in mind framing for content as well as framing for access.

Framing for Content

The very difficult challenge of media advocacy is to reframe the dominant view of health problems from individual matters to public issues. The media advocate's goal is to frame the content of the story to reflect the social justice perspective. Table 4.3 summarizes some basic steps in framing for content.

The alcohol and tobacco advocates have been very successful in re-framing issues to a public policy perspective. The tobacco industry, once seen as invincible because of strong support from politicians, has suffered several serious setbacks in recent years on the policy front. Things that we take for granted now seemed highly unlikely just a few years ago. The smoking ban on airplanes, continuing expansion of policies to limit indoor smoking, and increases in excise taxes are just a few examples of hard-won victories by advocates. These policy changes would not be seen as necessary or even relevant if the tobacco industry had been allowed to get away with framing smoking solely as an issue of individual choice and personal courtesy. The effective use of the mass media has been instrumental in resetting the agenda, reframing the issue, and promoting public policies for tobacco control.

The first step in framing for content is to translate what are commonly seen as individual problems (e.g., alcoholism) to social or public policy issues (e.g., promotion and availability of alcohol). The focus shifts from

Table 4.3 Framing for Content

- Translate individual problem to social issue
- Shift primary responsibility away from blaming the individual
- Present solution
- Make practical or policy appeal
- Develop story elements
  Create compelling pictures and images
  Do the social math
  Identify authentic voices
  Identify compelling symbols
- Tailor to audience

---

the person with the problem to the way that we as a society organize the environment through which alcohol is made available. For example, the Marin Institute issued a news release about drinking patterns in Marin County. Journalists wanted to interview an alcoholic to provide some pictures for the story. A recovering alcoholic agreed to an interview but immediately shifted the focus onto the behavior of the alcoholic beverage industry and its advertising practices. Framing for access—localizing and personalizing the story with a face of the victim—was transformed into framing for content.

The second step is to shift primary responsibility for the problem to the industry or other institutional or environmental actor or factor. The purpose of this is to counter the blame-the-victim strategy of the industry, which capitalizes on the same tendency in the larger society. An advocate's effort to focus on the activities of the alcoholic beverage industry as contributory causes to alcohol problems may be interpreted as absolving the individual of responsibility. On the contrary, the advocate's goal is to emphasize the shared responsibility and the unfair distribution of the burden for change. Thus the response to the commonly asked question "Well aren't the parents really responsible for kids' drinking?" is "Sure, they have a shared responsibility, but parents need help. Their children are barraged repeatedly with messages to drink through advertising and promotion. These messages are crafted by highly skilled people who have the single goal of making money. What parent can hope to compete with the glitz and sophistication of a multi-million dollar advertising campaign?"

The third step, presenting the solution, usually involves undertaking a broad-ranging approach to policy. Whatever your issue, there is seldom a single answer. The solution must fit your overall policy goals. In the alcohol control field, the surgeon general's recommendations to reduce drunk driving serve as a general blueprint. Depending on the specific topic being addressed, however, there should be a practical appeal to promote a specific policy—the fourth step. For example, one practical appeal on alcohol availability might be zoning limitations on the number and type of liquor outlets in the community. Tobacco control advocates want to support a ban on vending machines, which provide an easy way for youth to obtain cigarettes. Framing for content requires you to think though your overall goals and decide on the specific, tangible actions you want your target audience to take to advance those goals.

In considering how you will approach and interact with the media it is critical to remember that your strongest and most important asset is your credibility. You need to be very careful to provide accurate information and respect the conventions of journalistic practice. Journalists have information needs, and you can be a valuable resource by anticipating and responding to these needs. Information is a form of currency, and you want make sure you do not provide any $3 bills! Numbers, analogies, pictures, images, and symbols can all be used to convey your story, but they must be internally consistent and support your overall point. These can be very powerful in telling your story, but if misused, or not fully understood, they can end up distracting from your argument. These tactics include social math, media bites, authentic voices, symbols, shaming, and visuals.

Social Math

Numbers are one way to substantiate claims about the importance or magnitude of a problem or issue. Generally, the larger the number of people affected, the more likely a problem will be defined as newsworthy by journalists. Big numbers are better than little numbers, official numbers are better than unofficial numbers, and big, official numbers are superior to all (Best, 1989). Big numbers, however, are effective only if they can be made meaningful to the audience. We are continually bombarded with numbers too big to comprehend, such as trillion-dollar budgets, billion-dollar deficits, and millions of people affected by a specific problem. The numbers are overwhelming and numbing. The challenge is not so much to emphasize big numbers as to produce meaningful numbers.

Michael Daube, an Australian tobacco control activist, introduced the concept of creative epidemiology as a way of making data interesting to the media and understandable for the audience. It requires the marriage of the solid science of the researcher with the creativity of the advocate to meet the needs of the audience (Advocacy Institute, 1989a). The concept of creative epidemiology makes some people uncomfortable because *creative* might be construed as an inappropriate manipulation of data. On the contrary, because using data this way draws more attention to them, advocates should expect journalists to scrutinize them even more closely than usual. Hence, more than the usual care and attention to detail is essential to confirm the scientific basis of the point being made. Overall, "social math" might be a more appropriate rubric than creative epidemiology because the point really is to understand numbers and issues in their broad social context.

Pertschuk and Wilbur (1991) specify three approaches to the process of making large numbers meaningful: localization, relativity, and effects of public policy. Localizing involves taking large numbers and applying them to a particular community. For example, tobacco control advocates might talk about the number of people in a particular area dying per day or week from smoking rather than using the national statistic of more than 400,000 deaths per year. Advocates in Australia developed a death clock, prominently displayed, which showed the cumulative number of people who had died there from smoking. Localizing cost data is also important. Advocates can translate billions of dollars of annual costs of major health issues into how much these cost people in a particular region, state, city, or town. You can emphasize the point by comparing the sums to what the money could have bought.

Relativity refers to the comparison of the number with something that is easily identifiable to the audience. For example, a recent study on college drinking reported that college students consume 430 million gallons of alcoholic beverages per year at a cost of $5.5 billion. To convey these data more clearly, it was noted that enough alcohol was consumed by college students to fill 3,500 Olympic-size swimming pools, about 1 on every campus in the United States. It also was estimated that college students consumed approximately 4 billion cans of beer annually, which if stacked end-to-end on top of each other would reach the moon and go

70,000 miles beyond (Eigen, 1991). Although the reader, listener, or viewer may not know whether this level of consumption is good or bad or if it is a problem or not, they will know that it is a lot of beer. The researchers made another powerful comparison: The overall amount spent on alcohol per student exceeded the dollars spent on books and was even far greater than the combined amount of fellowships and scholarships provided to students (Eigen, 1991).

Advocates in South Central Los Angeles seeking to limit the number of liquor stores in the community produced another good example of relativity. After some research, they found that South Central Los Angeles had more liquor stores (728) than 13 individual states combined. Furthermore, the state of Rhode Island, with three times the population of South Central Los Angeles, has just 220 liquor stores (Johnson, 1992). This comparison powerfully makes the point—there is a high concentration of liquor stores in this area!

The creative use of data to promote better understanding of problems is certainly not new. In 1897 Brain included a section about this strategy in his book. Here are three interesting examples:

- Allowing eleven feet frontage for each, the saloons of this country would line both sides of a street reaching from Washington, DC, to Kansas City, Mo.
- The world's production of beer for 1894 was . . . nearly five and one-half billion gallons. Beer-kegs sufficient to hold this quantity would belt the earth seven times at the equator.
- Christendom has introduced into Africa 70,000 gallons of rum for every missionary sent. (pp. 48-49)

One variation on relativity is to make numbers smaller and more familiar. For example, the alcohol industry spends more than $2 billion every year to advertise and promote consumption. This amounts to approximately $225,000 every hour of every day. This latter characterization of the data is no less accurate but probably more understandable and meaningful to the audience. You might want to remember that $1 billion a year translates into roughly $2.7 million per day, $114,000 per hour, and $1,900 per minute.

Another way to highlight a large amount of money is to compare it with the amount being spent on your issue currently. For example, the tobacco industry spends more money promoting smoking in a week than the entire federal government spends on preventing smoking in a year.

One form of relativity that needs careful thought involves comparing your issue with another major health issue to establish the greater importance of your issue. For instance, tobacco control advocates designed a poster noting that tobacco is responsible for more deaths than AIDS, homicide, suicide, traffic crashes, and other forms of death combined. This kind of social math may make the point but miss the larger issue. Coalitions are the key to success in changing public policy and by implicitly minimizing or competing with another health problem you may be alienating a potential ally or undercutting another important effort to promote health.

Using creative epidemiology or social math in the public policy context requires converting the potential policy into some quantitative result. For example, proposed increases in excise taxes could be framed in terms of the large amounts of revenues generated or the relatively small cost per person. Changes in policy regarding alcohol can easily take advantage of extensive economic research that has translated policy changes into lives saved.

However, if numbers are used they must be reliable and you must be able to document where they came from. Creative epidemiology is not playing with numbers; it is the careful application of numbers to enhance the role of research in the public policy process. Numbers that lack a strong scientific basis can detract from your point and damage your credibility. One example of this is the claim that children see 100,000 beer commercials on television by the time they finish high school. Generously assuming that they see equal numbers of commercials over each of their 18 years this would require them to see slightly more than 15 beer commercials per day. Given that sports programs, which have the heaviest concentration of alcohol ads, contain about 7 per event (over usually at least 2 hours), it would probably be impossible to see 100,000 ads even if someone tried. This number, however, was placed in the preamble to a piece of federal legislation to require health messages on alcohol advertising. In his testimony, the president of the Beer Institute ridiculed this number and used its specious nature to cast doubt on the overall legislation. He was right, and it reminds advocates to "know thy numbers" and anticipate an opponent's response.

Using numbers treads a fine line between highlighting a problem and exaggerating a problem. Public health advocates want to increase the perception of risk based on the assumption that this will motivate individuals to take protective action and encourage the media and opinion leaders to pay attention. For example, a strategy commonly used to increase awareness about the risk of HIV infection is to convey information that suggests everyone, and not just some parts of the population, is at high risk. This can backfire if, in fact, the differences between the risks faced by different groups are minimized when the risk is not equal.

One example of risk maximization that created problems was in the area of breast cancer. The last thing a media advocate would want to see is the following headline in the Sunday *New York Times:* "Faulty Math Heightens Fears of Breast Cancer" (Blakeslee, 1992, sec. 4, p. 1). But this did happen and the all-important first paragraph of the story indicated that the risks have been so greatly exaggerated that many women were needlessly exposing themselves to powerful drugs and even surgery. The American Cancer Society used the conventional wisdom that 1 in 9 women will get breast cancer to motivate women to have mammograms. The odds represent a cumulative total. More accurately stated, the data indicated that by the time a woman reaches age 85 her risk will be 1 in 9. Women at age 40 face about a 1 in 1,000 chance of having breast cancer in the next year. This kind of controversy confuses people and causes anxiety, and, regarding media advocacy, it may adversely affect the credibility of the source.

Another problem that media advocates face is using comparisons that do not clearly convey the point they intend. In 1992, California had a deficit of more than $10 billion. A news story indicated that the deficit was larger than the gross national product (GNP) of Ecuador and Tunisia for 1991 (Rheinhold, 1992). It would be interesting to see how many people who read this article could locate these countries on a map much less know what a comparison to their GNP means.

In sum, if you are using math for advocacy, you must be able to understand and defend the data and the way you are presenting the information. It is hardly worth risking your credibility and the importance of your issue to just make a point with data. The opportunities for creative, accurate use of data are considerable, and the value of this tactic is great. Use it with care.

Media Bites

In the 1988 election, the average time that presidential candidates spoke without interruption on network news was 9.8 seconds (Adatto,

1989); in the first 6 months of the 1992 campaign, the average candidate sound bite was 7.3 seconds (Kurtz, 1992). Apparently the key to free speech is short speech. Unfortunately, the need to reduce difficult concepts into a sentence or two risks trivializing important issues and reinforcing superficial understanding. For this reason, the process of developing sound bites may seem distasteful to some advocates. Media biting needs to be seen as part of the overall process of agenda setting and framing. It can be a means for gaining more air time for an issue, and if done well may actually increase audience understanding of the advocate's position.

Media bites are short, concise summaries of your issue or position that can be conveyed in a few sentences or less than 10 seconds. If presidential candidates average under 10 seconds, you should not expect to do much better. Pertschuk and Wilbur (1991) explain that "the media bite can serve to encapsulate both information and effective symbols for an audience that is increasingly used to quick bursts of information" (p. 19). They provide a number of basic points to consider in developing media bites, with the most important being always to keep in mind that the purpose of the media bite is not to make you look clever or good but to advance your policy goal. With the overall goal in mind, media bites should reinforce the important, longer points that you want to make; should avoid moralizing, sloganeering, and sounding contrived; should carefully use humor so as to not detract from the gravity of the problem (irony is probably the best kind of humor to use); and should be clear and authoritative.

The best way to develop media bites is to role-play with your colleagues and develop ideas off your key points. Some people are wonderful at coming up with media bites, but for most people it takes some work. Expect that your media bite may be the only sound bite of you on the news or the only quote in the newspaper. In your interviews repeat it as often as you can fit it in. Here are some examples of media bites:

- "You face more danger with the 20 cigarettes that are in your pocket than any six bullets in somebody's gun" (Ken McFeeley quoted in Shales, 1988, p. D1).

This media bite uses the imagery of a deadly weapon as a chilling comparison for smoking. The source of the quote, a retired police officer who was dying of lung cancer, provides additional power to the bite.

- "Would you want the Mafia underwriting anti-crime programs?" (Andrew McGuire quoted in Abramson, 1991).

This media bite is a response to the efforts of the Century Council, an alcohol industry-sponsored organization, to launch a new alcohol education initiative. The bite points to the irony that the people trying to do something about the problem really have other interests. The reference to the Mafia makes use of a powerful symbol.

- "To claim now that its dangers could not have been foreseen . . . would be like professing surprise that a rifle that could kill a deer could also kill a priest." (Selikof, 1991, p. B7)

In this media bite, Irving Selikoff, of Mount Sinai Medical Center in New York and an authority on asbestos-related diseases, uses a simile to ridicule an assertion that the asbestos in Kent cigarette filters could not be foreseen as a potential health risk. It suggests that the relationship should have been obvious. While this media bite conveys an interesting image, it lacks the clarity, conciseness, and immediacy of the McFeeley and McGuire bites. You have to think about the Selikoff bite, sorting out its logic. On the other hand, the use of the Mafia in the McGuire quote is a symbol that conveys enormous meaning because it serves as shorthand for so many people.

In California, the State Department of Alcoholic Beverage Control was facing a severe budget cut that would severely curtail its efforts to enforce laws prohibiting sales to underage youth. During a brainstorming session, an advocate came up with the following: "Tomorrow your 14-year-old turns 21." This bite was later used on a local newscast. It is an effective summary of the issue even though it is only a 2-second sound bite composed of seven simple words. It suggests that anyone, no matter how young, would be able to purchase alcohol because of the lack of funds for enforcement and conveys an appropriate sense of urgency about the proposed budget cut.

Media bites, by the way, are certainly nothing new. Some may be timeless. A temperance book from the 19th century contained the following under the heading "Quotations": "Grape-juice has killed more than grape-shot" (Brain, 1897, p. 42). Structurally, this is a short, concise quote that makes its point by juxtaposing grape-juice (alcoholic beverages) with grape-shot (warfare and combat).

One way to get the hang of media bites is to study television and print news stories more closely. Notice the media bites and ask yourself how well the bite conveys an image and what other symbols or other words might have been used. Also keep in mind the words of President Clinton's 1992 campaign media strategist. When asked to describe his job, he replied, "Let's say you ask a politician what time it is. Some pol[itician]s will tell you the time. Some will tell you how to build a clock. Bill Clinton will tell you how to build a Swiss Village. The consultant's job is to say: 'Governor, just tell them it's time for a change' " (Kelly, 1992, p. A9).

From the Face of the Victim to Authentic Voices

The media in general and television in particular define the newsworthiness of an issue by how visual it is and by how much human interest is involved. Hence, in putting together a story, the media often try to show the face of the victim. Stories on alcohol or other drug issues usually feature someone in recovery. A story on teenage drinking inevitably will include a teenage alcoholic in recovery. Stories about other drug addiction will focus on people's personal stories. The face of the victim is important because it personalizes the story for the audience, stimulates interest, and usually portrays the person with the problem in a sympathetic light. The problem with this, however, is that this type of framing tends to focus attention on personal problems and not on the social policy approaches that have the greatest potential for adequately addressing the problem. Also, from an ethical perspective, media exposure for people in recovery can add stress to their situation, with potential unintended consequences both positive and negative.

Advocates can broaden the concept of *face of the victim* to *authentic voices.* This term includes people who are deeply involved in the issue in any number of ways and who have essentially won their credibility through their experiences; people who are defined not as victims but as advocates. These people may have been victims in the past, but define themselves on what they are currently doing. Although it may be important to provide an authentic voice to meet the needs of the journalist, it is important to move quickly beyond the personal to the social. For example, one broadcast news story on drunk driving started out with a teenage girl who had been hit by a drunk driver. The teenager worked as an advocate in the story: After establishing her credibility as an authentic voice/victim, she quickly moved on to discuss the policy issues involved in the problem.

Symbols

An Advocacy Institute booklet (1989a) notes that "in scientific journals, *science* frames the issue. In the courts and in scholarly policy debates, *facts and arguments* frame the issue. But in the mass media, science, facts, and arguments are compressed into *labels* and *symbols:* labels and symbols frame the issue" (p. 30). People resonate to symbols that stand for larger ideals and issues. These symbols may be abstract, such as freedom of speech, or concrete, such as a school notebook with a Joe Camel cover. What they have in common is that they stand for something larger and elevate the debate to broader issues.

Politicians make excellent use of symbols and are constantly engaged in positioning themselves around them. An incumbent president might use a "Rose Garden" strategy, employing the symbol of the White House to convey importance, competence, and leadership. In the conflict between the alcohol and tobacco industries and public health advocates, great use is made of symbols. The tobacco industry characterizes itself as an advocate of free speech, supporter of personal choice, and promoter of cultural diversity through sponsorship of community events. Recently Philip Morris captured one of the most powerful symbols in the United States by renting the Bill of Rights from the National Archives for a national tour (see Chapter 6). By associating itself with such a significant symbol, the company acquired a kind of "innocence by association" (a term coined by Michael Jacobson, director of the Center for Science in the Public Interest), presumably resulting in increased public goodwill toward the company.

The alcohol and tobacco industries use highly charged and symbolic issues like paternalism, freedom of choice, freedom of speech, freedom from discrimination, and free enterprise to place themselves in a positive light. Advocates, on the other hand, emphasize freedom from addiction, a fair chance for children, the personal right to be healthy, freedom from secondhand smoke, freedom from drunk-driving crashes, freedom to work in smoke-free workplaces, and the consumer's right to information about the risks associated with products.

The use of symbols in statements such as "This group is really more concerned with censorship than health" and "When it comes to the health of children, people can either believe the surgeon general or the alcoholic beverage industry" can convey a larger reason why people should be concerned about an issue. The symbol of the surgeon general, for example, is a shorthand for medical credibility and legitimacy. Caring professionals such as doctors, nurses, and teachers are viewed very positively by the general public. Fortunately, these groups are extremely supportive of health and are often willing to lend their legitimacy to important public health and social issues.

The use of a visual symbol can convey a broader image in a more powerful way. For example, to stimulate discussion about the surgeon general's recommendations about advertising directed at youth, advocacy groups used a Spuds MacKenzie toy dog, which had a label indicating that the product was for children aged 3 or more years old. This dog served as a symbol to illustrate the vulnerability of youth and the deceptiveness of the alcoholic beverage industry.

Shaming

Tony Schwartz has made extensive use of shaming as a media advocacy tactic. Schwartz believes that shame is a powerful motivating force. He argues that making public the behavior of individuals can serve the same function as the public stocks did in colonial America. Schwartz has used a small filler ad on the front page of *The New York Times* to tell readers that "Lincoln Center Supports Addiction" and to encourage them to call an 800 number for further information. A call to this number elicits a taped message, explaining that Lincoln Center takes money from the tobacco industry to support the presentation of cultural events. Schwartz also has developed a series of radio advertisements that speak to single individuals whose behavior he found offensive. One spot questioned the intelligence of a man whose dog fouls the public sidewalk.

The paid advertising of the Canadians for Non-Smokers' Rights described earlier also used shaming. Their newspaper ads pointed out the relationship between the prime minister and a chief lobbyist for the tobacco industry. The ad clearly stated that the health of thousands of Canadians was in the hands of these two men, and that Canadians for Non-Smokers' Rights hoped they had the integrity to make the right decision.

Visuals

A picture is worth a thousand words. Broadcast journalists need pictures to illustrate stories. Try this exercise: Watch the news and look at how the verbal script is very much secondary to the pictures being shown. The pictures can contradict a story, overwhelm it, or reinforce it. Leslie Stahl, reporter for CBS News, did a story critical of President Reagan's policies. After the story, she received a phone call from a Reagan aide who surprised her by praising the story. Although Stahl's verbal narrative was critical of President Reagan, the pictures showed him in positive, supportive settings. The aide believed that people paid more attention to the images and the message they conveyed than the specific words of the story (Jamieson, 1988).

Advocates have learned that no verbal presentation of advertising issues can rival the showing of just one beer ad adorned with bikini-clad women or with race cars speeding across the screen. Generally, pictures of people, places, or things enhance the newsworthiness of a story. When Wallack appeared on the *Today* show to comment on youth and alcohol, he was pleasantly surprised 2 days later when the live-to-tape interview aired. Over comments he made about the images in advertising, the story's producer had added a brief collage of alcohol advertisements. This served as an exclamation point to Wallack's critique of alcohol advertising and greatly enhanced the overall value of the interview. Though the editing, of course, was not something he was able to influence, it demonstrates the importance of thinking of ways to make stories more visual.

When the United States placed an embargo on all agricultural imports from Chile because of the presence of cyanide on two grapes, tobacco-control advocates used this breaking news to gain access to the media. Groups in several cities used a strong visual image to highlight the inconsistency in government policy on the fruit versus cigarettes. At their press conferences, advocates placed several bushels of grapes on a table next to a pack of cigarettes to show the amount of grapes you would need to equal the cyanide in one pack of cigarettes. The image was compelling.

Another tobacco example comes from Vallejo, California. In a sting operation underage youth purchased more than 250 packs of cigarettes and smokeless tobacco. The group then faced the problem of how to dispose of all the cigarettes. The local paper, in a large front-page photograph (6.5 by 9 inches) featured their solution: Two of the high school students who participated in the study dumped the cigarettes into a hazardous waste disposal container at a local hospital (de la Torre, 1989, p. A1). The visual image linked general concern about toxics with tobacco products. The involvement of high school students enhanced the photo opportunity by including the authentic voice of a vulnerable population, while at the same time highlighting tobacco's toxicity.

More Lessons From Tony Schwartz

It is a virtual certainty that public health groups will have less money with which to promote health than those who contribute to illness and death. For example, when more than a million Californians signed a petition to place an initiative on the ballot to increase the excise tax on alcohol, the equivalent of 5 cents a drink, the alcohol industry spent between $30 and $40 million to urge people to vote no. The pro forces had a total of $1 million, and in the end the alcohol industry won.

Advocates have fewer financial resources, less time, and many other obstacles to overcome. They must take advantage of all possible tools. Schwartz explains that you cannot win today's battles with yesterday's ideas, especially when it comes to using media. He urges, "Use media to fight and remember that it is a fight and it's guerrilla warfare" (Varied Directions, Inc., 1988).

Schwartz sits in the first-floor studio of his New York City townhouse and cranks out ways to use media as weapons for social change, a process that he likens to guerrilla warfare. He has done product advertising, political advertising, and advocacy advertising and is known for his ability to perform surgical strikes on individuals and organizations that stand in his way. His radio and television spots have focused on topics as diverse as city crime, tobacco control, and nuclear war. He has provided media advocates with several vital lessons for getting the job done.

Schwartz says you need to be prepared to use paid media to get your message out. Free time or public service advertisements, he explains, are spots that warn children not to take rides with strangers which are shown at 3:00 a.m. when only the strangers are watching! Using free time, there is no way to guarantee that the message will reach the audience you want to reach.

You do not always have to air the ads, however. Schwartz has some-times allowed the targets of his spots to hear a message before it was to be broadcast. Sometimes just the possibility of a spot being aired was enough to reach his objective. Policymakers reacted and acted on policy, to avoid being publicly shamed by the ad.

Schwartz's second lesson is that radio is an underutilized medium. This is ironic, considering that radio is pervasive and found in many more places than television and the production of radio spots uses relatively low technology and is inexpensive. Also, actual air time for radio spots is much cheaper than television and can be better targeted to the people you want to reach. In addition, interesting radio spots can generate news coverage, which can further highlight your issue.

Schwartz's third lesson is to think of your audience in *narrowcast* rather than *broadcast* terms. You may only want to speak to one person or one group. One famous Schwartz spot addressed the CEO of McDonald's by name and told him he could be a hero to children all over the world if he just changed the way his company fried its food. Schwartz explains that when people hear their names or the names of their organizations mentioned in a spot, they not only pay attention but imagine everyone else hearing the spot is paying attention as well. Schwartz wanted to change the behavior of only one man; his radio message had an intended audience of one. Yet because that message was broadcast across the airwaves, many people besides his intended audience of one heard it. The broadcast put pressure on the narrowcast target.

Schwartz's fourth lesson is that shame is a strong motivator for people, especially when the embarrassing message is traveling around the city, state, or region at 186,000 miles per second. Shaming, however, can be a high-risk strategy, and the structure of the shaming message must be in line with community norms, not be overly personal, be done tastefully and honestly, and generally be positive in nature. The key is to be strong enough to make the target person or group pay attention but not so strong as to outrage the person and the general public and risk negative feedback for your cause.

Schwartz has developed many useful strategies for using media but has tended to downplay the importance of community involvement and community organization. For Schwartz, media can be necessary and sufficient for change. Most social activists, however, would argue that media advocacy will only be effective to the extent that it is embedded in community advocacy.

Conclusion

Media advocacy, far from being a science, is an art. As with most arts, mastery of media advocacy will improve with practice. In this chapter we have reviewed many of the basic building blocks of gaining access to the media and framing issues from a policy or community perspective. The next two chapters illustrate in more detail how different groups are effectively using media to promote policy change.

To make effective use of the media you would do well to remember these key points:

- Understand the needs of journalists in identifying and reporting news.
- Set media objectives that relate to your overall policy goals.
- Be on alert for stories on which you can piggyback your issue.
- Never do anything that would compromise your credibility.

5

DOING MEDIA
ADVOCACY

The purpose of media advocacy is to use the media to stimulate broad-based coverage that will reframe health issues to increase community support and mobilize community action to change policies affecting health. In using media advocacy, the first point to remember is that it is not an approach to be taken lightly. It has considerable payoffs, as many who have successfully used this approach can attest. However, substantial thought and effort are required and significant risks are always present. It is not for everyone or every situation. Media work easily takes on a momentum of its own, and you can lose your own agenda in the face of the media's timetables and need to build on their conventions of newsworthiness. Your media advocacy activities should frequently be measured against your organization's goals and objectives to promote healthy public policy. The media are a valuable resource but should always be used with a clear purpose in mind.

A prerequisite to media advocacy is a willingness on the part of your organization, coalition, or you to engage in public controversy. Controversy is fundamental to media advocacy. It is one of the most commonly used access strategies. If an issue were not controversial, it is unlikely that media advocacy would be the chosen strategy—other media strategies, such as social marketing, might suffice.

However, discomfort with controversy on the part of members of your organization or coalition is not a good reason to abandon media advocacy. For example, local and state health departments may need to avoid controversy, but can provide important support to those in the community who can afford to do battle more openly. Background materials such as fact sheets and survey results, current media lists, suggestions of expert spokespeople and resources can be made available to advocacy-oriented community groups. Financial and logistical support for media advocacy training and funds for media advocacy staff positions in private organizations that contract with public health departments are examples of the kinds of assistance health departments can and do provide, without having to take a position on the front lines. The point is that other members of the coalition can play the lead role in a media advocacy campaign. Simply because your organization cannot play the lead role does not mean that you should sacrifice the opportunity to take advantage of the power of media advocacy to support the development of healthy public policy.

Planning for Media Advocacy

Media advocacy generally promotes policy. Any specific action, however, may focus on short-term goals such as getting on the media agenda, building public awareness, alerting opinion leaders to the importance of an issue, discrediting the opposition, stimulating community concern or mobilizing community resources. Media advocates are opportunistic: They monitor the media, looking for opportunities to make their issues part of the daily news. Because the news is often unpredictable, media advocates cannot always plan their initiatives. But, like any other media initiative, media advocacy efforts work best if they are well planned. Even in the case of fast-breaking, opportunistic media advocacy efforts, if a group has discussed in advance the basic elements of its media advocacy strategy, the chances are much greater that its response will contribute to their overall goals.

Monitoring the Media

The purpose of monitoring the media is to know and understand the outlets and gatekeepers that you are trying to influence and to be able to speak to them in the language of their interests.

The minimum level of monitoring is reading your local daily newspaper with a specific eye to which reporter is covering which topics. A step up from this is keeping up with local television and radio newscasts as well. Almost every news broadcast includes stories on health, and many stories that do not obviously have a health angle could be given one. This level of monitoring opens up the possibility of identifying reporters who might be interested in your issue. For example, a reporter on a San Francisco network affiliate did a story on risk factors for breast cancer in which she acknowledged her own family history and personal concern. Advocacy groups concerned with the inadequate level of funding for breast cancer research, the high cost of mammograms, and the lack of treatment for uninsured women would likely have a willing ear from this reporter if they wanted to pitch a future story.

Monitoring the media can also open up immediate opportunities for the media advocate. An editorial or opinion piece that does not mention the health aspect of a particular issue can provide the opening for a letter to the editor or a guest op-ed piece. For instance, the dominant frame for the war on drugs in the media has not been health but rather criminal justice and the legalization/criminalization debate. In a San Francisco area paper, an editorial supporting repeal of antidrug laws provided health advocates in the area with the opportunity to write guest editorials chiding the paper for leaving health out of the picture and calling the legalization approach a "quick fix for a complex problem." Placing the problem within a health frame also created an opening for one of the main criticisms of the war on drugs, namely, that it has been a war on only some drugs and that two legal drugs that were left out, alcohol and tobacco, also are the two most lethal drugs in the United States, dwarfing the death toll from illegal drugs.

Monitoring the media can provide advocates with a picture of the community's concerns at any given time. Though the media set the agenda for community discussion, thus opening up a window on community life, the view from the window changes constantly and rapidly. Knowing the events that are in the window increases one's ability to gain access. Advocates in northern California used two recent alcohol-related fires as news pegs for their local news conference on behalf of a proposed 1990 alcohol tax increase. *Recent* in media terms is usually quite short, which makes steady monitoring fundamental to media advocacy.

To work with the media with any kind of regularity, you must use your information from monitoring the media to develop a good media list. Media lists need to be maintained and updated regularly, because newspeople are constantly shifting assignments. The list should be divided by areas of interest—health, business, local news, sports, and entertainment—because many health stories overlap with other beats. For instance, although the Marin Institute's study "Beer and Fast Cars: How Brewers Target Blue-Collar Youth Through Motorsports Sponsorships" (Buchannan & Lev, 1990) was built on the health issue of high drinking-and-driving rates among working-class youth, one natural target—and the place where the story received a lot of play—was the sports section. The point of maintaining the media list is to be ready to take advantage of the situation when media opportunities arise.

A good media list is more than simply a set of names, addresses, and phone and fax numbers of local outlets and contact people. Ideally, media lists combine the basic facts with information gathered from monitoring the media and noticing who writes what. Knowing the interests of different reporters, producers, and editors permits you to target story ideas at a particular outlet or reporter. Careful attention to the media puts an advocate in a strong position to undertake the next step in doing media advocacy: developing working relationships with journalists.

Electronic Networking

Because of the amount of work that can be involved in good media monitoring, advocates have begun trying to divide the tasks among themselves. One community organization or government agency can take on the task of maintaining a good media list as a service to others in the community. Another can maintain press clipping files for all to use; a third may have a resource center that can help with background research.

To help smoking-control and alcohol-policy media advocates keep up with the national press, the Advocacy Institute (for tobacco control) and the Marin Institute (for alcohol control) developed two on-line computer networks, the Smoking Control Advocacy Resource Center Network (SCARCNet) and the Alcohol Control Network (ALCNet), accessible at modest cost to advocates with a personal computer and a modem. Both of these networks include national clipping services. Every day, staff from each institute read and summarize news stories relevant to tobacco control or alcohol policy from five major national newspapers and post these on-line. The news summaries are also placed in a data base that can be searched by subject, keyword, or date, enabling advocates to be up to date on breaking stories and review past stories rapidly.

Because the information in the alcohol industry press is so vital to health advocates, the Marin Institute developed an on-line data base for ALCNet. This data base consists of indexed abstracts from alcoholic beverage industry publications. The industry abstracts have two important functions: They help advocates monitor the biggest player in the alcohol field and they organize the information so that it is quickly accessible, permitting advocates to use it to support building relationships with the media. When journalists call advocates who are on-line on ALCNet, a quick search of this and the news summaries data base can provide invaluable background information on whatever issue the journalist is interested in, with the speed that journalists require.

Another feature of the two networks is a set of strategy exchanges, in which advocates share information and provide each other with strategic counseling on issues breaking in the media and in public policy. The strategy exchanges are small conferences in which activists pool their best ideas to respond to the multibillion-dollar marketing efforts of tobacco and alcohol producers. The beauty of the exchanges is that people from around the country converse without ever having to be in the same place at the same time.

Tobacco activists relied heavily on the SCARCNet strategy exchanges to plan a response to Philip Morris's sponsorship of a national tour of the Bill of Rights (see Chapter 6). ALCNet helped activists organize their media strategy against PowerMaster.

ALCNet and PowerMaster. On June 17, 1991, ALCNet ran an extensive news summary of a *Wall Street Journal* article titled "Potent, New Heileman Malt Is Brewing Fierce Industry and Social Criticism" (Freedman, 1991b). The news summary detailed Heileman's plans to launch a malt liquor with 7.4% alcohol content (by volume) targeted at African-American men. The response was immediate. Activists on-line downloaded the summary and began faxing it to other advocates in Chicago, Philadelphia, Dallas, and other cities across the country. That same day an Advocacy Institute staffer started a strategy exchange, allowing advocates to compare notes on media interviews and framing strategies and share updates on local action. Active participants in this strategy exchange included much of the ALCNet subscriber family, with computer dialogue flying fast and furious between the Advocacy Institute, the Marin Institute, and a group of activists around the country.

As a result of the strategy exchanges, advocates across the country had up-to-the-minute details on every facet of the campaign as it developed—and could comment on them. Almost daily, the Marin Institute would upload summaries of strategy sessions occurring among the quickly forming national coalition of African-American groups against PowerMaster, thus giving ALCNet users access to grassroots activists who were not on-line. ALCNet users could then provide useful feedback on the efforts going on in other communities that could be relayed back to those who were strategizing off-line.

ALCNet offered 30 news summaries and morning briefings on PowerMaster during the 3-week campaign. Each day, advocates could look forward to reviewing at least one source of news on the campaign and then downloading articles for circulation to staff and other advocates in their local communities. This service proved invaluable for organizations who, because of geographic or financial barriers, did not have access to many of the news sources cited in the summaries.

After more than 2 weeks of steady news coverage by the media, ABC's late-night news show, *Nightline*, featured PowerMaster as its topic for the evening. Advocates watched Chicago-area activist the Reverend George Clements speak on the issue along with Surgeon General Antonia Novello and Dewitt Helm, Jr., a representative from the Association of National Advertisers. One advocate wrote down the questions asked of Clements in the *Nightline* interview and posted them on ALCNet's strategy exchange the next day. Advocates then made comments, suggested alternate frames and discussed how they should deal with the morality of industry targeting of racial and ethnic communities. The discussion prompted advocates to reframe the issue to focus more on equal application of the relevant BATF code and less on the morality of targeting vulnerable populations. These shifts, as well as other lessons processed from the interview, enabled advocates to answer industry criticism more effectively and more cohesively.

Advocates stayed tuned to ALCNet and started a new strategy exchange that focused on another malt liquor advertising campaign. St. Ides malt liquor presented advocates with some of the most blatantly irresponsible advertising ever. Targeted to young African-American males, St. Ides ads used direct appeals to sex ("Get your girl in the mood quicker, get your jimmy thicker"), underage drinking ("I've been drinking ever since I could swallow"), heavy consumption (a 40-ounce container was portrayed as a single serving), and youth gang imagery to get the drinking message across. The St. Ides issue has been a continuing topic on ALCNet. Advocates have worked through the media to focus attention on this issue and have won several significant victories, including BATF sanctions (see Chapter 6).

Cultivating and
Supporting Journalists

Relationships with journalists are the stock-in-trade of good media advocates. Journalists spend much of their time talking to people on the telephone—they might as well be talking to health advocates. Anyone who has worked with the media knows that one can often feel like a supplicant, begging for coverage. We often underestimate our importance to journalists. They need us for the stories we can provide to them, for our expertise on health issues, and for our firsthand experience of the impact of health problems on community life. Some advocacy groups, understanding this need, have regular "story conferences" around particular times of year when they know journalists will be looking for certain types of story ideas (see Chapter 4).

A journalist's primary interest is in getting the story and getting it right. This usually means providing objective coverage and balance, that is, offering both sides of an issue. Thus, no matter how sympathetic journalists may appear to your cause, you must bear in mind that they have to speak to the other side and have to maintain their objectivity, regardless of how they may feel personally. For a journalist, writing a well-balanced story is more important than presenting your side of the issue in exactly the way you want it told.

Pitching the Story

Making the first contact with a reporter, editor, or producer can often be intimidating. It can be helpful actually to script and practice with colleagues the *pitch*—a summary of your story that emphasizes its newsworthiness and is designed to sell it to the journalist. When you call a reporter, usually the first question to ask is, "Are you on deadline?" For instance, most morning newspaper reporters face a late-afternoon deadline. Calling them to pitch a story that is not breaking (not happening on that very day or soon after) is better done in the morning. If the journalist is on deadline, you may have a better chance of selling your story idea if you offer to call back later.

Once you begin your pitch, if you do not know the journalist, you will need to establish your credibility and let him or her know that your story is worth listening to. Establishing credibility could entail providing professional credentials if you are an expert or community credentials if you are a community activist. You could say something like this: "I represent the Healthy Organization, which has X number of members." Then you could relate something your group has done that received news coverage recently. If someone known to the journalist has suggested you call about the story, you should certainly mention that as well. Sometimes, the power of the story itself may be sufficient to get the journalist's attention.

Constructing your pitch entails using everything you know about framing for access: emphasizing what is unique about it, what is controversial, how it is a milestone or a watershed, and how it relates to other events in the *media window* if you are trying to piggyback your story on some other breaking event. The questions you need to answer in the journalist's mind reflect the multiple motivations of the media: "Why would I want to write about this? How will this satisfy my editor/producer, sell papers/win ratings, get my story prominently placed in the newspaper or on the newscast? How does following up on this story fulfill our outlet's mission of letting the community in on significant events happening in and around it?" Think about these questions in planning your pitch.

Working with a journalist only begins with the pitch. A good media advocate is then poised to follow up. Being able to provide journalists with exactly what they will need to write the story you want written will increase the likelihood that that is what they will write and will win their respect and favor as well. Journalists are usually extremely busy people who appreciate reliable and thoughtful assistance. They value people who can help them do their job well. You can fill this role. It is rare that a journalist will have the luxury to delve into a health issue as deeply as health advocates do. Thus it is part of the advocate's job to distill the issue for them, including providing well-researched and documented fact sheets, suggestions of visual or sound images for broadcast journalists (and, increasingly, color stills for newspapers), and lists of spokespersons (and their phone numbers) on both sides of the issue.

Giving the media the names of the best spokespersons for the other side has two advantages: First, it increases your own credibility with the journalist, because it shows that you are aware of the major players in the issue, including the opposition; that you have confidence in your own position; and that you are not reluctant to provide the journalist with the best spokespeople the other side can offer. Second, it can give you an opening to inoculate the journalist against the other side's arguments. For example, after describing the credentials of the spokesperson for the other side, you can tell the journalist what his or her arguments are likely to be, what your responses to those arguments are, and suggest key questions for the journalist to ask of the other side. In fact, the journalist may have the opportunity to ask questions of the opposition that you would like answered but are not in a position to ask. For example, the distilled spirits industry seeks credit for voluntarily keeping their product advertising off television and, at the same time, claims that advertising has no effect on consumption. A useful question for a journalist to ask would be why that industry wants to be congratulated for not advertising on television, something that they claim does not work anyway!

Credibility and "one-stop shopping" are essential to building good relationships with the media. The more that they can come to depend on you to give them an accurate and timely story, the more likely they will be to come back to you, eventually conferring on you one of the badges of the successful media advocate: They will begin to treat you as a source. Instead of calling them to pitch story ideas, they will begin to call you for comment on breaking stories. When Anheuser-Busch announced a multimillion-dollar campaign promoting moderate drinking, the advertising columnist for the *San Francisco Examiner* called the Marin Institute for comment. What ultimately appeared in print was far from the public relations coup Anheuser-Busch had probably expected. Instead, the article took the company to task for using public relations to mask its ad campaigns targeting young people (Marinucci, 1992).

Media Kits

Different kinds of media initiatives call for and permit different levels of preparedness. When targeting a breaking story at a single journalist, it probably will not be possible or necessary to develop a full media packet of background materials. Nonetheless, one should be ready with relevant data and spokespeople, including authentic voices (see Chapter 4) if possible. Whenever possible, media advocacy campaigns should be planned in advance. Calls or meetings with journalists to pitch the story should be cemented by delivery of a media packet and provision of visuals to television journalists.

A good media packet will include a news release. When you write a news release, keep in mind that this is another opportunity to sell the journalist on your story. A catchy headline and a strong opening, or lead, paragraph will draw the reader in. This can be followed by a quote from a key spokesperson and whatever other background information is crucial to communicate the importance of the story. Try to keep the news release to one page, remembering how busy journalists are and how many such releases come across their desks daily. The news release should include a release date and a contact name and phone number. Write a model of the story as you want it written or told. Although most major outlets will only use sections or quotes from it or simply use it for reference, some smaller outlets may print the news release nearly verbatim.

Fact sheets providing any statistical background to your story should also be included. A good fact sheet is brief—no more than one page—but referenced. As in a news story, list the facts in declining order of importance, with the most striking facts up front. Printing the facts on the front and the references on the back in smaller type is a good format. Whenever possible, references should be from high-credibility sources, such as government reports or scientific journals. A brochure or one-page summary of your organization will give the journalist background on who you are. Finally, recent news clippings that mention your organization or are relevant to your story can also add credibility and cachet to your story idea or event.

Structuring the Initiative

*What Are Your Media Goals
and Objectives?*

There are a number of different ways to think about goals and objectives. You might want to think of your overall goal as the key thing that you want to accomplish through media advocacy. For example, you might want to advance a specific policy or set of policies to limit alcohol availability or cigarette sales to youth. Your specific objectives might be to gain access to the media, create news stories that frame alcohol or tobacco as a community availability issue, and gain general public and key opinion leader support for your overall program goal. While the ultimate goal of media advocacy initiatives is some kind of specific policy change, media advocacy can accomplish a great deal on other fronts along the way.

Most groups, organizations, or coalitions have an overall goal that they are pursuing. For example, after the uprising in South Central Los Angeles, community groups mobilized to reduce the concentration of liquor licenses in this neighborhood. Their overall goal was to reduce social disruptions associated with alcohol; their immediate objective was to develop policy initiatives that would prevent the rebuilding of liquor stores that had been destroyed. It is then necessary to ask, "What role do we want media to play in helping us to accomplish our overall goals and immediate objectives?" The media advocacy plan addresses the specific role that media will play in meeting organizational goals.

Who Is Your Target Audience?

In media advocacy, because the ultimate goal is changing policy, the target audience is usually those policymakers who have the power to enact the policy initiatives being advanced. Another audience frequently targeted by media advocacy includes those who shape or influence public opinion, often the media themselves. Sometimes the audience for media advocacy is the voting public, active or potentially active citizenry, or that segment of the public that we are trying to organize to support our policy initiative.

Determining the target audience affects everything about a media advocacy campaign: the message(s) of the campaign, the channels through which the message is transmitted, and how we seek to frame ourselves and the opposition. Influencing policymakers usually means placing our message in that part of the news to which policymakers pay the most attention: the front section of the newspaper, the first portion of a newscast, the op-ed section of a newspaper, or influential talk radio or television shows in that media market.

Sometimes we want to influence a single policymaker or group of policymakers. In that case, we need to target our message at the channel or channels those policymakers are most likely to attend to, sometimes a single station or newspaper. Narrowcasting relies on paid media and, as discussed earlier, has been heavily used by New York media advocate Schwartz (see Chapter 4). Taking advantage of relatively inexpensive rates for radio advertising, Schwartz has targeted key decision makers. He developed a radio ad designed specifically to tell the mayor of New York City that he should not allow tobacco advertising on city property, because the ads were "selling death." An "earned media" variation of narrowcasting is to create news in specific congressional districts or near the corporate headquarters of major companies.

If our goal is to change public opinion more generally, then we can broaden our channels to include the features page and more general human interest stories, as long as the messages maintain the focus on policy and do not shift the issue back to the level of individual behavior.

What Is Your Message?

When answering the question "What is your message," the rubber meets the road and media advocacy becomes an art. The central message of media advocacy campaigns is that problems are socially generated and involve institutional actors—government, industry, the media, churches, and sports organizations—who have the most influence over the environments in which individuals make decisions affecting their health. Developing a consistent media advocacy message begins with framing the story itself and answering these two questions: "On what part of the environment do we want media attention focused?" and "What stories will best demonstrate the health hazards of that environment?"

Media advocates constantly make decisions about which stories to follow up, which to let pass, and which angles of a story to emphasize. The introduction of Black Death Vodka and its endorsement by rock guitarist Slash of the group Guns N' Roses offered a clear opportunity for advocates to highlight how alcohol marketers target youth already at risk for destructive behaviors, in this case heavy metal rock fans. Advocates, from local prevention organizations to the surgeon general, spoke out against and generated negative media coverage about Black Death Vodka. In contrast, the introduction of Jack Daniels's Country Coolers, a new line of low-alcohol whisky products targeting youth but lacking Black Death Vodka's level of outrageousness, offered a lesser opportunity and passed without specific comment from advocates.

The situation in South Central Los Angeles following the uprising in the spring of 1992 offers a host of lessons in the importance of clarity regarding one's overall message. Journalists were ready to write about South Central, and many stories could have been generated. Advocates in South Central worked very hard to keep journalists on the alcohol availability issues by turning down media requests when they strayed too far from their priority issue. They also kept the alcohol issue alive, by publicizing the area's historical problems with availability, highlighting milestones along the way to a healthier process for licensing outlets, soliciting opinion pieces from politicians favoring more control of alcohol availability in the neighborhood, and framing the release of new research to show its relevance to the issues faced by the community.

Another aspect of framing the story involves defining *we* and *they* for the media and the public. Who is the villain of the piece? Who is going to be charged with responsibility for the problem that your policy change seeks to alleviate? There are many actors in the environment, but sharpening the focus of who *they* are will strengthen your group and increase the public's ability to grasp and act on your issue. For example, when the Oakland Athletics agreed to give out Bud Lights, flashlights with the Bud Light logo on them, to all fans age 16 and over attending an A's baseball game, local advocates knew that it would be a mistake to place the A's in the *they* category. The popular team had recently won the American League pennant and had earned a very positive reputation in the community. Also, the Oakland Coliseum, where they played, had an excellent set of alcohol policies governing availability at sports events.

The advocates' plan was to speak directly to the Oakland A's executives, by letter and through the media so everyone else was in on the conversation, and show public concern for their behavior. The objective was to generate public support for the goal of changing the A's policy regarding the flashlight distribution and also to question the credibility and ethics of Anheuser-Busch, which was sponsoring the promotion. The way to gain the greatest public support was not by targeting the A's but by showing them to be unaware collaborators in Anheuser-Busch's scheme to market to underage youth. The letter from a local health official to the A's, released to the media along with a media advisory announcing a news conference of community groups and officials concerned about the promotion, highlighted the A's history of responsible actions regarding prevention. The letter began, "The Oakland Athletics organization deserves a great deal of credit for the concern it has shown for safe and responsible alcohol use in conjunction with Oakland Athletics baseball games." It portrayed the flashlight giveaway as "surprising and inconsistent." In interviews with the media, spokespeople from the coalition carried forward the theme that Anheuser-Busch, and not the A's, was at fault. The Alameda County deputy director of Alcohol and Drug Programs, Robert Matthews, was quoted as saying, "We are not really criticizing the A's. We see the A's as being part of our community. We saw the entire thing as part of Anheuser Busch's push to market alcohol to underage people, which if not illegal is certainly unethical" (Wong, 1989, p. D1).

The point of carefully planning one's message is to ensure that all members of the group understand and communicate the same message and all materials going to the media support that message. For instance, if a group's campaign to eliminate alcohol- or tobacco-industry sponsorship from a local college sporting event chooses to frame the event organizers as innocent or uninformed and the industry sponsor as a cynical marketer trying to circumvent restrictions on marketing to young people, then no one from the group should criticize the event organizers in the media.

As the Bud Light example above demonstrates, clarity about one's overall message should be carried through to the microlevel. In media advocacy this translates most often into the words and pictures of the story—the quotes and visuals that a group provides to support its framing of the issue. Those of us who have planned social marketing campaigns are accustomed to developing messages, often in the form of slogans, and testing them with small focus groups drawn from the target audience. This model does not translate easily into media advocacy. First, individual messages in media advocacy generally should not sound planned. Media bites need to sound spontaneous even if they have been practiced many times.

Second, the target audience for media advocacy is often not available for focus group testing. It is rare that one can call together a group of policymakers and test different media bites or other issue frames on them. In media advocacy, often the best we can do is to test out our messages on each other. Role-playing with one's colleagues can be extremely helpful in selecting media bites and has prevented more than one poorly conceived bite from appearing in print.

Media bites are not the only form in which messages are communicated in media advocacy. Particularly for television, it is crucial to collect or identify visual images that express one's message. There is no more powerful statement of how alcohol marketers target young people than a photograph of Anheuser-Busch's Budman (a costumed superhero character) shaking the hand of a 4-year-old child at a public event. The Marin Institute used this photo repeatedly in its efforts to call attention to how the brewers use motorsports events to target young people. The institute also collects marketing paraphernalia of the alcoholic beverage industry, including a baby's bib with a beer logo on it, candy packaged as beer cans, and stuffed animals used to promote beer. The institute had the most illustrative examples photographed in black and white and in color, for journalists to take with them for use in their print or broadcast stories.

Talking With Journalists. Talking directly to journalists, on camera, into a tape recorder, or on the telephone as a reporter types away at his or her terminal recording your every word, can be intimidating. Giving interviews is, however, an essential part of media advocacy. It becomes easier with experience, as you come to understand how the process works and build confidence. The more you know about the situation, the easier it will be to take charge of it and turn the interview opportunity to your group's advantage.

The first point to remember is that every time you or someone in your organization is interviewed it is an opportunity to get your story out to a broader audience. The audience can vary from a small well-defined group such as those watching a local news or talk show, to 19 million people who might be tuning in to *The Oprah Winfrey Show, Nightline,* or the *Today* show. Each time the phone rings it may be an opportunity to highlight social and economic aspects of key health issues and help build support for healthy public policies in the general population. Also, each time you talk to journalists you have an opportunity to educate them on the public health perspective by bringing up important aspects of health issues such as community action, corporate behavior, and current political and policy issues.

When the phone rings it might be any one of a number of people. A television journalist, news producer, or newspaper reporter might want to talk to you about a story. Also, a radio news reporter might want to tape you during the call for your reaction to a story or might ask you to go on the air live. Unless you are well known to the person calling, the interview probably will serve as a miniaudition or preinterview to see if you have something interesting to say, can say it well, and might be available for an interview. Especially for the electronic media, how you tell your story is almost as important as what you say. Don Hewitt, creator and producer of *60 Minutes* says, "A guy may have a great story to tell, but if he's not a sparkling character who speaks articulate English, he's not going to tell it on *60 Minutes*" (quoted in Hertsgaard, 1991).

There are a number of things to consider when a journalist calls. The most important thing is to relax, and remember he or she is are calling you because of your expertise or your experience and that this is an opportunity to get your message out. A reporter will usually ask you if it is a good time to talk. If you feel uncomfortable or simply want time to collect your thoughts you can put the person on hold for a minute or tell him or her you will call right back.

Basic Questions

Generally, the more information you get from the journalist about the overall focus of the story the more likely it is that you can frame your response in a way that can promote your key points. Table 5.1 lists the basic questions to ask when contacted by a journalist. The first question, "What's your story?," will help you figure out how the reporter has framed the issue. The reporter has probably called you to provide a particular perspective on a story. The frame may have already been set. Your comment can fill in a space the journalist has already outlined, or you can help draw the outline yourself. Hearing from the reporter first can help you decide whether to accept or question the reporter's frame on the issue. For example, in Chapter 6 we tell the story of how a call to the Marin Institute transformed a frame from a controversy between two rap stars to alcohol-industry marketing to youth.

The next question to ask is "Who else have you talked to?" This question gives you more information about how the journalist is framing the issue. Are there heroes and villains? This may be a good time to educate the journalist on the sides of the issue as you see them. You can get a sense of what arguments are being presented and shape your comments accordingly.

You also might ask "Why call me?" It might be that in the course of doing the story your name has been mentioned as someone who knows the area or that the reporter is looking for someone who can speak to a

Table 5.1 Responding to Media Requests

What to Ask Journalists
What's your story?
Who else have you talked to?
What do you need?
What's your deadline?

very specific point. A follow up on this question is "What kinds of things do you want to know?" This helps you to get a sense of whether you or someone else might be the best person to do this interview. For example, a producer for a national prime-time news program asked Wallack to talk about two issues: the presumed health effects of wine and the effects of malt liquor advertising in low-income minority communities. Wallack explained that he could provide a general public health perspective on the former and raise some additional points that had not been aired on the issue, but that the latter issue should be addressed by a person whose community was more directly affected by the marketing practices being reported.

Knowing what the reporter or producer is after provides the advocate with an opportunity to broaden the journalist's perspective. For example, a local news show was doing a special series on teenage drinking. The producer called Wallack to talk about advertising research he had recently conducted. Wallack was able to expand the story by suggesting that the producer also talk with another group concerned with marketing to youth in communities of color. He provided a name and phone number (making it easy for the producer to follow up) and material on that related issue, which the producer subsequently used in the story. (When you refer calls to someone else, it is a good idea to give that person a call so he or she can prepare.)

Many people's initial response is to try to please a reporter and go to great lengths to do an interview. It is fine to decline an interview, but to be prepared for the reporter to pressure you by emphasizing the important things that you have to say. It helps if you can provide the name of someone else to be interviewed in your place.

Advocates who want to become sources will ask, "What do you need?" Journalists may be looking for general background, for specific facts, a quotable comment, or a person to interview. Sometimes it is difficult to be responsive to the needs of the journalist because you have your own responsibilities and deadlines. On the other hand, the time spent with the media can help further your organization's goals and contribute to long-term relationships that can be very valuable in the future. Having a plan for how media fits into your organization's goals can provide guidance for responding to media requests. Sometimes you have to be selective.

For live interviews, other questions will be appropriate, such as "Who will interview me?" and "Will other people also be interviewed?" Knowing who will be doing the interview can help you prepare. You may already be familiar with the interviewing style of the person; if you are not, you can tune into the show and get a feel for the context. If you will be doing a talk show it is essential that you know who the other guests will be so that you can plan for their arguments. If you will be on a panel with representatives from the advertising industry and the tobacco industry, you might want to review particular materials such as recent studies on key health and marketing issues. You should call around to see if any of your colleagues have appeared with these people and get as much background as possible. For example, spokespersons for the alcohol producers and advertisers routinely misrepresent a key Federal Trade Commission report. Knowing this will enable you to challenge them and expose the misrepresentation. If panel members or other guests include teenagers, teachers, and politicians, you would prepare differently for the show by examining how these groups can more fully participate in the policy arena.

Getting Ready

Once you agree to do the interview you might have as little as 1 hour or as long as several weeks to get ready for your appearance. It is hoped that from your discussion with the producer you have a good sense of what questions might be asked of you. You are not limited to what the producer wants you to discuss, but you can use this as a starting point for organizing your approach. As much as you can, anticipate the questions you might get and think out your responses beforehand. Brainstorming and role-playing with your coworkers is one way to generate a list of potential questions. For example, if you are being interviewed about limiting tobacco or alcohol advertising, you can bet the interviewer (or another guest) will bring up censorship, First Amendment issues, and presumed lack of scientific basis for restricting advertising.

Live news interviews are excellent opportunities for getting your point across. You do not need to worry about being left on the editing room floor. There are some basic things to remember about live television interviews. First, develop a file of arguments and counterarguments on your issue and rehearse them with your colleagues. Second, get to the studio or wherever the interview is taking place early so that you have time to look around and check out the environment. Its important for you to be comfortable. Do not hesitate to ask questions such as "Where will I sit?" "Where will the camera be?" "Should I look at the camera or the person interviewing me?" Television journalists often want to convey a sense of an informal conversation and will usually have you look at the person conducting the interview. Third, sometimes it is possible to ask what the first question will be and then think about how to use that question to get to your key point. Even if they know what they *think* the first question will be, it may well be something else. Always have your initial response thought out and ready.

Fourth, television time, for some reason, seems faster than real time—much faster. Thus you need to stick to the point—remember, that great closing you are saving may never get used! Make your points early and often. Be able to tell your story clearly and succinctly. You should be able to present the problem and your solution in two sentences. Reinforce the few important points you want to make in your answers to other questions. Whatever setting, you will not be able to explain complex issues in a comprehensive way. Simply saying the issues are complex does not do much good either. You need to be concise and to the point. For example, you would not want to say something like, "Well, there are five reasons why people drive after they drink," and then go on to list the reasons. You might find that before you get to number three the interviewer has cut in and moved you to another question.

Fifth, to get your point across it is important to vary your speech and emphasize key words. Avoid jargon, technical terms, and acronyms and try to stick with short, concise sentences. Have your media bite ready. Numbers can work for or against you so know which numbers you want to use, but use them only when they can add to your point and do not need a lot of explaining.

Be aware that with a live audience the dynamic can change very quickly. With extremely controversial issues you may be yelled at or booed or, on the other hand, you might get a nice round of applause. It is a good idea to watch a few days' of the program you will be on to get a sense of the dynamic and how the host facilitates the flow of discussion.

If you are appearing on a talk show with someone representing the other side of the issue, keep in mind that the person you are appearing with is not your friend or your enemy—it should not be a personal issue. You want to get your side of the story out in a positive way; ridiculing or being rude (or overly nice) to the other guest(s) can work against you. Do not ask the other guests questions. Leave this up to the host. (In talking with the producer before the show, you probably suggested some good questions or issues that should be raised with the opposition.) Remember that when you ask the other side a direct question you are giving them a gift of airtime. They then have the floor and can ignore your question and say whatever they like. These people have probably been trained by public relations specialists and know how to get the most airtime, reframe questions, and highlight their own points—you do not need to serve up additional opportunities to them. It is fine to interrupt. It seems that some tobacco- and alcohol-industry people are taught to talk on and on as a strategy. They know that there is only so much time and the more they use the less time you have to get your points across. Anticipate the need to interrupt and develop a strategy for getting the discussion back on topic. Also, you can convey by your body language and facial expression your opinion of the talker while you are waiting. For example, gently shaking your head side-to-side will get your point across if the camera moves to you during your opponents rambling.

When you have finished your interview you can be assured of two things. First, you will probably feel that you did not do as well as you could have. You will replay your responses to the questions and remember all the things you forgot to say. It is only now, after the interview is over, that you probably feel absolutely ready to do an interview. Second, you performed much better than you thought. You made some good points, you looked good, and you sounded knowledgeable. Also, no matter what show you were on, do not expect the phone to ring off the hook with calls from long lost friends or family members. Even though a few hundred to many millions of people might have seen you, do not expect much. Personal fame was not the point anyway, reframing the issue was the point.

Tape your appearances and review these by yourself or with someone who can give you objective feedback. Did you got your key points across? Were you able to frame the interview around your issues? Did you look comfortable and knowledgeable? Did your posture complement your message? And the two most important questions: What did you learn from the experience? and How can you improve in the next interview?

Keep in Mind . . .

You are potentially a valuable source of information and ideas for newsworthy stories. You need to develop confidence that you can work with the media to communicate your public health perspective and make it better understood. When working with reporters or talk show producers remember that you are an important variable in their story and that you can make a contribution. *You* are the expert, not them. Be sure to follow these rules:

1. Be honest. Fortunately we have truth, science, common sense, and fairness on our side. We do not need to be untruthful or dishonest; by doing so we can only lose. Our reputation as a news source totally depends on our ability to produce accurate, reliable data and clear ideas.
2. Educate the press. When journalists call, help them to better understand the issues by broadening their perspective on the story. Learn what makes stories interesting and newsworthy (see Chapter 4), and build your communication around these factors.
3. Know your limits. Do not blow your credibility by talking about issues on which you are not adequately versed. Refer the reporter to other people, and do not be pushed into responding to questions that you do not feel comfortable answering. Saying "I don't know" may be difficult, but dealing with the aftereffects of an inaccurate or inappropriate answer could be far worse.
4. Be on guard. Everything is on the record. Even if you offer something as off the record, you have no guarantee that it will not show up in a news article. Do not say anything that you are not comfortable having attributed to you. Be very careful about flippant statements and casual remarks. You need to be focused and on when you are being interviewed. If you are having a bad day it might be a good idea to call the reporter back later or reschedule the interview for another day if possible.

Evaluation: Did You Contribute to
Your Overall Goal?

Media advocacy is part of a long-term process to promote policy change. Such change is difficult, time-consuming, and complex. Seldom can you find a direct cause and effect relationship. Because resources are so scarce, there is little chance of a formal evaluation. Nonetheless, it is important for you to take some time to get a sense of your accomplishments. Feedback is critical in determining whether your results were worth the effort and can inform future strategy and tactics. In fact, you simply *cannot afford not to* do some basic evaluation.

Below are some basic questions to guide you in evaluating what you have accomplished. First, did you achieve your objectives? This can be answered on three levels. (a) Were you able to gain access to the media and, if so, how much coverage did you get over what period of time? Were you able to generate new spin-off stories? (b) Was your story told in the places you wanted so that it reached your intended audience? (c) Were you able to tell your story the way you had hoped? Did your frame define the story?

Second, did the media initiative help build community support for the overall program goal? For example, when a group in Milwaukee set out to gain media attention to highlight the number of alcohol and tobacco billboards in the African-American community, they held a large community picnic as part of the billboard counting procedure. Community involvement in this process thus contributed to the support base for future media initiatives.

Finally, a long-term evaluation question is to ask if you or your organization has become a source for the journalist. This question will be answered over time as you practice media advocacy.

Overall, evaluation can generate useful information and ideas for future advocacy. It does not have to be expensive, time-consuming, or strictly scientific. It does have to be thoughtful and tailored specifically to your program needs.

In the next section we describe how all the elements of media advocacy, from planning to evaluation, came together in an initiative that focused attention on policy solutions to drinking and driving.

Surgeon General Koop, Drinking and Driving, and San Francisco

In August 1988, the Senate and a unanimous House of Representatives passed concurrent resolutions calling on Surgeon General C. Everett Koop to declare drunk driving a national crisis, and to focus national attention on "this slaughter on our highways." Koop responded in December of that year by inviting more than 100 experts on public health and traffic safety to a workshop on drinking and driving. Representatives of the broadcasting and advertising industries were invited to participate; however, the alcoholic beverage industry was not. On reviewing the list of participants, both broadcast and advertising industry representatives staged a unanimous pull-out. The National Beer Wholesalers Association then filed suit in the U.S. district court to postpone or cancel the workshop, charging that the meeting violated the requirement that government-sponsored meetings be open to the public.

The suit was settled at the last minute, and the meeting was allowed to proceed when Koop agreed industry representatives could attend as observers and submit comments on the workshop's recommendations. The public health and traffic safety experts produced more than 230 recommendations for the surgeon general's consideration. Assuming that Koop endorsed these recommendations, they would constitute the most comprehensive blueprint for addressing alcohol-impaired driving ever produced by a federal agency. For the first time, the recommendations included many of the environmental measures public health advocates had sought for years, including calls for increased excise taxes, health and safety counteradvertising, and greater controls on alcohol availability and marketing.

Federal staffers thought that media coverage of the Koop workshop was curiously subdued, given the controversy it generated. Although they were not sure why there was so little media coverage, they wondered whether the alcoholic beverage industry had somehow influenced the media to forestall coverage. At the close of the December workshop, Koop agreed to study the recommendations and release and promote them aggressively within 6 months. He said, "I will see that these recommendations reach the widest possible audience, because we *all* must be advocates" (Advocacy Institute, 1989b, p. 1, emphasis in original).

Responsibility for dissemination of the recommendations was placed with a group of federal employees from the departments of Defense, Education, Health and Human Services, Justice, and Transportation. The Office for Substance Abuse Prevention (OSAP) took the lead role in this group. To bring the recommendations the highest possible visibility, the group decided to reallocate the resources for a Washington-based media strategy and try something new: media advocacy. They decided that in addition to the traditional public relations channels to be used by Koop and his staff they would identify and provide limited support to pilot media advocacy groups in three different regions: Atlanta, Detroit/Lansing, and San Francisco.

Koop was slated to release the recommendations to the media in May 1989. Representatives from all three regions met with OSAP staff in late March to plan strategy. One of their first tasks was to identify facilitating and inhibiting factors for getting media coverage. Positive factors included Koop's enormous name recognition and high credibility among health professionals and the general public—he was newsworthy no matter what he was saying. Second, public opinion polls had shown a high level of public support for the kinds of control measures being suggested. Third, the unanimity of Congress in calling for an all-out effort against alcohol-impaired driving brought additional weight to the recommendations. Fourth, a growing body of research and an increasingly articulate cadre of community-based advocates able to use this research provided important support. Finally, the controversy surrounding the meeting itself could be turned to health advocates' advantage if played properly.

On the negative side, local advocates faced a number of significant barriers. First, they had limited experience in working with the media and had few existing media relationships. Second, drunk driving was widely perceived as old news, something that had already received more than its fair share of media coverage. Third, the report contained more than 230 recommendations, running the gamut from law enforcement, educational, and judicial measures to pricing, availability, marketing, and advertising. Fourth, the apparent success of the alcohol industry in downplaying the initial workshop in the media showed the industry's high level of access and sophistication in working the media, in contrast to the advocates limited experience. Fifth, there was no clear congressional advocate willing to take on the whole package, and Koop was a lame duck; it was well-known by then that he would be leaving office by the fall of 1989 at the latest. Finally, the 60 days between the planning session and Koop's national news conference seemed like little time for the groups to learn the principles of media advocacy, build relationships with local media, and pull off a successful campaign.

The San Francisco working group was particularly skeptical about the project's chances for success. California is a major wine-producing state, and the alcoholic beverage industry's influence in the state capital was well known. It was also assumed that the alcohol industry would have considerable influence with local media outlets. Attempts to pass health-oriented legislation on alcohol issues had been blocked in the legislature for years. Other barriers facing the San Francisco group included the fact that there was no obvious local angle to the story—from California, this looked like just another boring report emanating from Washington. Mothers Against Drunk Driving (MADD) had begun in California and had made drunk driving a big story in the state in the early 1980s. However, by the late 1980s, the story had crested and was now old news at the state level. Finally, the long shadow of prohibition still clung to every effort by health advocates to promote greater local control of the alcohol industry and made it difficult to escape the neoprohibitionist label.

Planning the Initiative and
Identifying the Target Audience

The working group in San Francisco included one professor (who had participated, as an invited expert, in Koop's December workshop); two graduate students from the University of California at Berkeley's School of Public Health; and two staff people from the Marin Institute. To help the group establish relationships with local media quickly, a local person with extensive media experience and contacts was hired as a media consultant. This person knew the media extremely well and had a reasonably good background in alcohol policy issues. He was critical to gaining access to the media world and conveying to advocates the norms of the profession. In effect, the working group purchased his contacts and credibility with local health reporters.

The overall goal of this media advocacy initiative was to set the media agenda on a comprehensive public health approach to alcohol-impaired driving. At its first meeting in early April, the working group set four specific objectives for the campaign:

1. Gain access to the media and localize the story.
2. Use this as an opportunity to reframe the drunk-driving story from a focus on individual behavior—drunk drivers and victims—to the community factors and social policies contributing to the problem.
3. Extend coverage of the story over a longer period of time than the usual 1 or 2 days of exposure such a report might receive.
4. Establish the Marin Institute as a credible local source for stories and information on alcohol and other drug issues.

In keeping with the second goal and remaining cognizant of the media's limited capacity for detail, the group initially chose 4 recommendations from the original 230 (the 4th one listed below would later be dropped, as group members discovered that 3 recommendations were as much as the media could handle). These included:

1. An end to alcoholic beverage industry sponsorship of events aimed at underage youth, including the elimination of advertising and promotion on college campuses.
2. An increase in excise taxes (a statewide ballot initiative calling for a nickel-a-drink tax increase was in the offing, and the San Francisco group assumed that Koop would highlight the recommendation to increase state excise taxes in his national news conference releasing the recommendations).
3. Equal time on broadcast airwaves for public health-generated counteradvertising to balance alcoholic beverage advertising.
4. Safer serving, including mandated server and manager training and elimination of happy hours.

The target audience for the effort was the voting public in northern California. The group was specifically interested in building support for the tax increase planned for the November 1990 ballot but also wanted to begin to change the climate of public opinion to support a wide variety of local alcohol control initiatives.

Framing for Access

In its early meetings, the San Francisco group brainstormed about how to make the issue attractive to the media. The members began with the barriers, focusing on how to reframe each barrier into a means for stimulating interest. For instance, the alcohol beverage industry's opposition to the recommendations turned into "these are the recommendations the industry didn't want Americans to see." The claim that the initiatives were the first stage in a campaign to bring back prohibition was countered with "these recommendations are prohealth, not anti-alcohol." Koop's lame duck status also became a strength that was used to attract media attention: The group's news release would eventually begin with the phrase "In what may be his last significant act as U.S. Surgeon General." The sheer number of recommendations permitted advocates to call them "sweeping" and "the first truly comprehensive effort to reduce the carnage caused by drinking-driving."

Members of the working group monitored the local media for any potentially alcohol-related stories throughout April and May. Without any obvious local news pegs, they used a national one: May 1989 happened to be the 25th anniversary of the surgeon general's report on smoking, which had served as the federal kickoff to a successful movement to reduce smoking in America. So the working group framed the drinking and driving recommendations as "a watershed, the equivalent for alcohol of the 1964 Surgeon General's report on smoking. In twenty-five years, people will look back on this as the start of a whole new approach to alcohol and health in America." Although then in its 3rd year, the much-ballyhooed federal war on drugs also provided a bit of a peg, and advocates described the recommendations as treating alcohol as the serious problem drug that it is.

Cultivating Journalists

To the working groups, the less than 2 months from the date of the workshop to the day of Koop's news conference did not seem like much lead time, but actually it is quite long in terms of media advocacy. All three working groups recognized that the best way to counter any efforts on the part of the industry to squelch the story would be to begin work early, and each of the groups developed different strategies for getting to journalists. Atlanta and Detroit/Lansing both planned events to bring groups of journalists face to face with advocates and experts. In Atlanta, a breakfast briefing was held, and in Detroit/Lansing, two news conferences were called—one in mid-May and the second simultaneous with Koop's national news conference in Washington on May 31.

Concerned about its ability to make the story of much local interest without a tremendous amount of effort and networking, the San Francisco group elected not to put on a single media event but rather to meet individually with key journalists and pitch the story to them one to one. To this end, the group poured most of its energy into creating a comprehensive news packet that could provide everything a reporter might need in pursuing the story.

To increase the odds that the stories generated would actually focus on the recommendations selected by the working group, "key facts" sheets on the priority recommendations were developed. Ultimately, fact sheets were developed on drinking and driving in California, alcohol industry marketing on college campuses, promotions at sporting events, and state and federal excise taxes. All fact sheets contained basic bullets highlighting important numbers on one side and specific references for each fact on the reverse side. In addition, the media packet contained recent articles relevant to the issue, one from *The New York Times*, focusing on a server training program and quoting the Marin Institute program director, and one from *Sports Illustrated* about the sports promotions issue.

The working group also put together a list of public health spokespersons from a wide variety of constituencies: health advocacy groups, youth and groups that work with youth at both high school and college levels, government officials, and representatives from some of the Bay Area's racial and ethnic communities who were working on alcohol policy issues. Each spokesperson received a copy of the media packet and a briefing packet with more background materials—key pieces of research and a list of difficult questions and model answers—to help them frame their answers to the media, should they be called.

The goal with the journalists was to make the story easy for them to write or shoot. This meant providing them with whatever they needed to produce a good story that reframed drinking and driving from a law enforcement issue to an environmental and public health problem that required changes in public policy regarding marketing, taxation, and alcohol service. For television, the group put together the visual side of the story: The graduate students went to local beer distributors and told them they were interested in beer marketing, could they have some samples? They returned with posters, displays, and the prize find—a talking Spuds McKenzie stuffed dog, with a tag around its neck saying "suitable for ages 3 and up."

About 2 weeks before the national news conference, the Detroit/Lansing group held its first news conference and reported a higher-than-expected response. Based on the Michigan group's success, the San

Francisco group changed course midstream and decided to put on a local news conference following Koop's national event. The group promoted the news conference as one-stop access to spokespeople on the issue and as an opportunity to get local comment on the heels of the national event. San Francisco General Hospital would be the site of the news conference, and the anchor would be the head of surgery at the hospital, providing local mainstream credibility to the group and the recommendations.

The group also continued its original strategy of meeting with journalists and pitching the story individually. More than 100 news packets went out in the mail in the 2 weeks before the news conference. Group members then formed teams to meet with key journalists. Marketing posters showing young, fresh-faced models and steamy, sexy imagery were mounted on foamboard and taken along to meetings at the television stations, where TV crews filmed them in advance to hold for the day when the story would break.

A casual conversation between a Marin Institute staffer and a local high school alcohol and drug prevention coordinator led to a youth news conference to follow the local news conference. The working group now had a one-two-three punch lined up: the national, local, and youth news conferences, supported by the campaign of individual contacts with journalists well in advance of the event.

The young people would function in the stories that followed as authentic voices, recognizable faces of the problem who, in a few words, could reframe the issue from individual behavior to the environment. An interview with a young woman who had survived a drunk-driving crash led off the first local television news story that aired, *nearly a week before* Koop's national news conference that was to release the recommendations. Her words told the story. After she described her crash, the reporter narrated: "She survived, but her attitudes about alcohol did not." The young woman then said, "You watch TV commercials, movies—there's always young people drinking, showing them that's the way to have a good time." The shift in frame had been made.

Framing for Content

Carefully chosen spokespeople such as the young woman described above helped frame the message, as did visuals designed for television. The media bites used to gain access also framed the message. The Marin Institute's executive director would eventually be quoted in print as saying, "It's historic. The Surgeon General in 1989 is about to do for alcohol what the Surgeon General did for cigarettes—wake people up to the possible dangers and deaths" (Haddock, 1989, p. A1). A working group member used the phrase "these recommendations are not anti-alcohol, they're prohealth" in several television interviews. Advocacy Institute codirector and long-time antismoking advocate Michael Pertschuk contributed another media bite: "We've allowed Spuds McKenzie to become the leading alcohol educator of America's youth, and now the Surgeon General wants his turn."

The group worked to make the news conference a visual extravaganza embodying the message. The marketing posters, set up on easels, formed the backdrop, while in front of the speakers, a "Price Is Right" table showed how alcohol products have become price-competitive with soft drinks by placing price placards in front of six-packs of beer and soda, fortified wines, and wine coolers. The talking Spuds doll also sat on the table, available for filming.

Speakers at the news conference also told the story. Each of the speakers had received in advance a loose script of brief talking points that their statement was expected to cover. The event began with a welcome from the Marin Institute's program director, who would frame the theme of the news conference using the comparison with the 1964 surgeon general's report on smoking. He called on California policymakers at every level to support the Koop recommendations. San Francisco General Hospital's chief of surgery followed, establishing the severity of the problem by talking about the carnage coming into the emergency room as a result of alcohol use. The surgeon, in his white coat in the lobby of the hospital, also provided strong symbolic value, firmly establishing this as a serious health issue. The University of California professor who had served on the Koop panel then moved into the recommendations themselves, speaking as a public health expert and Koop adviser. Students from two local universities then discussed alcohol issues on college campuses locally, good and bad, and were followed by a local organizer from the African-American community who brought issues of targeted marketing to light.

Evaluation: What Happened?

In San Francisco, 6 days before Koop's national news conference, coverage began with a substantial story on the evening news by one of the most interested reporters. The story reported authoritatively that Koop's recommendations would focus on three areas: higher excise taxes, an end to promotions on college campuses and sporting events, and equal time for public health and safety counteradvertising. For the health advocates, this story was a clear victory, despite the fact that the anchor felt obliged to balance the story by remarking that controls on alcohol price and advertising had not prevented alcohol problems in the Soviet Union. The story met the group's goal of focusing attention on the recommendations that would have the greatest impact on the alcohol environment.

The next big story came on Sunday, May 28, when the Bay Area's major Sunday paper, the combined *San Francisco Examiner/Chronicle*, carried the story on the front page, with the headline "Surgeon General Joins War Against Alcohol" (Haddock, 1989, p. A1). The story was written by a reporter who had had minimal contact with the working group. The group had, however, met with two of her colleagues, and her piece quoted a Marin Institute spokesperson, included a chart of Bay Area drinking-and-driving deaths (with a credit to the Marin Institute), and drew heavily on the background materials that the working group had developed. The goal of positioning the institute as a key source on alcohol policy issues was being met.

May 31, 1989, the day of Surgeon General Koop's last news conference, was a very busy news day. House Speaker Jim Wright decided to resign under pressure, President Bush was proposing dramatic troop cuts in Europe, and students were taking to the streets in an historic uprising in China. Nonetheless, good preparation and the advance stories helped to build media interest for the news conferences. The Koop recommendations still won the number two spot on national and local newscasts. The ferment at the local level in the three cities helped raise the profile of the national event, as local editors alerted their national bureaus that something big was coming. In San Francisco, every major outlet attended the news conference.

Despite some bumps, the news conference ran smoothly enough to generate substantial television, radio, and print stories on the recommendations and about what local advocates were saying and doing. The follow-up youth news conference served to lengthen the television stories, providing more voices on the public health side. Two members from the planning group who participated in the news conference spent the rest of the day driving to television and radio studios, doing live on-air interviews. Other talk and interview shows had received advance media packets, and when the media coverage began to snowball, a flurry of media calls began coming to the Marin Institute. The advance materials continued to serve the health advocates well. In one talk show debate between a working group participant and representatives from the alcohol and broadcast industries, the "neutral" host settled a disagreement by reading from the fact sheets provided by the working group!

The visuals also proved to have a life long after the event they were designed to illustrate was over. The talking Spuds doll made numerous subsequent talk and news show appearances. Months later, young people in Oakland, California, used the doll in a news conference protesting the Oakland A's free Bud Light flashlight giveaway.

Overall, coverage in the Bay Area spanned 13 days and every outlet. Later that summer, the University of California professor who had been on the Koop panel (and the talking Spuds doll) appeared on *The Oprah Winfrey Show,* largely as a result of the controversy and media attention garnered by the issue of alcohol advertising in the course of the Koop project. Individual stories presented the public health side fairly and thoroughly. Some prime-time news stories ran as long as 6 minutes and were done by top reporters. Alcohol, advertising, and broadcast industry spokespersons were forced into a reactive posture. Early stories had no or little comment from them. In later stories, they appeared on camera or in print briefly, as commentators on the story but not shapers of it.

The San Francisco group exceeded expectations in terms of the coverage it was able to generate and accomplished its four goals to a greater extent than the members thought possible. The fact sheets, posters, and marketing paraphernalia were reused countless times in later years by Marin Institute staff and other advocates. Months later, a local print journalist told the Marin Institute coordinator of the working group, "Thank you for that story. You enabled us to do a local story on those recommendations. Without you, we would have had to go with the wire services. Wire stories don't sell papers." Another journalist remarked to an institute staffer casually that summer, "Oh, I don't have to remind you people—you're media savvy." The highest praise from reporters came in the form of repeated phone calls to the Marin Institute over the next year, requesting comments on alcohol stories, a sign that the institute had reached the goal of every media advocate: It had become a source.

The Koop initiative was the beginning of an extensive involvement in media activism for the Marin Institute. These kinds of activities are now an integral part of the mission of that organization. It is evident that organizations that are unwilling or unable to address media issues will be hampered in their ability to pursue their objectives. The credibility and legitimacy that the media can provide is far too important not to pursue actively.

Conclusion

Media advocacy can be done by community groups without benefit of huge media staffs, experts with advanced degrees, and slick public relations materials. What is most important is to be accurate, dependable, and true to your organization's and your community's goals. Even though it is not always possible to predict when the next media opportunity will occur, planning for it should be an ongoing process.

Planning can be guided by three general questions:

- What is the issue?
- What is the solution?
- Who has the power to make it happen?

The first question requires us to move beyond the notion of what is the problem. For example, the problem of concern to the surgeon general was obviously drinking and driving. However, the broader issue was the way the environment contributed to alcohol availability and to alcohol-related problems. Planning requires you to move from the discrete problem to the larger issue. The solution was the advancement and ultimate implementation of several policy initiatives. There were many solutions specifically detailed in the report. The working group chose three: no more sponsorship on college campuses, increasing excise taxes a nickel a drink, and equal time for counteradvertising. The policy solutions were specific, direct, and could be expressed succinctly. In this case, the power for change was defined to be the general population, which was seen as a vehicle to pressure those who had the power to move the policy agenda. Other initiatives might name more directly those who have the power to enact the solution. For example, your advocacy approach could use the media to speak directly to the mayor, city council, director of the alcoholic beverage control department, or an executive of the alcohol industry.

The failure to attempt to make effective use of the media will be far more costly than dedicating the time and effort to understand the media and to participate in the media arena. Much of what we have written here was gleaned from our experiences. But no amount of advice will compare with the actual lessons you will learn by seeking out and interacting with the media. In doing media advocacy, you can begin to shape the landscape of the news media and claim its power for health issues.

6

MEDIA ADVOCACY
CASE STUDIES

An eighth grader in Pojoaque, New Mexico, decides to "just say no" to alcohol and tobacco billboards near her school; a family physician in Davis, California, prepares to go jogging so that he can come up with a plan to put attention on handgun deaths among children; executives at a giant tobacco company think they have anticipated all potential problems and get set to introduce in Philadelphia a new cigarette developed for the African-American community; a community activist in San Diego comes across a letter to the editor criticizing Anheuser-Busch's plan for a beer garden at its newly acquired Sea World location; an advocacy group in Hawaii wants to reverse a legislative decision and needs to get the state legislature to reconvene—something that has never been done; one of America's most powerful corporations takes the Bill of Rights on tour and tobacco activists all over the country formulate a plan to respond; a nonprofit agency wants to change the frame on a story of malt liquor to focus on the policy issue rather than the celebrity issue; and in Washington, DC, AIDS activists mobilize to pass legislation to provide care for people with AIDS. These are the beginnings of media advocacy initiatives, and this chapter will use each of these examples to illustrate the tools of media advocacy.

In most cases, the people involved in these stories did not define themselves as media advocates. They just knew that they had a story they wanted to tell, a point that they wanted to make, and/or a policy issue they wanted to advance. The advocacy actions were similar in that they had extensive community support (with one exception), achieved some degree of success (in several cases 100%), and made excellent use of the media. Those involved may not have known it at the time, but they were a vital part of the emerging process of media advocacy.

Lydia's Decision: New Mexico Youth Battle Beer Billboards

Lydia Encinias was having a hard time deciding on a community improvement project focused on the theme "say no to drugs." Lydia was an eighth grader at Pojoaque Middle School in Pojoaque, New Mexico, a community of just over 1,000 people located about 10 miles north of Santa Fe. Every year, students in New Mexico participate in community improvement projects sponsored by Future Homemakers of America/Home Economic Related Occupations (FHA/HERO). Lydia's teacher urged her to think about a possible project over the weekend.

The Story

On Saturday morning, as she and her grandmother drove past her school, Lydia noticed two billboards for alcohol, one for Hamm's and the other for Budweiser. She realized that her fellow schoolchildren had to see the ads on their way to and from school, and that one of the ads was visible from the school windows:

> We saw how close the billboards were to each school. They were both advertising beer and they were both facing the school. I thought that was kind of strange, so I decided to do something about it and try to get the messages down.[1]

This would be her project to improve the community and help kids say no to drugs. The project gained the backing of the Middle School principal and Lydia's teacher. In addition, two sixth graders, Maya Salazar, 11, and Jacqueline Benavidez, 13, volunteered to help Lydia.

The three students began by asking who controlled the kinds of advertisements that were placed on the billboards. First, they called the alcohol companies advertising on the billboards. The companies told them that they did not own the billboards but simply rented the space from the billboard company. The students discovered that a local real estate manager, Joseph Martinez, was responsible for leasing the Pueblo land to the billboard companies. They called Martinez several times, but received no response. They decided to pay him a visit.

Martinez would not talk with or see them. Discouraged, the students were tempted to give up; however, they had taken the project on, and they were determined to see it through. The students researched local laws that governed the billboards. Lydia's uncle, Judge Art Encinias, a municipal judge in Santa Fe, told them that because the billboards were located on Pueblo land, they were governed by Pueblo law and not by the state of New Mexico or by local laws or regulations.

A few days later, Lydia's teacher, Glenda DePaula, ran into Felix Benavidez, a member of the school's Substance Abuse Advisory Committee. She told him about the students' difficulties. He replied that if the students were encountering resistance, they must be on the right track. He explained that they needed broader community support and suggested that if the students could demonstrate grassroots involvement in their issue, the billboard company and the real estate agent would have to respond.

Getting Grassroots Support

The students acted on Benavidez's suggestions and began to mobilize the support of the other schools, other students, and the community at large. First, they contacted the New Mexico Records of Vital Statistics and other agencies to find out how many deaths in their county were alcohol-related, what percentage of those deaths involved underage drinkers, how much the town was spending on drug education, and so on. Armed with facts, they visited the other schools to tell them about the project and gain their support. They also went door to door in their neighborhoods, asking residents to sign a petition calling for the removal of the alcohol ads on the billboards. They collected 260 signatures—a quarter of the town's population.

Getting Media Attention

In mid-February, Maya's mother mentioned her daughter's project to a friend, Tom Sharpe, correspondent for the *Albuquerque Journal*, the largest daily newspaper in New Mexico. Sharpe decided to do a story on the girls' project, but warned them that his editors in Albuquerque would make the final decision about whether the story would be published. It also occurred to Maya's mother that her employer was related to the editor and publisher of *The New Mexican*, a local paper. She mentioned the project to her employer and told him that the *Albuquerque Journal* was working on a story about it. She also encouraged the three students to get in touch with *The New Mexican* themselves.

T. J. Sullivan, the education reporter for *The New Mexican*, called Maya's mother 2 days after she had spoken with her employer. Sullivan wanted to interview the students and their teacher. On March 7, *The New Mexican* ran a front-page story with the headline " 'What Kid Can Resist That?' Students Declare War on Booze, Tobacco Ads" (Sullivan, 1992, p. A1). The article described the three students as "crusading to get billboards advertising alcoholic beverages and tobacco products banned from areas near schools." It went on to say that they were seeking a legislative sponsor for a bill prohibiting alcohol and tobacco ads within view of elementary and secondary schools. As a quote from Lydia put it, "They show money and cars and women. What kid can resist that? . . . We spent $11,000 [in Pojoaque] trying to promote drug education and here's what we're talking about right across the street," referring to the beer ad near her school.

On March 10, the *Albuquerque Journal* ran Sharpe's (1992b) article on the project in a special section circulated only in northern New Mexico. This time Jacqueline's quote gave the students' message: "It's dumb to have the billboard for beer right by the school because it's like encouraging the kids to drink beer" (quoted in Sharpe, 1992b). Sharpe had managed to reach Richard Zanotti, general manager of Gaechter Outdoor Advertising, the company responsible for placing specific ads on the billboards. Zanotti told Sharpe he was unaware of the students' project and that the two billboards were not in violation of the company's code requiring that alcohol and cigarette ads be placed at least 500 feet away from schools.

In the next week, the Budweiser ad disappeared, replaced by a public service ad from National Council of La Raza encouraging Latinos to stay in school. On March 16, the headline "Beer Ads Canned" topped the front page of the *Albuquerque Journal* (Sharpe, 1992a, p. A1). The story told of the replacement of the Budweiser ad and said that the other beer ad would be taken down soon. This time, Zanotti said the location of the signs was "an oversight . . . we usually don't put them near schools or churches."

On March 17, "Students Win Battle Over Billboard" (Easthouse, 1992) was the headline in *The New Mexican*. *USA Today* ran a short paragraph on the story that same day ("State Round-Up," 1992). The three students' project won first place in the local and second place in the statewide FHA/HERO competition. As Lydia put it, "I felt good about myself because I had succeeded in getting the billboards down and reaching our goal, making the community more aware and having their support."

The Lessons

This case provides a dramatic example of how the media can bring an issue into the light of day, thereby making it impossible for people not to pay attention. Before the newspaper story, the issue was invisible. The people who had the power to make the change necessary refused to see the issue. The newspaper coverage made that impossible. On the other hand, three things made the newspaper pay attention: young people taking on a big issue, the irony of beer ads close to the school, and the large base of community support. Finally, access was gained because someone had the confidence to pitch the story.

The project was a success, but the work is not done. The billboard company's action was voluntary, and the beer ads could come back at any time. According to Maya's mother, "The next step is to involve the Pueblos in getting a policy made saying that these billboards cannot be used for alcohol and tobacco."

When Children Shoot Children,
the Media Pay Attention

Garen Wintemute is a family-practice physician on the faculty of the University of California Davis Medical Center in Sacramento, California. Garen has conducted research and worked in the emergency room through much of his career, where he has seen the deadly consequences of firearms. He decided he wanted to use his research to do something about firearms.

The Story

Garen knew he wanted to bring attention to injury and death from firearms, and focus attention on the need for policies restricting access to handguns. At the same time, he wanted the research to be newsworthy enough to attract substantial local and national media coverage. He wanted more than the usual amount of attention—or inattention—afforded to stories on medical research. Garen had two goals—policy significance and newsworthiness—and needed to design research that would accommodate those goals. He wanted a research topic on gun deaths "so compelling that nobody could walk away" from it.[2]

Before Garen went running one day, he decided to concentrate on this problem during the run. It worked. By the end of the run he had the idea for his research and the study's title all at once. "When Children Shoot Children" (Wintemute, Teret, Kraus, Wright, & Bradfield, 1987) was published in the *Journal of the American Medical Association* (*JAMA*) followed by extensive local and national media coverage. The coverage brought attention to the issue of childhood deaths from firearms and precipitated local and statewide policy on replica guns.

The Study

Garen and coworkers (Wintemute et al., 1987) examined the deaths in California of children shot by other children. Their study found that over a 6-year period, 88 children in California, ages 0 to 14 years, were unintentionally shot and killed by other children or themselves. Handguns were involved in 58%. The topic was so compelling that *JAMA* offered to produce a video news release, which was subsequently aired nationally. Locally, the public relations office at the medical center coordinated a news conference.

Garen used the news conference to highlight one aspect of why children shoot children: real guns that look like toy guns. Several shooting deaths occurred because children mistook a real gun for a toy and shot a playmate.

The Visuals

For the news conference, Garen mounted real guns paired with their toy replicas on plywood. During the news conference, he challenged the reporters to identify the real guns, a difficult task, even on close visual examination. The visual image was striking, the effect on the reporters themselves impressive, and the resulting coverage extensive. Some reporters used the images from the news conference to package a dramatic story. Garen remembered that

> part of the fun from my point of view is watching the finished product, watching how much the reporters get to sandwich a few brief clips from the press conference with material which enhances the effect greatly. One guy here in Sacramento, a consumer reporter, got clips from [the movie] *Rambo*, and clips of little kids, little kids 3 to 5 years old, watching *Rambo* in utter fascination, and then cut to clips of the matched pairs. It was very powerful.

The compelling visuals attracted newspaper and television coverage and made it easier for reporters to reinforce the points that Garen was trying to make.

The Lessons

"When Children Shoot Children" succeeded in bringing national attention to the issue of injury and death from firearms. We can draw several lessons for media advocates from this case about framing research and the importance of visuals.

Framing Research

Researchers can choose projects that will attract attention to policy. Garen and coworkers chose to do research that was interesting to them and that they knew would have policy implications. Garen's specific intent was to design research that would bring attention to the need for changes in firearm policy.

> The larger goal of the press conference [was] to build awareness in the public and in the public's representatives of the conclusions and the policy implications of the research. In this field, the conclusions are sometimes very straightforward. Descriptive epidemiology is usually pretty simple. The difficulty is whatever interventions are suggested by those conclusions usually involve legislative or at least regulatory action. [Thus] the press conference serves primarily an advocacy role . . . to advocate for the interventions which are suggested by the results of the research.

Garen ended up doing an extensive research project that could pass the scientific review of one of the country's leading medical journals. Others, however, have been able to conduct less-sophisticated research and still make the point (see CSPI example in Chapter 4).

The Importance of Visuals

The visual image of the toy guns next to the real weapons was stunning and frightening. The very simple juxtaposition had tremendous power. Reporters were personally affected when they could not tell the difference between the toy and real gun. Garen explained:

> I talked, but the image that was broadcast first locally and then nationally, because the networks picked that up, was these guns that nobody could tell apart when they are seeing them on TV. . . . More specifically, the reporters and cameramen, they're a cynical bunch, couldn't tell them apart in a room with bright lights and the tape rolling. So they got the message personally and that personal sense showed up in their reporting.

Reporters can be cynical. Winning them over, evoking their *personal* reaction, can translate into enthusiasm and support for your story and your point of view.

Framing Messages:
Arguments and Counterarguments

There were several audiences for Garen's project. The first was the medical research community. For them, the topic had to be framed as objective research. Before *JAMA* published the study, it sent the paper out for two blind reviews, to be sure the research was sound in the opinion of other scientists. Garen's study was carefully designed and written to meet *JAMA*'s stringent criteria. It was worth it. Publishing in such a prestigious journal gives weight to the findings and draws media attention in and of itself.

The medical community was only one audience, however. Another was the toy industry. If the industry would cease manufacturing the replica guns, children's lives could be saved. Garen parlayed the credibility of the study published in a prestigious journal, with the visibility and legitimacy gained from the media coverage to pressure the toy industry.

To pressure the toy manufacturers into making a policy change at the corporate level, Garen wrote to Charles Lezarus, president of Toys "R" Us, the nation's largest retailer (November 5, 1987). He described the problem and asked him to stop the sale of the replica guns in his stores. Garen noted that he would check the Sacramento store himself and have volunteers check other locations nationwide. Garen also wrote to Douglas Thomson, president of the trade association Toy Manufacturers of America, challenging him on the toy gun manufacturers' inadequate attempts to differentiate the replicas from the weapons (November 5, 1987). In his letter, Garen enclosed color photographs of pairs of guns, one real and the other a toy. He asked the president of each company to identify which was which. The letter went on to say,

> It's hard to tell, isn't it? The toy gun is the one on the left, and I purchased it at your toy store recently [here he gave the address of the store]. The other gun was used in a residential shooting death here in town; you ought to do something about this.

Anticipating the Arguments

Garen received a long letter of response from Thomson. Like the alcohol and tobacco industries, the Toy Manufacturers of America argued in the name of individual rights against public safety regulation, emphasizing the industry's right to sell a legal product and its duty not to interfere with the marketplace. "Legal products can enter the market and the public rejection or acceptance determines what goes from there," Thomson wrote (November 13, 1987). It is the family's responsibility to instill good values that is key, according to Thomson. Furthermore, he stated,

> toy guns are legitimate legal products and have been for hundreds of years. Manufacturers have a right to produce them, at the same time producing a product which the public perceives to be a safe and decent play-thing.

In communicating with the toy industry Garen effectively framed the issue. In his letter (November 20, 1987) back to the president of Toys "R"

Us, Garen confronted his arguments, sent copies of his research papers, and said that

> for the toy industry not to do something would be to reveal that they really are anti-kid, when you come right down to it. Which was not a position they were willing to be put in, so Toys "R" Us to begin with, to their credit, said "Enough! We're not going to purchase any more, and when we exhaust our current stocks, we'll stop." And in fact, I doubt they exhausted their stocks. At least locally they got pulled off the shelves.

Being antikid was the last thing the nation's largest toy supplier wanted to be associated with. And putting pressure on the largest member of the industry had a ripple effect throughout the rest of the industry. It is now much more difficult to find a toy gun that looks real.

Philadelphia Puts Uptown Out of Town

Although it has been said throughout this book, it is worth repeating: The media are only one set of tools for effective advocacy. There are times when media can divert energy from, and even be a barrier to, advocacy goals. An experienced advocate knows that sometimes it is better to say no to certain media requests and appearances if they do not contribute to the overall plan. This lesson is powerfully illustrated in the effort to stop the release of Uptown cigarettes.

The Story

RJR Nabisco (RJR) was planning to launch a new cigarette brand called Uptown. The menthol cigarette, targeted to African-Americans, was to be test marketed in Philadelphia, home of the famous Uptown Theater, which (like New York's Apollo Theater) was an important institution in African-American history. In fact, Uptown's tag line was to be "The Place. The Taste." RJR was proud of its marketing effort and announced in mid-December its intentions to launch Uptown on February 5, 1990, during Black History Month (Heller, 1990). However, RJR had not anticipated the activism of the Philadelphia African-American community.

The Coalition Against Uptown Cigarettes quickly formed after news spread of RJR's plan to test market Uptown in Philadelphia. The coalition was an extremely diverse gathering of health, religious, and community organizations led by African-Americans working in Philadelphia. They held their coalition together by agreeing on a number of basic principles, including organizing broadly in the African-American community and including smokers, placing the focus on RJR and not other African-Americans or African-American organizations that might be on the "wrong" side of the issue, stopping RJR from test marketing the product locally, and mobilizing the African-American community around this issue, which was the primary goal.

This understood, the coalition saw the media chiefly as a tool to mobilize their community. Local media was more important than national media, and local media outlets that spoke to African-Americans were more important still. Even though these principles were clear, it still was not easy.

Immediately after the first coalition meeting, the American Cancer Society (an Uptown Coalition member) received a call from *The New York Times* requesting a list of the organizations that joined the coalition. Some members thought the coalition should comply with *The New York Times* request right away. After all, this was *The New York Times*, the newspaper of record and a media opportunity that they should not pass up. For others, it seemed too soon to publish the list. Most African-American organizations needed time to go through their organization's endorsement process to be able to lend their formal support to the effort. The coalition, at that time, consisted primarily of groups in the classic tobacco control movement (i.e., American Cancer Society and the American Lung Association) and was not yet representative of the broader African-American community. There was concern that the story would be that this coalition was made of the same old players and that the issue had gained little attention among broader segments of the African-America community.

The group decided to wait to release the list at an upcoming news conference when more organizations could be announced. "And sure enough," says Charyn Sutton of the coalition, "we got other African American organizations and the *Times* didn't go away. They understood."[3]

The group faced a similar decision when ABC's *Good Morning America* called requesting that a representative come on the show to debate a marketing expert on the Uptown issue. The marketing expert was African-American, and it was strictly against the coalition's principles to engage in any activity that would pit it against other African-Americans or African-American institutions in public. It was a simple decision for the coalition, but less so for other tobacco-control activists nationwide who thought the *Good Morning America* appearance would have been a good opportunity to promote the Uptown issue to a wide audience. The coalition was firm and the answer was no.

Good Morning America booked instead Dr. Harold P. Freeman of Harlem Hospital. Freeman focused on the poverty and lack of education of African-American smokers and the ethical responsibilities of African-American companies on this issue. This was directly opposite to the coalition's principle of keeping the focus on RJR and off those in the African-American community. However, many believed that given the show's setup, there was no way to avoid being boxed into framing the issues in that way. The coalition held to its belief that it was better not to appear on the show at all than to appear under those circumstances.

In addition to turning down *Good Morning America* because of the show's setup, the coalition also turned down that show (and other national shows, including the *MacNeil, Lehrer* news hour) because the group's focus was on the local community. As coalition member Charyn Sutton said,

> We would go to a local newspaper before we would go national. Even though there was more glamour in the national media, it was a diversion. Our task was the local piece. Our audience is in Philadelphia. The test market was in Philadelphia and if we could win it, we would win it in Philadelphia.

The Lessons

The Uptown Coalition was able to do what many other groups would find difficult. It resisted the pull of national media coverage for its issue. It did this for a very simple reason: It was not in line with the overall strategy the coalition had developed. Members had decided to gain the support of local organizations and build their coalition before getting widespread media attention.

Campaign goals informed members' choice of audience, media outlets, and the composition of their coalition and coalition leadership. They did not veer from those choices. This kind of clarity in goal setting was key to the coalition's success in keeping Uptown cigarettes from ever seeing the light of day.

Spuds McKenzie to Shamu the Whale: "This Bud's for You"

James Baker had a little extra time and was going through a file of news clippings about alcohol in San Diego County. He found a letter to the editor complaining about changes at the Sea World amusement park since its purchase by Anheuser-Busch, the makers of Budweiser. Baker, a long-time community organizer and newly appointed head of the San Diego County-funded Media Resource Center on Alcohol Issues, tracked down the original inch-long article that had generated the letter and began to ask other local alcohol policy activists about what was going on at Sea World. A media opportunity was quickly coming into focus.

The Story

Purchased by Anheuser-Busch in 1989, Sea World of California in San Diego is a premiere tourist attraction, offering marine life exhibits, ecology education, and family entertainment. The park sits on 166 acres of city-owned land, and hosts daily shows of dolphins, whales, sea lions, and otters as well as bird, water-skiing, and boat shows. It also houses a creative playground structure, known as Cap'N Kids World. Busloads of school groups, church groups, and conventioneers attend the park throughout the year.

Sea World of California sold alcoholic beverages before the Anheuser-Busch purchase. However, California's tied-house law prohibiting alcohol producers from retailing alcoholic beverages would have forced the park to go dry after the purchase. To avoid this, Anheuser-Busch installed a demonstration minibrewery, bringing the park under another state law allowing brewers to sell beer at the brewery site. The state tied-house law still prevented sale of any other alcoholic beverages at the park. This was a problem for Anheuser-Busch, which sought to attract large corporate conventions to the site.

As reported in the tiny article located by Baker, Anheuser-Busch announced plans in September 1991 for a multimillion-dollar expansion of the theme park, putting their stamp on Sea World of California. The plans included a 30,600-square-foot Anheuser-Busch Hospitality Center with a beer garden, two restaurants, gift shops, an exhibit explaining the history of the Anheuser-Busch company, group banquet space, a small auditorium, and bakery facilities. In addition, a stable was to be built for six Clydesdale horses, the signature trademark for Budweiser beer. To make room for the new Hospitality Center and brewery, the company bulldozed a park landmark: a large-scale map of the United States across which San Diego children had walked for years.

The Goal

Baker's goals in the Sea World effort were much larger than simply changing beer marketing practices at the park. He saw in Sea World a potential focal point around which to build a countywide environmental prevention coalition:

> The alcohol prevention providers had been working in their own communities on individual projects. Sea World offered us an opportunity to come together around a county-wide issue. We had to build a coalition and bring people together. We were looking for ways to work together that would be interesting and fun. We wanted to bring discussions of alcohol policy into a public forum. We had a feeling the situation at Sea World could help us do that.[4]

Baker wanted more information. He used local libraries to research the history of Sea World and to answer questions he had about Anheuser-Busch. Did it own other theme parks? What were the company's beer promotion activities? How much money was spent on advertising? What was its overall budget? How has it reacted to community alcohol prevention/policy groups in the past? When he brought his findings to the monthly meeting of county-funded prevention agencies sponsored by the Media Resource Center, group members decided to send a team to Sea World to see what was really happening.

Judy Winston, a long-time alcohol control activist from the North Park Prevention Project; Karen Zaustinsky, director of the Lemon Grove Prevention Project, a community-based alcohol prevention education program; and Linda Miramontes, also of the Lemon Grove Prevention Project, each visited Sea World to assess the situation there. They found a variety of promotional items carrying the Anheuser-Busch symbols and logos, including candies shaped and packaged to look like tiny Budweiser beer cans, child-size T-shirts and jackets with Anheuser-Busch symbols, cartoon character "BUD Man" magnets, salt and pepper shakers in the shape of Budweiser beer cans, stuffed Clydesdale ponies in various sizes, and expensive beer steins with the Anheuser-Busch name. All the eating establishments featured Anheuser-Busch promotional placards on every table, and the food shop menus highlighted Budweiser beer in large red letters but displayed other food items in smaller, white letters.

Word spread among the prevention community about the Sea World effort, and by March 1992 the coalition had grown to 15 community groups, including the countywide PTA council; alcohol recovery and prevention programs from throughout the county; advocates for youth, gay, and lesbian community projects; and local alliances for drug-free youth. Casual conversations with friends indicated to coalition members that the issue touched a nerve among San Diegans. According to Pamela Rahn, a coalition member from a gay and lesbian alcohol prevention services agency,

> This was something the whole community could relate to. There was the appeal of instant rapport that people already had with Sea World. People love the park. Whenever I talked with friends about what was going on, I never heard anyone ever say that Sea World should be giving away free beer. And all the promotional things, that kids would go home with BUD t-shirts and not whale t-shirts was wrong.

Getting Media Attention

The group decided to use the media to bring to the public's attention the fact that many of the promotional items Winston, Zaustinsky, and Miramontes had found at Sea World targeted children and youth. The focus was made larger than Sea World; Baker explained,

> Our goal from the beginning was to bring to the citizenry and the public officials of San Diego county an awareness that they could participate in establishing alcohol policy in their own community. And we knew we could do this by using certain examples that were fun and interesting.

Before going public, Winston and Baker met with Dan LeBlanc, Sea World's public relations representative. They explained that they were from a community coalition concerned about alcohol promotion at Sea World and interested in knowing more about the changes Anheuser-Busch planned for Sea World. LeBlanc told them that Anheuser-Busch would be opening a temporary hospitality center in late April where adult visitors to the park could sample two free 10-ounce glasses of beer and attend an exhibit on the Budweiser brewing process as well as a display of Anheuser-Busch's "Know When to Say When" campaign.

With this information in hand, the coalition set about trying to place a major news article about what it had found. It wanted to give the issue the legitimacy of media exposure, bringing its findings to the community in a responsible, factual, intelligent, and sensitive way. Coalition members turned to Winston, who had a reporter in mind to write the first story:

> We knew that this [child-oriented promotional items at Sea World] was a big issue. So I put together a news sheet about what we found at Sea World and I sent one to Barbara Fitzsimmons, a reporter from the *San Diego Union-Tribune* with whom I had done a lot of work in the past. At the time though, we didn't really know if we had a story, because we couldn't get any school boards to come out and say they were concerned about it. All we had was our loose coalition. So I said to Barbara, "I don't know if this is a story." And she said, "*This* is a story."

Winston knew that Fitzsimmons was interested in and sympathetic to health and family issues. Fitzsimmons met with, interviewed, and photographed several members of the coalition. She also sent a photographer to the park to shoot the beer-shaped candies sitting on the shelves in the gift store. Fitzsimmons's article, "This Bud's for . . . Who?", appeared on April 11, 1992, on the front page of the "Currents" section of the Saturday *San Diego Union-Tribune,* a long feature article with color pictures. The piece gave a sympathetic and vivid description of the effects the changes at Sea World were having and would have on the theme park and the community.

Creating a Media Event

Fitzsimmons mentioned in the article that members of some community groups planned to picket at Sea World during the upcoming Easter week. The coalition targeted its main action for Friday, the day on which Sea World officials planned to open the temporary hospitality center, where two free 10-ounce glasses of beer would be available to every adult. To ensure a good media turnout, coalition members sent out news releases a few days before to all the major news outlets in town and made many follow-up phone calls. It alerted specific reporters, editors, and producers that group members had worked with in the past, sent announcements to the assignment editors at all the television stations and to city and general assignment editors at the local newspapers. The group wanted a media event; as Baker recalled:

> We know from media advocacy training that you don't just step out and have a news conference. That's not what news media personnel need to do their job. They need something with glamour and excitement and interest, because they are in the entertainment business. . . . We wanted this event to be alive, we wanted sunshine, palm trees, sea life, community members, lots of expression, lots of movement, lots of freedom. And, we wanted to be ready to give them lots of information.

More than 40 protesters came out on Friday, some in colorful costumes, one dressed as a shark, another as a penguin, and many with placards expressing their dismay at the "beerish" image of Sea World. Sea World officials nixed the group's original plans to stage the protest in front of the ticket booths at the main walk-in entrance but gave them an even better backdrop by moving the group to an area near the parking entrance where, on a nicely manicured stretch of grass with flowers and tall palms, stood the biggest Sea World sign in town.

Media Coverage

Reporters came from all the major television stations, a few radio stations, the *Los Angeles Times*, the two principal local newspapers, and a couple of community newspapers. Baker deemed the protest a huge success:

> Coverage was immediate and extraordinary. One radio station did a live broadcast from the scene, and we were sort of aghast because as we all drove off to our businesses in the middle of the day, we all tuned in and we could hear the story moving across the air waves. At almost any point on the radio dial, it was mentioned as news. And one . . . talk and news station, devoted the rest of its day to the events at Sea World.

Saturday morning, the story made the front page of the two major San Diego dailies and the front page of the "San Diego Section" of the *Los Angeles Times*. As a result of this coverage, the Media Resource Center and other coalition members began receiving phone calls from other community groups and individuals wanting to know more about what was happening at Sea World. The first goal, attracting new coalition members, was already being accomplished.

One of the phone calls to Baker shortly after the Sea World protest came from the producers of the Ross/Hedgecock show, a locally produced hour-long afternoon program with a news and talk-show format. Roger Hedgecock, former mayor of San Diego, hosted the talk-show portion of the program and invited groups to address controversial community issues. The show initially wanted Media Resource Center staff to participate in a discussion of another alcohol-related issue; Baker agreed but also pitched the Sea World story. Producers for the Ross/Hedgecock show decided to do a whole program on the situation at Sea World and scheduled it for the end of April, just a week or so after the Sea World protest. Two Anheuser-Busch spokespersons flew in from St. Louis to participate, arriving in the Whale Plane, a huge jetliner painted black and white to resemble Shamu, the killer whale.

Zaustinsky along with Holly Richardson, a student from San Diego State University and an intern at the Media Resource Center, volunteered to represent the coalition on the show. Both had been involved with the Sea World campaign since the beginning and understood the broader alcohol policy issues the campaign was trying to address. Holly had some prior experience in front of a television camera; Zaustinsky had almost none.

Members of the coalition worked together to help Zaustinsky and Holly prepare for the show. They got together the weekend before and practiced role-playing. Zaustinsky described it this way:

> James acted as the host and he threw questions at me. At first I was very scared, all I could do was laugh and giggle and joke about things with him. I was too scared to respond, to really get into the role. Then, little by little I did it. I thought, what is my goal and if I could pick only one thing to get across to the audience what did I want it to be.

An overflow audience turned out for the show, the highest attendance ever for a Ross/Hedgecock show. Many coalition members came, joined by representatives from their communities. Holly and Zaustinsky stressed the changes at Sea World and the subtle and not-so-subtle proalcohol messages that were directed at children. The Anheuser-Busch representatives, Francine Katz, a parent and director of Consumer Awareness and Education for Anheuser-Busch, and Susie Busch-Transeau, direct descendant of the founder of the company and the company's executive in charge of National Advertising and Product Development, defended the beer sampling. They repeatedly insisted that giving away free samples of Anheuser-Busch products was pure hospitality and not irresponsible marketing.

Audience participation was lively; toward the end of the show, Alma, a 15-year-old who had come to the show along with other youth from the San Dieguito Alliance for Drug Free Youth, summed up her view of the situation:

> San Diego county is filled with places and things to do for adults. Sea World is one place where kids can go. Parents have always felt that this is a safe and healthy environment for us, and now it is changing and you are taking away one of those healthy environments for kids, and changing it into another place for adults. Why don't adults just go to a bar? Don't mix it here with Sea World.

Consequences of the Coverage

In May 1992, the alcohol promotion items targeted for children disappeared from Sea World gift shop shelves. Beer give-aways continued, however. Sea World officials told coalition members that servers in the Hospitality Center were trained to know when a customer had consumed the allotted two-beer maximum. Zaustinsky did her own personal test and succeeded in obtaining five free beers in a 35-minute period, just 1 hour before the park closed. "If I had consumed those beers, they would have clearly put me over the legal limit, and then I was supposed to get in my car and drive home!" remembered Zaustinsky.

The extensive media coverage caught the eye of State Assemblywoman Dede Alpert of San Diego. She contacted several coalition members and, after being briefed by them, offered to host a meeting between Sea World General Manager Mike Cross and other Sea World officials, her aides, staff from the county public health department, and coalition members. The goal of the meeting was to negotiate agreements between Sea World officials and the community.

In the meantime, the coalition had been in contact with activists nationwide via ALCNet to gather information and get feedback on its tactics along the way. Someone on ALCNet referred them to Common Cause in Sacramento, Common Cause in Washington, and Consumers Union in San Francisco. Common Cause, a government watchdog group, proved an invaluable ally to the coalition. According to its research, Anheuser-Busch had donated almost $500,000 to legislative campaigns in California over the previous 5 years. Common Cause also reported that Anheuser-Busch spends more than $125,000 a year to lobby the legislature. Finally, Common Cause records revealed that California Governor Pete Wilson held more than $100,000 in Anheuser-Busch common stock. Common Cause staff member Kim Alexander agreed to write an op-ed piece about Sea World, Anheuser-Busch, and the pending state legislation connection with help from Baker.

The coalition strategized about how to place the piece. Literally while the piece was being written, Baker hosted a media seminar for the coalition and invited editors from two or three newspapers in San Diego. During the seminar, he posed a hypothetical question to the editorial page editor of the *Union-Tribune*, "If you received an op-ed piece from Common Cause in Sacramento on the issues we are discussing with you today, and you know they are a fairly progressive group, that is, not in line with some of the conservative positions your newspaper takes, what would you think?" The editor indicated he would look at it favorably. When the editorial was ready to go, a phone call went to this editor, Common Cause sent in the piece, and then followed up with another phone call.

Much to the surprise and delight of the coalition members, the Common Cause editorial appeared on the same morning of the meeting hosted by Alpert and influenced the tone of the meeting. "The editorial added depth to our position," Baker said. "It was excellent. For the first time we were joined by quotable, notable, and formidable out-of-towners, who were interested in our issue for a variety of ethical reasons, all of which were positive for our community."

Coalition members brought with them a list of carefully considered requests, which had been reviewed not only by the coalition but also by advocates nationwide over ALCNet: (a) the immediate cessation of beer give-aways in the park; (b) no ads within the park that promote the use of alcohol; (c) no children in the Hospitality Center (perhaps turn it into a marine life exhibit per the park's mission); (d) no education about the glories of beer or alcohol industry-based propaganda on "Know When to Say When"; (e) Sea World to join the San Diego-area Responsible Hospitality Council and be certified as a responsible server of alcohol; (f) no distilled spirits to be served for anything except a special event or private party; (g) no marketing of any items associated with the use of alcoholic beverages that might appeal to young people; (h) no use of Anheuser-Busch names, symbols, or logos in Sea World and no cross-association of Anheuser-Busch and Sea World in ads outside the park; and (i) no Clydesdales in the park.

In person, Cross stonewalled the group's requests. In a subsequent letter to the meeting's participants, he reiterated Sea World's plans to continue beer selling and sampling and pointed out that Sea World currently sells beer in fewer locations than before Anheuser-Busch purchased the park (today the park has alcohol available at 9 locations, versus 18 in 1989). He also noted that all Anheuser-Busch logo merchandise is sold "largely" in the temporary hospitality center and denied that Anheuser-Busch made, or that Sea World sold, any candy, toys, or children's clothing displaying beer logos or names. Finally, he wrote, "Sea World continues to stand up to the test of responsibility in our sales and sampling of our Company's quality beverages, and continues to be willing to have discussions with any individual or group who have any concerns whatsoever" (Cross, 1992).

Despite his apparent unwillingness to address some of the coalition's requests, Cross did attend a Responsible Hospitality Council meeting. The Anheuser-Busch merchandise, which he stated did not exist, disappeared from the shelves. More important to the group than the changes at Sea World, however, were the changes occurring among San Diegans. Everyone seemed to know about what was going on at Sea World, and the coverage was influencing how people thought about the park. Rahn recalled:

> One day I was at the park with some friends, just there for fun. I was in one of the gift stores and a man in front of me was trying on a hat that said "BUD" on it. He was there with his young son. He turned to me and said, "This doesn't give the right message, does it?" I wondered if I had it written on my forehead that I was part of the coalition! I thought, it's successful if people are wondering "is that okay or not?", if people question what they are doing.

Zaustinsky summarized the impact of the campaign so far from her perspective:

> People were able to see in this issue the relationship of alcohol to the problems the community faces. The relationship of alcohol promotion to how they are targeting youth. It wasn't just about Sea World, it was about being able to focus attention to the broader alcohol-related problems. We used Sea World as a vehicle to engage the community. They can see the implication of the alcohol industry using our healthy environments for their own agenda.

A permanent lobbying coalition, the San Diego County Council on Alcohol Policy, grew out of the Sea World effort to address a range of alcohol policy issues in the San Diego area. Future activities regarding Sea World were to include an 800 number to encourage Sea World staff to blow the whistle on predatory marketing practices and a "red ribbon around Sea World" event to tie in with October's red ribbon week for alcohol awareness.

The Lessons

The Sea World campaign proved an invaluable learning experience for coalition members, a living primer in media advocacy. Baker reflected on the experience:

> We discovered that a media advocacy campaign is in every sense of the word a living "beast." It changes and breathes and moves. It disintegrates and heals and evolves. Its members come and go, some get stronger, some get weaker, some get afraid, and some get brave on a daily basis, on an hourly basis. To the extent that you try to plot it from the beginning and confine it, it's going to be unsuccessful. It has to have intentions, but it cannot have restrictions.

The campaign worked as a vehicle for community organizing around alcohol policy in San Diego. Clarity about the group's goal—to bring to the citizenry and public officials of San Diego County an awareness that they could participate in establishing alcohol policy in their own community—kept the campaign on track even when events proved unpredictable.

Coalition members approached the media with high ethical standards. They were uniformly committed to seeing that the truth came out and to ensuring that both sides had a chance to be heard. This meant two things: First, coalition members agreed that they would always tell media people the truth. As Zaustinsky cautioned, "Don't say you can provide them with information you can't. If you say you are going to get back to them with something, do it." Second, this commitment to truth meant that they needed to know the people who could accurately represent the views of the other side. They directed media personnel to different Sea World and Anheuser-Busch officials, being sure to give phone numbers and any other necessary information. They knew who the experts were on the issues being addressed and made the names and numbers of these people available as well. They wanted the whole story told, as accurately and truthfully as possible. Because they felt strongly that this campaign was a worthy and morally justifiable one, they believed that having both sides come out would further their cause.

The coalition took the time to do thorough research on the situation at Sea World before contacting the media; members gathered information from libraries, newspaper clippings, ALCNet sources, and key individuals. Coalition members analyzed the situation from different angles. They also researched how Anheuser-Busch had reacted to community alcohol prevention groups in the past.

The Sea World experience became a springboard for other community alcohol awareness and prevention activities. It showed that everyone can play the alcohol policy game, not just executives from Anheuser-Busch and politicians. Conscientious use of the media brought questions of alcohol policy into the open, making it possible for everyone to take part in seeing that the community's interests were addressed. According to Baker,

> We see the entire campaign, both to date and yet to come, as a functioning alcohol policy tool which is already extremely useful to the people of our county. We've used the Sea World experience as an example to loudly and publicly raise other alcohol issues that need to be approached all over the county.

MADD Fixes the "Flaw in the Law"

The Hawaii Mothers Against Drunk Driving (MADD) chapter saw the prospect of all their hard work to pass a new drunk-driving law going down the drain. To make sure the law was enacted as they had intended they would have to challenge the political establishment. The state legislature would have to convene a special session to fix the "flaw in the law," and this had never happened before. Indeed, the outward facts suggested that the prospects were virtually hopeless.

The Story

The central problem was that the legislature, influenced by a system that gave committee chairpersons (in this case, the Senate Transportation Committee chair) extraordinary powers, had deleted the "implied consent" provision from Hawaii's new drunk-driving law.

This provision, which had been in Hawaii law since 1967, allowed for virtually automatic license revocation for refusal to take a Breathalyzer test when stopped by the police. The deletion would have made Hawaii the only state with such weak sanctions against drunk driving. The legislature had adjourned on April 28, and the new law was to take effect on July 1.

Most observers, including the governor, agreed that something should be done. But doing something would have meant convening a special session just to restore the implied consent provision. It would have also meant challenging the authority of a committee chairperson. No party—the governor, the speaker of the House, the Senate president—seemed ready to get involved, despite the considerable publicity given the situation in the media.

MADD probably would not have taken its plunge without the political intelligence it developed from friends within the legislature and the executive branch agencies—information that told them the situation was not quite as hopeless as it appeared. According to Carol McNamee, MADD's legislative chairperson, "The Governor had said enough publicly that we were not worried about him. He knew something should happen but did not want to get involved until the House and Senate had taken action." [5]

The key person was Senate President Richard S. H. Wong because he was the one who could reconvene the session. However, to do this he would have to overturn the decision of the Transportation Committee chair, which would involve some political risk. Wong was somewhat harder to pin down on the issue, but McNamee's sources convinced her that the senator "perhaps needed something to help him take some action." In other words, Wong needed a face-saving reason for overriding the position of one of his committee chairpersons.

"Positioning ourselves required a lot of deliberation," McNamee said. "We did not want to look like MADD against the world." This, plus the belief that Wong was not so much an enemy as a politician needing cover, led MADD to adopt a less strident tone in its public statements than it might have.

Although MADD identified Wong and the governor as the primary targets of its campaign, it depicted Wong as a person waiting to hear from citizens that they cared. MADD's approach thus concentrated almost exclusively on generating a grassroots movement to show Hawaii's political establishment the extent of citizen concern about the flawed law. At no point in the campaign did MADD criticize Wong's position. "We wanted him to look good," said McNamee.

Getting Media Attention

MADD originally believed the publicity given to the need for a special session would quickly convince the governor and the legislature to reconvene for a quick fix. It took 2 weeks after the legislature adjourned for them to realize that the governor and the legislature would not act without being prodded. By this time it was late May, and the law was due to take effect on July 1.

MADD decided to use the observed Memorial Day, May 27, to launch its campaign. This choice had obvious symbolic value. In addition, MADD's planners realized that the holiday is a slow day for news, so both TV and print media would be likely to give the opening salvo prominent coverage.

In a scene that must have made assignment editors' jobs a little easier that day, MADD staged its action in front of Hawaii's Eternal Flame war memorial. McNamee pointed out that Hawaiians should remember those killed not only in war but on the highways. A 2-foot-high sign attached to the speakers' podium carried the governor's and Wong's telephone numbers.

On the actual Memorial Day, MADD started collecting signatures for a petition that it would present to Wong. Again, the press and TV cameras were invited to show up at the shopping malls and parking lots where the MADD volunteers were working. Again, the 2-foot-high sign showed up to drive the point home that this was a grassroots campaign and there was something individuals could do to help.

This tactic, asking all Hawaiians who cared to call or write Wong and the governor, became MADD's primary and almost exclusive message. The rationale given for the campaign—"After July 1st, most drunk drivers will not lose their license to drive. They will be legally sharing the roads with us and our families"—was equally simple.

The first Memorial Day ceremony generated more than 3,000 telephone calls to Wong's office—a record number—and a record number of letters as well. But these calls and letters all came within the first week, and it was clear to MADD strategists that the furor would quickly die down unless something were done to sustain the effort and interest in calling for the special session.

Sustaining the Coverage

Much of MADD's planning after Memorial Day centered on generating events that would catch the interest of the media and thus keep up the pressure on the governor and Wong. MADD started a letter-writing campaign to local newspapers. MADD's president also appeared on several talk shows. In every television appearance, McNamee carried the sign with the 2-foot-high telephone numbers of the governor and Wong. The sign showed up on the front of podiums, beside interview chairs, and on top of petition desks.

In a ceremony at Wong's office on June 4, a delegation of MADD state and chapter leaders presented petitions. Each member of the delegation wore a bright yellow T-shirt with "Fix the Flaw in the Law" on the front and "Ring Wong" (with the telephone number) on the back. This parade of visual effects paid off, as the event was covered in full by the media.

In one event that evoked a Hawaiian political tradition, MADD organizers took to the road. Hawaii law prohibits billboards, so political advertising is often done from commuter roadside, with candidates and volunteers holding signs bearing the candidates' names. With TV cameras nearby, MADD volunteers took to heavily traveled commuter routes during several rush hours and flashed signs with the governor's and Wong's telephone numbers.

MADD's chief ally, the Hawaiian Medical Association, also paid careful attention to visual effects during its opening news conference. Hawaiian Medical Association President John McDonnell described the setting:

> We had an ambulance in front of the building. We invited the Hawaii Nurses Association and the Emergency Physicians Association. We also happened to have the coincidence of a victim: a former world class swimmer, still in the hospital, who had been hit by a drunk driver while jogging. We were unashamed. We all wore white coats and stethoscopes, although we never wear them at work.

Broad Community Support

The allies that MADD recruited became an important, even vital, force in giving legitimacy to the grassroots movement calling for a special session. The Hawaiian Medical Association, for example, purchased a full-page ad in the local newspaper. According to McDonnell, it also "called in a couple of markers" with Honolulu's main morning newspaper so that the paper would print letters supporting the campaign. It coordinated news events with MADD so that interest in the issue would be sustained throughout June.

MADD also targeted as coalition partners law enforcement agencies, insurance groups, the Hawaii Convention and Visitors Bureau, and the chamber of commerce—any group, according to McNamee, that could conceivably have an interest in the legislation.

MADD's approach to the chamber of commerce typified the recruitment effort. MADD knew the chamber's executive director and staff, having worked with them previously. McNamee telephoned the chamber, asking to be invited to a board meeting to present MADD's case. The pitch to the chamber centered on Hawaii's unique stigma as a state with weak drunk-driving laws, and framed this in terms of the harm this could do to the image of the state as a safe place for tourists. Once the chamber agreed to back the campaign, McNamee asked the board to issue its letter of support as a news release.

The final countdown started when a delegation from MADD presented the petitions to Wong. At that time, the senator spoke with the media and indicated publicly his concern about flaws in the new law. Throughout the following 2 weeks, Wong showed that he was intent at least on exploring all possibilities: He visited the Transportation Committee chair, he convened a caucus of the Democratic leadership, and on June 20 he convened a caucus of Senate Democrats.

This was encouraging news to the MADD leadership, which by this time had made personal contact with each senator. While not all of them had committed themselves, MADD had a nose count indication that a majority of Senate Democrats favored convening a special session.

Nevertheless, MADD was not leaving things to chance. It decided that the caucus, which was certain to be covered by the media, gave the organization a good opportunity to garner attention through good visuals. The particular medium chosen also reflected MADD's deliberate positioning: a positive attitude and no casting of stones.

MADD volunteers were at the state capitol at 7:00 on the morning of the Democratic caucus to present "balloon-a-grams" to each senator. Each helium-filled balloon was tied to a gold key with the inscription "You are the key." A note of appreciation ("We thank you for coming back to the caucus.") was also attached. MADD made a statement to the media along the same lines shortly before the caucus convened. MADD members held a highly visible vigil outside the caucus room during the session.

The Democratic caucus broke up 2 hours later with the announcement that a special session would be convened to address the drunk-driving law. There were still many obstacles to overcome, inasmuch as the entire administrative license revocation bill, which had taken 7 years of intense lobbying to enact, was again placed before the legislature. MADD followed through by being active in the necessary, conventional legislative work such as drafting committee testimony, preparing witnesses, and so on. By the end of the special session, an amended bill with the implied consent provision had passed both houses with only one dissenting vote.

The Lessons

The day after the Democratic caucus, Wong told a reporter that "MADD is a giant killer. . . . MADD started something that was totally different in the history of Hawaiian politics" ("MADD Gets Mad," 1991). The senator's administrative assistant, Yen Lew, distinguished MADD's campaign from the kind he often sees in the Senate. "We get a lot of computer generated letters on various issues," said Lew ("MADD Gets Mad,"

1991). What Lew saw in the MADD campaign, on the other hand, was a large volume of calls and letters in which voters "had some strong feelings and had paid some attention" to getting these thoughts through to Wong.

MADD had a specific, clear goal and used the media surgically to advance their desired policy outcome. Their excellent visuals got the media's attention and, at the same time, promoted the phone numbers citizens could call. They used a holiday to peg their story and garnered wide community support.

Though the issue was politically delicate, MADD effectively navigated the sensitive territory to achieve their goal and not alienate politicians with whom they might need to work in the future. MADD used narrow-casting to focus wide media exposure on two men, thereby bringing those men's actions into public view. Whatever Wong's decision, the public would know, and he knew they would know. MADD used the media to apply pressure to a specific target, and he responded.

Nicotina Meets Philip Morris:
The Battle of the Symbols

In the summer of 1990, the Philip Morris Co. announced plans to sponsor a national tour of an original copy of the Bill of Rights. Philip Morris's announcement of the tour came several months after it launched a joint project with the National Archives, backed by a televised advertising campaign, to commemorate the 200th anniversary of the Bill of Rights at the national level.

Tobacco-control advocates saw Philip Morris's involvement with the Bill of Rights as more than just a strategy to improve their public image in general; they also suspected that Philip Morris wanted to encourage the public to associate "rights" with smoking, as in "people should have a 'right' to smoke" and "the government should not take that 'right' away from them."

The Story

When Philip Morris's joint project with the National Archives had first been announced it had been met with widespread expressions of concern and condemnation. Hearings were held before the U.S. House of Representatives. However, no voice of protest was able to establish or sustain any momentum and the project continued.

In August 1990, the Advocacy Institute, a Washington, DC-based public interest consulting group, obtained an advance schedule of the national tour, including dates and specific locations for each of the tour's 52 stops (every state, including two stops each in California and Texas). According to the schedule, the tour was to open in Barre, Vermont, on October 11, 1990, and conclude in Richmond, Virginia, on February 10, 1992.

Copies of the tour schedule were distributed at a national tobacco-control, grassroots, and community organizers' conference held in Boston that month. There, activists recognized the tour as a golden opportunity to protest this national campaign at the community level. Two early-morning meetings were held during the conference to brainstorm and share ideas on tactics and arguments that could counteract Philip Morris's presumed goals.

It was quickly agreed that a countersymbol should be developed to accompany the tour from state to state as a focal point for local efforts. Suggestions included a "death clock" to update continually the number of tobacco victims in the country, a scroll of tobacco victims, and a Vietnam Memorial-style wall inscribed with the names of victims. Some suggested that activists rename the tour the "Bill of Wrongs" tour. Others suggested more caution and warned that attacking anything connected to the Bill of Rights could backfire. Everyone agreed that any counter-events or countersymbols must be carefully designed to focus protest on Philip Morris's exploitation of the Bill of Rights and not on the Bill of Rights itself.

Although many other ideas were recorded and enthusiasm was high, activists left the meetings with no clear next step; no organization or individual had volunteered to take charge of any of the responsibilities involved in creating and managing a national tour for a countersymbol.

However, the brainstorming that started at the Boston conference continued over the next days and weeks (and, eventually, months) via the tobacco-control electronic network, SCARCNet (see Chapter 5). Ideas continued to be developed, themes tested, and data gathered. Dr. John Slade of the Robert Wood Johnson Medical School calculated a day-to-day total of the number of tobacco-related deaths that would occur during the course of the tour. The Advocacy Institute developed a pamphlet listing examples of how Philip Morris had squelched the free speech of others. And a Seattle-based physicians activist group, Washington DOC (Doctors Ought to Care), began to build Nicotina, a movable countersymbol designed to travel with the Bill of Rights tour.

At a news conference unveiling Nicotina in Seattle, Bob Jaffe (the president of Washington DOC) described the statue as follows:

> Nicotina is modeled off of the Statue of Liberty. She's holding a cigarette in her upheld hand, instead of a torch, and her eyes are closed, the symbol of shame that she's been exploited by the tobacco companies and made a symbol of tobacco. The chains from her cigarettes in the pack help to illustrate to all of the children who are going to see the Bill of Rights tour that this is a dangerous, addictive drug. At her feet are the words, "Give me your poor, your tired, your women, your children yearning to breathe free." . . . She's standing on the base of cigarettes, most of which were bought by 14-year-old children around this area. . . . And in the front is a clock that states, "Since the beginning of the Philip Morris Bill of Rights tour, 38,195 people have died of tobacco-related diseases." About every 70 seconds, it goes up another notch.

The first few stops on the tour were scheduled before Nicotina was completed and featured more traditional protests from activist groups. In Barre, Vermont, the tour opened with a lot of media attention focused on the patriotic spectacle that Philip Morris had staged (including a parade through town and a custom-designed armored vehicle, accompanied by retired Marine honor guards, to carry the Bill of Rights into town).

Media attention in Vermont and the next few states on the tour was highlighted by innocuous feature pieces, including the following:

- "High-Tech Exhibit Displays Bill of Rights in Positive Light" (October 11, 1990)
- "Bill of Rights Rises in High-Tech Splendor" (October 18, 1990)
- "Bill of Rights Arrives in Albany" (October 22, 1990)
- "U.S. Bill of Rights Will Visit Augusta" (November 5, 1990)

Some articles focused on those protesting the tour—not on their message or on their target of protest, for example:

- "Protesters Greet Opening for Tour of Bill of Rights" (October 11, 1990)
- "West Warlock Police Prepare for Bill of Rights Tour Protest" (October 17, 1990)
- "Gay Rights, Anti-Smoking Activists to Protest Philip Morris' Bill of Rights Tour" (October 17, 1990)
- "Activists Protest Bill of Rights Display" (October 21, 1990)

News coverage and photographs gave as much attention to protesters from ACT-UP, an AIDS activist group that was calling for a boycott of Philip Morris products because of their support of homophobic Senator Jesse Helms, as they did to antitobacco health groups.

Activists across the country shared summaries of news stories from the first several states of the tour via SCARCNet, discussed reactions to protests, and modified their tactics.

By the time Nicotina was unveiled 6 weeks later in Boston, the message of the antitobacco activists had changed. A simple slogan was developed to clarify that protests were directed toward Philip Morris and not the Bill of Rights: "Bill of Rights Yes/Philip Morris No." The slogan was put on buttons and pamphlets that were distributed to the mostly school-aged viewers of the tour.

Media coverage, reflecting the change in strategy, began to focus on the health messages of the antitobacco activists and on the general controversy surrounding Philip Morris's sponsorship of the tour, for example:

- "Philip Morris Taking Heat as Sponsor of 'Bill of Rights Tour' " (November 28, 1990)
- "Tobacco Company Criticized for Bill of Rights Tour" (February 19, 1991)
- "Anti-Tobacco Group Hails Exhibit, Assails Sponsor" (February 19, 1991)
- "Tour Sponsorship Draws Fire" (April 23, 1991)
- "Anti-Smoking Coalition Looks Askance at Philip Morris Gift" (May 14, 1991)
- "Bill of Rights Stirs Free Speech: A Protest Against Cigarette Maker" (July 13, 1991)
- "Tobacco-Funded Rights' Display has Anti-Smoking Forces Fuming" (July 10, 1991)

When the tour stopped in California, the *Los Angeles Times* (May 9, 1991) accompanied a story with a close-up photograph of a "YES Bill of Rights,

NO Philip Morris" button. Overall, the advocates changed their strategy and tactics to make sure their story was being told. The headlines presented above provide clear evidence of their success. `

Throughout most of the stops on the tour, the statue of Nicotina served as a focal point for media coverage of health groups' counterefforts. As such, the statue helped ensure clarity and consistency in health groups' messages as the tour progressed from state to state. In many tour stops, health groups unveiled Nicotina the day before the Bill of Rights arrived, thereby gaining maximum control of the news coverage of the event; by the time Philip Morris arrived, many newspapers had already featured Nicotina in prominent stories. The statue also served as an organizing tool as community groups in each location took on the logistical responsibilities (with support from Washington DOC in Seattle) of transporting the statue between sites, sometimes hundreds of miles.

In early 1991, perhaps in response to the well-coordinated efforts of the health groups, Philip Morris quietly changed the schedule of the remaining stops on the tour. Many stops were shortened, reducing the overall length of the tour by 2 months, and several dates and locations were changed. Philip Morris also stopped some of the national public relations support it had been providing for the tour, including a toll-free hot line that had been providing information on tour dates and locations.

Even at this early point in the tour, it was clear that Philip Morris had not created the public relations masterpiece that it may have originally expected. Instead of creating the public image of a patriotic, charitable, civic-minded corporation, the tour served to reinforce images of Philip Morris as a cynical, exploitive producer of an addictive, lethal substance. Health groups achieved this turnaround by carefully creating messages to frame the tour from a health perspective, preempting Philip Morris's attempts to frame its own message.

The Lessons

Make Good Use of Intelligence. Like everyone else, health advocates do not operate in a vacuum and must know and understand their targets plans and strategies. Even before Philip Morris had publicly announced the Bill of Rights tour, health advocates had found early schedules of the tour and distributed them to their colleagues across the country. This early intelligence gave advocates the time they needed to plot counter-strategies.

Learn From Your Mistakes as Well as Your Successes. Early in the Bill of Rights tour, press coverage was not as good as some had hoped. Messages were diffused or ignored altogether. Potential coalition members were scared away or uninterested. But the experiences of the early states helped teach the later states what they should and should not do when Philip Morris came to visit them.

Capture the Symbols. Before the Bill of Rights tour even started, health advocates were at a disadvantage. There are few symbols more sacred to Americans than the Bill of Rights, and Philip Morris had already owned it. Any attack launched at Philip Morris risked being seen as an attack on the constitution itself. However, health advocates paid close attention to the symbols and chose their words carefully. YES Bill of Rights, NO Philip Morris made it clear what the health groups were, and were not, protesting.

Halt the Malt:
Framing a Story Worth Telling

When the Marin Institute received a phone call from a CNN producer in January 1992, it was not so out of the ordinary. After all, the producer wanted (like many journalists who called during that time) to do a story on St. Ides malt liquor. This was a new potent malt liquor that was being targeted to young African-American males.

The producer had gotten interested in the story through the media coverage of rap artist Chuck D.'s lawsuit against the company and hoped to do a story focusing on the lawsuit as well as the contrast between Chuck D. (who was opposed to the use of rap to sell malt liquor) and rap artist Ice Cube (who had done numerous rap-oriented ads for St. Ides). This, to be sure, would have been an interesting story, the kind the media like best: two celebrities on different sides of a controversial issue. However, the reduction of such a serious alcohol policy issue to a disagreement among friends was not the kind of story a media advocate feels will advance the policy agenda. The Marin Institute wanted to pitch a new, more relevant frame for the story.

The Story

St. Ides's outrageous commercials and use of popular African-American rap artists had garnered much interest among the media before the CNN call. Articles on the ad campaign had appeared in *The Wall Street Journal, Chicago Tribune,* and *Washington Post,* not to mention the appearance of numerous stories via wire service in hundreds of newspapers nationwide. Surgeon General Antonia Novello had been particularly outspoken on the campaign as were other civic leaders in and outside of the African-American community, and with good reason.

St. Ides advertising featured popular rap music performers using lyrics that encouraged drinking the brew in unlawful and high-risk settings. One ad featuring female performer Yo-Yo, in a campaign targeting young women, suggested: "Tell your man to get you a six pack and don't be afraid of what it does to you . . . 'cause it will get you in the mood" Yo-Yo was 19 years old when this ad aired. Other ads featuring Ice Cube intimated that drinking St. Ides could "get your jimmy thicker" (sexually arouse a man) and "get your girl in the mood quicker."

Action to curb these marketing practices had already begun. The Washington State Liquor Control Board banned the "Get your girl in the mood quicker" ad after members of the local African-American community complained about its obscenity. Oregon's Liquor Control Commission banned St. Ides posters featuring Ice Cube displaying a hand signal commonly used by gangs ("Oregon Bans," 1991) and the BATF had ordered fines and a 3-day permit suspension for ads found in violation of federal law ("BATF Imposes," 1992).

Yet there was more to be done. The company was currently engaged in an aggressive public relations campaign to clean up its image— particularly among African-American leaders. In December 1991 it announced new public service announcements that focused on drinking and driving and underage drinking. The company also began an aggressive sponsorship effort that included donations to a Medical Aid Fund to benefit the Drew-King Medical Center in the heart of South Central Los Angeles as well as donations to inner-city organizations in Baltimore and Los Angeles working with high-risk youth.

While these efforts were going on, McKenzie River Corp. (the company that markets St. Ides) had also produced commercials featuring The Geto Boys, a popular rap group whose leader Bushwick Bill was involved in a highly publicized alcohol-related shooting that resulted in the loss of his eye. Details of the incident appeared in a number of publications, including *Rolling Stone* magazine in which Bushwick was quoted as saying, "Whenever I keep mixing all these different liquors and get really, really drunk, I get depressed and suicidal" (DeCurtis, 1991). The new ads by St. Ides made direct reference to the shooting incident with Bushwick rapping, "This is Bushwick on the go with a blow to the eye show. . . ."

The Challenge of Reframing

The Marin Institute had hoped that CNN would frame the story around the unethical behavior of the company and the lack of regulatory redress available to police these kinds of violations. One thing was clear: Framing such a rich and complex issue that had captured the energy of so many nationwide as a conflict between two performers would trivialize the issue and deflect attention from the policy aspects of alcohol advertising targeting youth. After reviewing background materials including ad footage, relevant news clippings, briefings on the relevant regulatory issues as well as corporate documents sent by the Marin Institute, CNN staff began to look into framing the story in a more comprehensive way.

CNN became interested in how few regulations there were concerning youth targeting in alcohol advertising. The producer was thorough in his research, requesting copies of all relevant regulations, information on malt liquor availability on a state-by-state basis, and a list of people who might appear on camera. The Marin Institute staff was prepared and quickly downloaded information from its computer network ALCNet, its Alcohol Industry Materials Database and its Resource Center's large collection of materials by and about the alcohol industry. Fact sheets on malt liquor and its impact on inner-city communities had been prepared as well as a list of possible interviewees with contact information.

Providing Access to Credible
Authentic Voices

Marin Institute staff suggested that CNN go to Jamaica, Queens, a predominantly African-American community in New York City and interview staff and youth in treatment at the Jamaica Community Adolescent Program.

The youth spoke eloquently about the effects of the advertising on their own lives and the ease with which underage youth could purchase alcohol. Their statements provided convincing real-life examples of the human suffering, resulting from the alcohol industry's aggressive targeting of youth. Staff also provided expert testimony on the product's impact on their treatment facility. Marin Institute staff worked closely with the Jamaica Community Adolescent Program to ensure that it was comfortable with the interviews and to provide support as needed. This included fact sheets, background information, and sometimes simply a supportive ear to bounce off interview strategies.

In addition to suggesting to CNN whom it might interview in support of increased regulation, the Marin Institute also suggested names of those on the other side of the issue such as Minot Wessinger from MacKenzie River as well as key neutral players like BATF.

The Lessons

An 8-minute story on CNN's *Special Assignment* aired four times on "Super Tuesday," the day many states hold primary elections and thus a heavy viewing day for CNN. The piece was hard hitting and comprehensive, weaving together tough interviews with industry spokespersons with the Jamaica Community Adolescent Program staff and youth clients, kids on the street, ad footage, and a particularly revealing interview with BATF that clearly laid blame for the problem with the lack of regulatory power to police such advertising.

The story was reframed in a way that made the policy goal of more regulation for alcohol advertising clear and logical to viewers. However, no Marin Institute staff appeared in the story. In fact, the staff person involved felt very strongly that appearing on camera often weakens your ability to work effectively with the media because it gives the impression that your suggestions are calculated to publicize yourself or your organization. By not appearing in the story, the Marin Institute was in a more "neutral" position to provide the technical assistance and support needed to pitch CNN a more comprehensive frame.

Another important lesson is that the institute was not afraid to say to the CNN producer, "Hey, there may be another angle you might want to look into." Do not feel it is necessary simply to accept a reporter's frame on an issue. It may just be that the reporter has not had the benefit of the information at your disposal. Be sure to try to organize the information you provide so that it is easy to use. Always include a cover letter or memo that details the package contents. If the reporter made a request for specific information, be sure to identify it and place it prominently among the materials you send.

The CNN story was a real breakthrough in the St. Ides campaign, helping to recruit more groups to the network of activists working on the issue while bringing it to the attention of policymakers nationwide. The story was followed 3 days later by a front-page, hard-hitting piece in *The Wall Street Journal* on how malt liquor companies target the urban young ("Malt Liquor Makers," 1992). The reporter also called the Marin Institute for assistance, further solidifying the institute's reputation as a reliable, informed source on alcohol policy.

The Ryan White CARE Act

AIDS service organizations faced a terrible problem in 1990. A decade into the epidemic, services were stretched beyond their limits. The vaunted "San Francisco model" of care was crumbling under the weight of its caseload. Nationwide, at the end of April 1990, a total of 80,798 people had died, 51,712 had been diagnosed, and an estimated 1 million U.S. residents were infected with HIV.

At the same time, despite a few celebrity deaths, AIDS remained politically unpopular, particularly at the federal level. The vast majority of federal resources for AIDS before 1990 went to protecting the "innocent" public, with research and education receiving the lion's share of funding. Less than 5% of federal funding went to services for persons with AIDS or infected with HIV. Compassion fatigue was also beginning to show up in the halls of Congress, evidenced by rumblings that AIDS had already received more than its share of federal funding. The problem for the National Organizations for Responding to AIDS, the national umbrella and federal lobby organization for AIDS service organizations, and the AIDS Action Council, charged with handling Washington lobbying chores for National Organizations for Responding to AIDS, lay in how to frame a piece of legislation to break the Washington logjam on AIDS services.

The Story

In the second half of 1989, both Hurricane Hugo in the Gulf of Mexico and the Loma Prieta earthquake near San Francisco brought the specter of natural disaster home to the American public. AIDS Action Council member and San Francisco AIDS Foundation Executive Director Pat Christian was the first to seize on this as a potential frame for an AIDS services bill. Natural disasters still lay within the media window and the public consciousness. The frame also removed the stigma of guilt from AIDS, presenting the situation as an unpredicted disaster rather than the result of individual carelessness. Finally, stories documenting the inefficiency of the Federal Emergency Management Administration in responding to Hurricane Hugo and the Loma Prieta earthquake supported just the conclusion the AIDS Action Council wanted people to make about AIDS: Disasters demand a rapid response.

AIDS Action Council members framed their bill to reflect the disaster theme. The first portion of the bill would provide "disaster relief" to fund AIDS care in those cities hardest hit by the epidemic. The second created block grants for the states, combining existing federal programs in a package that would be attractive to conservative members of Congress like Orrin Hatch, a key member of the Senate Labor and Human Resources Committee, who would have to approve the bill. The third portion of the bill would fund states and private clinics to provide early intervention services, testing, counseling, and prescription drugs to infected people. According to AIDS Action Council Director of Public Policy Tom Sheridan,

> This was a compassionate bill. This was about care. This was about doctors and nurses and caring and hospital rooms and families—all the things that go into caring for people who are dying. It was a consensus for compassion. Even conservatives can agree on the morality of compassion.[6]

The bill focused on the health care crisis facing people with AIDS. "That sense of impending disaster . . . gave us the ability to fire it through Congress as quickly as possible," Sheridan said. In keeping with the frame, they called the bill the Comprehensive AIDS Resources Emergency Act, creating the acronym by which the bill became known, the CARE Act.

Attracting the Media

It was already relatively late in the legislative session when the bill was ready for introduction. The bill's backers needed to put the measure on a fast track. Senator Edward Kennedy would be on hand and would be quoted citing the national crisis of AIDS services. But communicating the frame to the Congress and the public would require a powerful media jump-start, and the AIDS Action Council looked to their strongest drawing card: Elizabeth Taylor.

The American Foundation for AIDS Research flew in Elizabeth Taylor, a coalition member, to anchor the news conference. Sheridan explained why:

> The media are interested in things that appeal to people in America. Elizabeth Taylor is news. Elizabeth Taylor doing something on AIDS is news. Tom Sheridan—no news at all. [Bill sponsor] Ted Kennedy—he does this all the time. [Ryan White's mother] Jeanne White—we feel sorry for her but just covered the funeral last week. Reporters are incredibly busy, overtaxed people who have to have a shove essentially. News is no longer substance, it's show. And quite frankly, we figured that if we have to put on a show, we're going to put on a damn good one. And she provides a great show.

Even with this strong and public start, the bill would have to overcome three major hurdles: first, attracting enough cosponsors—senators and representatives on record as committed to voting for the bill. In the Senate to reach the floor, over the certain objections of Republican Senator Jesse Helms of North Carolina, 61 cosponsors were necessary. Second, the bill needed to win approval on the floor ("authorization") of the full House and Senate and the signature of the president. Finally, it would have to weather the appropriations stage, in which appropriations committees in the two chambers would dole out actual dollars. Tie-ups would be most likely in the Senate, and activists aimed the bulk of their efforts there.

An unfortunate but serendipitous event occurred as the Senate Labor and Human Resources Committee was marking up the bill (preparing it for full Senate action). Hemophiliac Ryan White had become a popular symbol for the struggle for fair treatment for people with AIDS, standing up for his right to attend his Indiana grammar school like other children despite his illness. Ryan was in the national news that week, reportedly entering the hospital for his final stay there. Within a week, Ryan would be dead. Swept up in the moment, Hatch and Kennedy suggested and the committee agreed to name the bill for Ryan, as a memorial to his courage in standing up for the rights and dignity of people with AIDS.

The bill was now out of committee, but not yet on the Senate floor. Facing a tight agenda, and wanting to avoid a filibuster by Helms and his allies, Senate Majority Leader George Mitchell was unlikely to allow the bill to even come to the floor without enough cosponsors to secure a vote of cloture to head off a filibuster. The magic number of cosponsors needed was 61. To obtain that number, the AIDS Action Council once again looked to someone with immense popular appeal, both to members of Congress and the media: 3 weeks after her son had died, Jeanne White came to Washington to lobby for the bill. Sheridan described what happened:

> She was making a condolence call on [the Congress] essentially. Three weeks after her son's funeral, this woman was in town to ask for a very significant memorial, which was the piece of legislation. We felt that was newsworthy, and scheduled a press conference. Jeanne's a very simple woman, and in her simplicity there's a media brilliance. She said, "Look, I'm only here to ask people to support my boy's bill. I don't understand how all this happens . . . but I'm here with some friends who I know and trust and we're going to see if we can get this to happen." It was perfect. She didn't pretend to be anything different than what she was.

With the cameras in tow, White walked the halls of the Capitol. At the end of the day, White wanted to go to a hotel to rest her feet. But the tally of cosponsors still had not reached 61. Sheridan recalled:

> I gave her a tuna-fish sandwich and we went over to the Senate floor and I said, "we need to work here for an hour and we're going to pluck people off that I think you should talk to." So I stood at the elevators and literally button-holed Senators, one by one, and brought them in to talk to her. She was sitting at that point in the Senate anteroom because she couldn't stand anymore. Senators would come up and they would offer condolences—it was a bit like a wake. Jeanne, worn and tired, would ask for support on the Ryan White CARE Act. And people would co-sponsor, just like that. . . . We started the day with 32 cosponsors—and ended with 61.

Even with 61 cosponsors, the Senate leadership was still dragging its feet. After 3 weeks of waiting, the AIDS Action Council first organized a news conference outside the Capitol and a sit-in in the Senate gallery, with people with AIDS wearing T-shirts that said, "SHOW US YOU CARE." The next day, an AMTRAK car filled with mothers of people with AIDS came down from New York to show their support. And finally, on the 3rd day, White once again came to Washington and sat in the Senate gallery all day long, a one-woman vigil with the press corps duly notified and attentive. The next day, the bill came to the floor. Once there, it passed without event, on a 95 to 4 vote. In the House, the bill passed by 408 to 14. Passage of the authorization received extensive media coverage. Many of the stories quoted Kennedy, who continued to push the crisis frame: "Cities and states are struggling to keep their health systems from collapsing, and they deserve federal aid."

The next hurdle would be getting the authorized funds appropriated. In September, the crucial Senate Appropriations Subcommittee, chaired by Tom Harkin of Iowa, provided no new funds for the activities authorized under the bill. Funding was essentially frozen at the same level as the year before—a net gain of great publicity for Congress, and no new funds for AIDS.

Sustaining the Coverage

The AIDS Action Council and its allies mounted a major media campaign to reach the districts of the members of the full Appropriations Committees in both the House and Senate. San Francisco AIDS Foundation Public Policy Director Rene Durazzo described the campaign:

Volunteers identified the newspapers in the districts of members of key committees that we needed to influence and in the heavily HIV-impacted cities. We put together a packet of materials on the CARE Act, the controversy over it not getting funded and Congress welshing on its promise. We called up all the newspapers, identified either sympathetic or key editorial personnel on each of those newspapers, sent them the materials, and pitched the controversy over how Congress had passed this bill and decided not to fund it. The key was to make it a very controversial local issue, to drive the editorial. It came down to identifying the key writer and making insistent and persistent phone contact, and having a good strong controversial issue to put in front of those people. After that, the key was continued follow-up to make sure that they had run the piece. And we literally did that, with a checklist of newspapers that the volunteers called every day. Every time an editorial came in, it was circulated all over the hill to all the conference members and all the appropriations committee members in both houses.

Through their efforts, editorials calling on Congress to restore full funding appeared in papers in all 16 cities targeted for disaster relief and in numerous other areas as well. Unfortunately, the most important paper, Harkin's hometown *Des Moines Register*, editorialized against full funding, shoring up Harkin's reluctance, in a tight reelection year, to fund the act.

Once again, to attract media attention, White played a crucial role. On September 13, in Washington, the bill's sponsors, Kennedy and Hatch, joined by Senate appropriators Brock Adams of Washington, Frank Lautenberg of New Jersey, and Alfonse D'Amato of New York, held a news conference denouncing the subcommittee's failure to fund the bill. At the conference White said, "if you are not going to make this memorial to [my son] something that's going to help the people, then quite frankly I'd rather you not name it after him at all. Just take it off the bill" (interview by David Jernigan, February 13, 1991). In a piece of well-timed public shaming, White repeated her request to a national audience in an op-ed piece in *USA Today*.

The appropriations bill moved on to the full Senate Appropriations Committee, in which Adams, despite the fact that Seattle did not qualify for the disaster relief section, attempted a compromise. To create funds for the act, he proposed shaving 0.9% off of any of the other programs in the Labor, Health and Human Services, Education and Related Agencies section of the appropriations bill, which had an increase greater than the inflation rate. Head Start, worker training, and low-income home energy projects were but a few of the programs that would have been affected.

Needless to say, this compromise won the AIDS activists few friends in Washington and ultimately went down to defeat. The machinations of the Appropriations Conference Committee occurred behind closed doors, but advocates for the bill strove to keep the media spotlight on them. Elizabeth Taylor also published letters in *USA Today* and the *Los Angeles Times* (Taylor, 1990). Numerous other organizations worked to keep the issue in the spotlight, from ACTUP, which demonstrated in the streets, to health officials in the 16 hardest hit cities, who took out a full-page newspaper ad calling for full funding. If the bill went down, Sheridan wanted the public to know that Congress should not get away with getting all the publicity they got for helping when they weren't really going to provide any help, period.

On the final day of the conference meetings in mid-October, conferees somehow located funds for the bill, and it emerged and went to the president. It was funded at $350 million for its first year, which included $206 million for existing programs and $144 million for new services in the bill. This was substantially less than the $875 million originally authorized. The final outcome was a victory for AIDS activists—not all they had hoped for, but a victory nonetheless.

The Lessons

The campaign to pass and fund the Ryan White CARE Act used the news media extensively to pressure specific senators, win public support, and keep the bill in the public spotlight. Sheridan and colleagues tried to lead the media throughout the campaign:

> My goal as an advocate is to create systems and services that serve people better. But there are things you have to do to get that done in the political context, like manipulate the media, understand public opinion, know what wins and what loses, anticipate your opposition, answer their challenges, create the crisis so you can organize people around it and build a coalition. The CARE bill is a very good example of how all of that worked. We couldn't have done the CARE Act my first year at the AIDS Action Council because we hadn't built the coalition. And the coalition ultimately carried the bill.

This bill faced an image problem. People with AIDS were not universally seen as worthy of public sympathy or support. For the most part, gay men and IV drug users were on the margins of society. To gain support for this important bill, strategies to overcome these barriers needed to be developed. The use of Ryan's mother, Jeanne White, as a major spokeswoman and framing the services in the bill as disaster relief were two successful strategies. The themes contained in the framing and the use of symbols were consistently reinforced in all the coalitions activities. Finally, at a critical time, the coalition used the media to put pressure on Congress through shaming key legislators.

Conclusion

Groups across the country are using the media to advance specific policies to promote public health. From three schoolgirls pressuring a local billboard advertiser to a major Washington advocacy group lobbying the U.S. Congress to provide care for people with a serious illness, change is being advanced by creative use of media advocacy techniques.

In this chapter we have seen various groups clearly define their goals, deftly target the people they want to reach, finely craft their message, and successfully advance their policy. All of this is done with attention to gaining access to the media, shaping the debate, and advancing the policy or desired outcome. Each group set out to tell a story in its own way, different from the story that was most often told.

The groups used several journalistic conventions to gain access. For example, in New Mexico the irony of beer advertisements visible from the school coupled with young girls battling the large billboard companies made for a compelling story. In Davis, California, a family physician created a story that the media could not ignore and interested them in it even further by creating visuals that personalized the story and involved the journalists. In Hawaii, MADD linked the compelling emotion of a Memorial Day holiday to its issue of drunk driving and then combined their visuals with phone numbers to further advance their cause on the grassroots level.

Tobacco control activists created a symbol powerful enough to counter Philip Morris's multimillion-dollar campaign to link the Bill of Rights with the freedom to sell America's most deadly product. The activists carefully framed the debate so that it was Philip Morris that was under attack and not the Bill of Rights. Advocates for people with AIDS capitalized on current news reporting on a major hurricane and the Loma Prieta earthquake in San Francisco to frame the debate in terms of a crisis needing immediate relief. Alcohol-control activists reframed the St. Ides story from a controversy between competing rap stars to unethical corporate marketing practices. In each case, the advocates capitalized on what would attract media attention, and then turned that attention in the direction that would further their projects goals.

In San Diego, media attention brought new members to a coalition working on alcohol policy; in New Mexico, the offensive billboards came down; in Hawaii, the state legislature reconvened and passed the law—this time without the flaw; in Philadelphia, RJR withdrew its latest product; and in Washington, DC, the most comprehensive AIDS service funding package ever was passed.

In sum, these people had a story to tell and a goal to reach. They knew the media could amplify their power to do both these things effectively. In every case, they told their story and they reached their goal. On the surface, these groups appeared to be simply feeling their way along. In reality, the one thing they knew very well was that creative use of the media was necessary, though not sufficient, to accomplish their goals. What really made the media effort effective was the coalition and grass-roots support that each group stood on.

Notes

1. All the quotes from this case study are from interviews by Juana Canela and Marilyn Aguirre-Molina of the University of Medicine and Dentistry of New Jersey in their draft, "Pojoque, New Mexico—Media Advocacy Case Study," prepared for the Marin Institute for the Prevention of Alcohol and Other Drug Problems, San Rafael, CA, with support from the Center for Substance Abuse Prevention, U.S. Department of Health and Human Services.

2. All the quotes from this case study are from an interview with Dr. Garen Wintemute by Lori Dorfman, August 17, 1990.

3. All quotes from this case study are from an interview with Charyn Sutton by Makani Themba, December 27, 1992.

4. All quotes from this case study are from interviews conducted by Cheri Pies during September 1992.

5. All quotes from this case study are from "MADD Gets Mad" (1991). Reprinted with permission.

6. All quotes from this case study are from interviews conducted by David Jernigan on February 13, 1991, and February 1, 1993.

7
SUMMING UP

This instrument can teach, it can illuminate; yes, and it can even inspire. But it can do so only to the extent that humans are determined to use it to those ends. Otherwise it is merely wires and lights in a box.

—Edward R. Murrow (1958)

The media are seen by some as the source of society's problems and by others as the source of our salvation. The truth is, of course, that the media are a little bit of both. Coming to terms with the paradox of the media is essential to making appropriate use of this vital resource.

Since the late 1980s media advocacy has become an increasingly popular approach to using mass media to promote public health goals. This approach seeks to enhance the visibility, legitimacy, and power of community groups. Media advocacy represents more than just a different way of using mass media to promote health. It is an effort to shift power back to the community by cultivating skills that can enhance and amplify the community's voice. Instead of giving individuals a message about personal health behaviors, it gives groups a voice. It is based on the premise that real improvements in health status will not come so much from increases in personal health knowledge as from improvements in social conditions. It is the power gap rather than the knowledge gap that is the primary focus of media advocacy.

Media advocacy reflects a public health approach that explicitly recognizes the importance of the social and political environment and defines health problems as matters of public policy, not just individual behavior. Media advocacy attempts to help individuals claim power by providing knowledge and skills to better enable them to participate in efforts to change the social and political factors that contribute to the health status of all. The health of the community, not necessarily the individual, is the primary focus. Active participation in the political process is the mechanism for health promotion.

Media advocacy is a tool for mustering support in the social and political realms to change social conditions. It is a tool for advocates, activists, and organizers and as such contains basic elements of protest movements. Olien et al. (1989) have identified several principles of protest movements that are helpful for summarizing media advocacy. They found that protest movements aim to make legitimate an oppositional point of view, use drama to highlight their perspective, capitalize on media opportunities for gaining visibility and legitimacy, anticipate the arguments and actions of their adversaries, and build their own internal communication systems.

Legitimization

Media advocates work to legitimize the upstream view of health issues while highlighting the inadequacies of analyses that focus exclusively on individual responsibility. Every media event, every sound bite attempts to frame issues in terms of root causes rather than personal behaviors. No matter what the health issue is, you need to apply the concept of going upstream. What does it mean, in policy terms, when you take your issue upstream? What solution do you want to legitimize and make credible? What are the usual exceptionalist problem definitions, and how does a universalistic or environmental perspective improve on them? How do you gain support for moving your definition upstream? The point of advocacy, from our perspective, is to know the answers to these questions to make upstream problem definitions legitimate.

The Importance of Drama

To set the agenda for health issues and move it upstream, media advocates must get the attention of the media. Fortunately, most health stories involve personal and social drama and include controversy, injustice, personal struggle, and creative solutions. Journalists tell stories; therefore, media advocates must bring their issues to journalists in dramatic form. This means casting health problems in narrative form with characters, plots, villains, and heroes. The challenge for advocates is to understand the way the media works so they can craft stories that meet journalistic needs and contribute to the social good.

Opportunism

Media advocates use events, or create them, to attract media or illustrate a problem. Sometimes this is planned, but often it is not. Media advocates need to be opportunistic and take advantage of a wide range of events. They must be ready to respond to breaking news that presents an opportunity for media access and learn to interpret that news from the perspective of their policy goals. Tobacco advocates are practiced at this. They routinely use news events, such as a plane crash, a food contamination scare, or a news release from the tobacco industry, to create news of their own. Almost any news event is a potential opportunity to bring attention to your health issue. This is the day-to-day practice of media advocacy.

Anticipating the Reaction of Adversaries

Good journalists always want to know the other side of the story. So will a good media advocate. Responding creatively to the other side is part of the media advocate's work (another part is proactive, creating arguments to which opponents must respond). Media advocates need well-developed arguments and need to anticipate the reaction of adversaries. Media advocates should continually improve and reformulate arguments and counterarguments about their particular issue to account for new developments.

Media advocates must take seriously the challenge of counterarguing and reframing issues in a debate context. Gun control, alcohol, tobacco, and nutrition policy advocates routinely find themselves in direct debate with polished public relations people and must be skilled at handling symbols, themes, and slogans that these professionals use deftly.

Creating a Protest Controlled-
Communication System

Media advocates need an infrastructure to sustain a movement for social change. Advocates need to communicate, strategize, and develop their voices in a system under their control. Tobacco and alcohol advocates have done this using the computer networks discussed in Chapter 5 (alcohol) and Chapter 6 (tobacco). The important thing is that advocates be able to communicate with each other to strategize in a timely fashion. To take advantage of mass media, particularly news media, advocates have to be able to respond quickly to breaking issues as well as to create news. Fax machines, telephones, and computer modems can be important hardware in this process.

In sum, media advocacy tries to change the rules for working with the media. It moves the focus from public affairs to news desks to gain greater control over the way health issues are communicated. Media advocacy focuses attention on the behavior of those whose decisions largely determine the social and physical environment (e.g., corporations, government regulators, and politicians), which in turn defines the range of health choices available to the public.

Social and health programs generally tend to focus on giving people skills to *beat* the odds to overcome the structural barriers to successful and healthy lives. In the long run, it makes more sense to *change* the odds so that more people have a wider and more accessible range of healthy choices (Schorr, 1988). Media advocacy helps to emphasize the importance of changing social conditions to improve the odds. Media advocacy can be instrumental in escaping a traditional and limited focus on disease conditions and instead promote a greater understanding of the conditions that will support and improve the public's health.

A. J. Leibling said, "The power of the press belongs to those who own one." The challenge of media advocacy is to make this less true. In a way, the power of the press is being appropriated by those who understand how media work. The better you understand media, the more you understand your topic; the more you plan for your goals, the greater success you will have in harnessing media power and making news work for your issue.

The three stages of media advocacy might be best summarized as self-defense, reflection, and action. Self-defense means understanding the forces that shape the mass media and knowing how your issue is being portrayed to enable you to reframe the overall presentation to reflect your policy goals. Reflection involves blending knowledge of your issue with how the news media work in order to develop an overall media strategy. What is your overall goal, to whom do you wish to speak through the media, and what do you want to happen? Finally, action entails building your capacity to work with the news media, implementing your plan, and maintaining the power of media in your organizations efforts.

As you make use of the power of mass media, keep in mind the following guidelines for effective media relations and media advocacy.

Media Relations

Know Your Topic. Information is a form of currency in the news media. In large part your success in working with the media will depend on the extent of your knowledge about the issues you seek to influence. The more accurate, interesting, and timely the information, the more valuable it is to the journalist. Know your issue, the action you want taken, and who specifically has the power to make it happen. However, it is important not to go beyond your level of expertise. Refer any questions that you cannot answer with confidence and accuracy to others.

Be Confident. One of the greatest barriers to working with the news media is lack of confidence. Some people feel at a disadvantage or intimidated by journalists, even though they have more expertise on a given issue than the journalist. Community health issues are of great interest to the audience and what you have to say is important. As long as you stick to what you know best and follow your media plan you have every reason to feel confident about the value of your knowledge.

Be Scrupulously Honest. Never compromise the facts. Use accurate research studies and data to make your point. Common sense is also an important ally in helping to covey the essence of many public health issues. In many cases there is no clear truth and the struggle is to establish your interpretation of the facts as the truth of the story. Using misleading data or deliberately distorting a story will make your information the equivalent of valueless currency. In addition, your status and credibility as a source will be lost.

View the Media as a Partner, Not an Adversary. You are developing a professional relationship with the media. They need you for your ability to provide them with important facts, access to local programs and people, and story ideas. You need the news media to tell your story and highlight your solution. View every media contact as a building block for an ongoing relationship.

Ask the Right Questions. When a news person calls, ask the following questions: "What is your story?" "Who else have you talked to?" "What do you need?" and "What is your deadline?" Answers to these questions should provide you with a good overview of what you need to know to be responsive.

Be Creative. The news media, like other parts of the media, need to attract audiences and thus always have an eye toward entertainment values. Like it or not, this is the way it is, and you must be creative in shaping your story and presenting it to the news media. Especially on television, pictures are essential to telling your story. On the radio and the in the print media, the use of effective symbols and media bites is important.

Media Advocacy

Root Your Media Actions in Community Support. The basic legitimacy for media advocacy comes from community support. Keep community issues and values in mind. Cultivating local expertise, forming coalitions, and promoting local advocacy enhances the prospects for successful use of the media for social change.

Always Think Upstream. Focus as much as possible on the root causes of the problem and emphasize solutions that address these root causes. This is much harder to do than focusing on individual health habits or the struggles of people trying to overcome specific problems. Looking upstream involves integrating a social justice and fairness orientation into your understanding and presentation of the problem.

Emphasize Public Health Values. Public health tries to make the system more responsive to those most in need. This usually means a focus on those who are the least advantaged in our society. Values of fairness in sharing the burden for change, equity in receiving social benefits, and justice in having access to basic social goods such as housing and employment are central to public health. Emphasize the public health values underlying the specific action you are advocating.

Anticipate Opposition. Blending science, politics and activism to promote health creates a great deal of friction. Opposition emerges on practical and philosophical grounds, and you need to be well versed in the perspective of the opposition. Responding to the opposition on practical considerations means knowing your facts and understanding the broader issues that your problem involves. Responding on philosophical grounds means having a clear sense of your basic values and fundamental public health values.

Think Long Term. Media efforts of any kind need to be placed in the context of an overall plan for social change. If you do not know where you are going, then it does not make a difference which road you take. However, if you are advancing a policy and know where you want to end up, having an overall plan will provide important guidance.

Evaluate and Reflect. Take the time to measure your organization's goals and objectives against your media advocacy initiatives. Working with the media takes time and effort; you must be sure that you are using this resource in an efficient manner. Ask yourself whose agenda is driving your media activities. Is it your agenda or the media's agenda? You need to assess each media activity for how well it fits into your overall plan and contributes to your overall goal.

Final Thoughts

One of the basic messages about media advocacy is that it is important to learn the rules of the media to make appropriate use of this vital resource. As advocates, however, another purpose of learning the rules is to be able to change the rules. In this case, media advocates should think long term about changing rules that influence access and the presentation of news. Several important media policy goals that media advocates might wish to focus on include:

- Increased access to the mass media for nonprofit organizations, including reduced rates for paid advertising or a regular spot on local news coverage.
- Increased diversity of faces, voices, and sources in the news room.
- Greater community control of media outlets.

Public health is a struggle to eliminate the conditions that cultivate poverty, alienation, and disease in our society. The challenge for advocates is, to the greatest extent possible, to refocus attention upstream to put the spotlight on these conditions and those who benefit from the social arrangements that allow this to happen. Camus (1948) wrote in *The Plague:* "All I maintain is that on this earth there are pestilences and there are victims, and it's up to us, as far as possible, not to join forces with the pestilences."

We hope this book will make it more difficult for the pestilences.

Appendix
ORGANIZATIONAL ACRONYMS

ALCNet	Alcohol Control Network
ANSR	Americans for Non-Smokers' Rights
BATF	Bureau of Alcohol, Tobacco and Firearms
CARE Act	Comprehensive AIDS Resources Emergency Act
CCSAPT	Community Coalition for Substance Abuse Prevention and Treatment
CDC	Centers for Disease Control and Prevention
CSPI	Center for Science in the Public Interest
EPA	Environmental Protection Agency
FHA/HERO	Future Homemakers of America/Home Economic Related Occupations
INFACT	Infant Formula Coalition Action
MADD	Mothers Against Drunk Driving
NAAAPI	National Association of African Americans for Positive Imagery
OSAP	Office for Substance Abuse Prevention, now the Center for Substance Abuse Prevention
RJR	RJR Nabisco (formerly R. J. Reynolds Tobacco Company)
SCARCNet	Smoking Control Advocacy Resource Center Network
USDHHS	U.S. Department of Health and Human Services
WHO	World Health Organization

REFERENCES

ABC News. (1987, July 17). Nightline: *Slasher movies*. New York: American Broadcasting Companies.

Abramson, J. (1991, May 21). Selling moderation: Alcohol industry is at forefront of efforts to curb drunkenness. *The Wall Street Journal*.

Adatto, K. (1989, December 10). TV tidbits starve democracy. *New York Times*.

Advocacy Institute. (1989a). *Media strategies for smoking control: Guidelines* (NIH Publication No. 89-3013, for the U.S. Department of Health and Human Services). Washington, DC: Author.

Advocacy Institute. (1989b). *The media opportunities project: Localizing a national story* (Report prepared for the Office for Substance Abuse Prevention). Rockville, MD: U.S. Department of Health and Human Services.

Alexander, K. (1992, June 2). Sea World and alcohol don't mix. *San Diego Union-Tribune*.

Americans for Non-Smokers' Rights (ANSR). (1987, Winter). *Update*, p. 1.

Americans for Non-Smokers' Rights (ANSR). (1993). *Major tobacco control ordinances: Smoking and tobacco control* (Monograph No. 3). Bethesda, MD: National Cancer Institute.

Amidei, N. (1991). *So you want to make a difference: Advocacy is the key*. Washington, DC: OMB Watch.

Arbitron Company. (1991). *Radio Today 1990* [pamphlet]. Author.

Atkin, C. (1989). Mass communication effects on drinking and driving. In *Surgeon general's workshop on drunk driving: Background papers* (pp. 15-34). Rockville, MD: U.S. Department of Health and Human Services.

Atkin, C. (1992). *Survey and experimental research on alcohol advertising effects*. Paper presented to the Working Group on the Effects of the Mass Media on the Use and Abuse of Alcohol. Washington, DC: National Institute on Alcohol Abuse and Alcoholism.

Aufderheide, P., & Chester, J. (1990). *Strategic communications for nonprofits: Talk radio who's talking, who's listening?* Washington, DC: Benton Foundation and the Center for Strategic Communications.

Bagdikian, B. (1987). *The media monopoly* (2nd ed.). Boston: Beacon Press.

Barnouw, E. (1978). *The sponsor: Notes on a modern potentate*. Oxford, UK: Oxford University Press.

Barrett, J. (1992, June 15). Retailers and restaurants hard hit by L.A. riots. *Impact*.

BATF imposes three-day suspension on St. Ides producer's permit. (1992, January 13). *Kane's Beverage Week*, p. 3.

Baudot, B. (1989). *International advertising handbook: A user's guide to rules and regulations.* Lexington, MA: Lexington Books.

Beauchamp, D. (1976). Public health as social justice. *Inquiry, 12*, 3-14.

Beauchamp, D. (1988). *The health of the republic.* Philadelphia, PA: Temple University Press.

Bellah, R., Masden, R., Sullivan, W., Swindler, A., & Tipton, S. (1986). *Habits of the heart: Individualism and commitment in American life.* New York: Harper & Row.

Best, J. (1989). Dark figures and child victims: Statistical claims about missing children. In J. Best (Ed.), *Images of issues* (pp. 21-37). New York: Aldine de Gruyter.

Blakeslee, S. (1992, March 15). Faulty math heightens fears of breast cancer. *New York Times*, sec. 4, p. 1.

Blow, R. (1991). How to decode the hidden agenda of the partnership's Madison Avenue propagandists. *Washington City Paper, 11*, 29-35.

Blum, H. (1980). Social perspective risk reduction. *Family and Community Health, 3*, 41-61.

Brain, B. (1897). *Weapons for temperance warfare: Some plans and programs.* Boston: United Society of Christian Endeavor.

Buchannan, D. R., & Lev, J. (1990). *Beer and fast cars: How brewers target blue-collar youth through motor sport sponsorships.* Washington, DC: AAA Foundation for Traffic Safety.

Burns, K. (1989, May 14). "Moyers: A second look"—More than meets the eye. *New York Times*.

Camus, A. (1948). *The Plague.* New York: Modern Library.

Castillo, S. (1993, February 3). Personal communication.

Cohen, B. (1963). *The press and foreign policy.* Princeton, NJ: Princeton University Press.

Cohn, V. (1983). Views of scientists and journalists on how the media cover cancer. *SIPIscope, 11*, 1.

Communications Consortium Media Center. (1991). *Strategic communications for nonprofits: Strategic media—Designing a public interest campaign.* Washington, DC: Benton Foundation and the Center for Strategic Communications.

Comstock, G. (1991). *Television in America.* Newbury Park, CA: Sage.

Contra Costa County AIDS Program. (1991). *Quarterly report of HIV/AIDS statistics.* Contra Costa County, CA: Author.

Cook, F., Tyler, T., Goetz, E., Gordon, M., Protess, D., Leff, D., & Molotch, H. (1983). Media and agenda setting: Effects on the public, interest group leaders, policy makers, and policy. *Public Opinion Quarterly, 47*, 16-35.

Cross, M. (1992, June 8). Letter: To coalition members concerned about alcohol promotion at Sea World, San Diego.

Curtis, L. (1987). Policies to prevent crime: Neighborhood, family and employment strategies. *Annals of the American Academy of Political and Social Sciences, 494*, 9-168.

Dearing, J., & Rogers, E. (1992). AIDS and the media agenda. In F. Edgar & V. Freimuth (Eds.), *AIDS: A communication perspective* (pp. 173-194). Hillsdale, NJ: Lawrence Erlbaum.

DeCurtis, A. (1991, June 27). Geto Boy Bushwick shot in head. *Rolling Stone*, p. 17.

DeJong, W., & Wallack, L. (1992). The role of designated driver programs in the prevention of alcohol-impaired driving: A critical reassessment. *Health Education Quarterly, 19*, 429-442.

DeJong, W., & Winsten, J. (1990). The use of mass media in substance abuse prevention. *Health Affairs*, 30-46.

de la Torre, R. (1989, January 11). Students willing to help clear the air. *Vallejo Times-Herald*, p. A1.

DiFranza, J., Richards, J., Paulman, P., Wolf-Gillespie, N., Fletcher, C., Jaffe, R., & Murray, D. (1991). RJR Nabisco's cartoon camel promotes camel cigarettes to children. *Journal of the American Medical Association, 266,* 3149-3153.

Downs, A. (1972). Up and down with ecology. *The Public Interest, 28,* 38-50.

Dubos, R. (1959). *Mirage of health.* New York: Harper & Row.

Duncan, C., Rivlin, D., Williams, M., & Ogata, S. (1990). *An advocate's guide to the media.* Washington, DC: Children's Defense Fund.

Duhl, L. (1990). *The social entrepreneurship of change.* New York: Pace University Press.

Easthouse, K. (1992, March 17). Students win battle over billboard. *The New Mexican.*

Eigen, L. D. (1991). *Alcohol practices, policies, and potentials of American colleges and universities* [mimeo]. Rockville, MD: Office for Substance Abuse Prevention, U.S. Department of Health and Human Services.

Farquhar, J. W., Maccoby, N., & Solomon, D. (1984). Community applications of behavioral medicine. In W. Gentry (Ed.), *Handbook of behavioral medicine* (pp. 437-478). New York: Guilford.

Fein, R. (1992, November). Health care reform. *Scientific American,* pp. 46-53.

Fischer, P., Schwartz, M., Richards, J. J., Goldstein, A., & Rojas, T. (1991). Brand logo recognition by children aged 3 to 6 years. Mickey Mouse and Old Camel. *Journal of the American Medical Association, 266,* 3145-3148.

Fitzsimmons, B. (1992, April 11). This Bud's for . . . who? *San Diego Union-Tribune,* p. E1.

Flay, B. (1987). Mass media and smoking cessation: A critical review. *American Journal of Public Health, 77,* 153-160.

Florin, P. (1989). *Nurturing the grassroots: Neighborhood volunteer organizations and America's cities.* New York: Citizens Committee for New York City.

Freedman, A. (1991a, July 1). Malt advertising that touts firepower comes under attack by U.S. officials. *The Wall Street Journal.*

Freedman, A. (1991b, June 17). Potent, new Heileman malt is brewing fierce industry and social criticism. *The Wall Street Journal,* p. B1.

Freimuth, V. (1985). Developing the public service advertisement for nonprofit marketing. *Advances in Nonprofit Marketing, 1,* 55-93.

Galbraith, J. (1973). *Economics and the public purpose.* New York: Mentor.

Gamson, W. A. (1989). News as framing: Comments on Graber. *American Behavioral Scientist, 33,* 157-161.

Gerbner, G. (1992). The communications perspective. In *Environmental strategies to reduce alcohol, tobacco, and other drug (ATOD) problems: Summary report* (pp. 6-8). Rockville, MD: Office of Substance Abuse Prevention, U.S. Department of Health and Human Services.

Gerbner, G., Gross, L., Morgan, M., & Signorielli, N. (1986). Living with television: The dynamics of the cultivation process. In J. Bryant & D. Zillman (Eds.), *Perspectives on media effects* (pp. 17-40). Hillsdale, NJ: Lawrence Erlbaum.

Gitlin, T. (1980). *The whole world is watching: Mass media in the making and unmaking of the new left.* Berkeley: University of California Press.

Gitlin, T. (1983). *Inside prime time.* New York: Pantheon Books.

Glasgow Media Group (Philo, G., Hewitt, J., Beharrell, P., & Davis, H.). (1982). *Really bad news.* London: Writers & Readers.

Godfrey, J. E. (1991, July 18). Yo ho ho, a bottle of rum. *San Diego Tribune,* p. E4.

Green, L., & Raeburn, J. (1990). Contemporary developments in health promotion: Definitions and challenges. In N. Bracht (Ed.), *Health promotion at the community level* (pp. 29-44). Newbury Park, CA: Sage.

Haan, M., Kaplan, G., & Camacho, T. (1987). Poverty and health. *American Journal of Epidemiology, 125,* 989-998.

Haan, M., Kaplan, G., & Syme, S. L. (1989). Socioeconomic status and health: Old observations and new thoughts. In Bunker, Gomby, & Kehrer (Eds.), *Pathways to health: The role of social factors*. Menlo Park, CA: Henry J. Kaiser.

Haddock, V. (1989, May 28). Surgeon general joins war against alcohol. *San Francisco Examiner/Chronicle*, p. A1.

Hammond, S., Freimuth, V., & Morrison, W. (1987). The gatekeeping funnel: Tracking a major PSA campaign from distribution through gatekeepers to target audience. *Health Education Quarterly, 14*, 153-166.

Hawkins, J., Catalano, R., & Miller, J. (1992). Risk and protective factors for alcohol and other drug problems in adolescence and early adulthood: Implications for substance abuse prevention. *Psychological Bulletin, 112*, 64-105.

Hawley, A. (1973). Ecology and population. *Science, 179*, 1196-1201.

Heller, K. (1990, May 20). The slow burn: Cigarettes, cancer and blacks. *Philadelphia Inquirer Magazine*, p. 32.

Hertsgaard, M. (1991, May 30). 60 minute man. *Rolling Stone*, pp. 47-82.

Hilts, P. (1984, January 27). 6 1/2-year boycott of Nestlé is ended as firm adopts baby-formula code. *Washington Post*, p. A1.

How PR firm orchestrated the Alar scare. (1989, October 8) *Sacramento Bee*, p. D1.

In defense of virtue [Editorial]. (1989, March 2). *New York Times*, p. A26.

Institute of Medicine Committee for the Study of the Future of Public Health. (1988). *The future of public health*. Washington, DC: National Academy Press.

Iyengar, S. (1991). *Is anyone responsible? How television frames political issues*. Chicago: University of Chicago Press.

Iyengar, S., & Kinder, D. R. (1987). *News that matters*. Chicago: University of Chicago Press.

Jamieson, K. (1988). *Eloquence in an electronic age: The transformation of political speechmaking*. New York: Oxford University Press.

Johnson, C. (1992, July 1). A fight to keep liquor stores shut. *San Francisco Chronicle*, p. 1.

Johnson, J. (1989a). Horror stories and the construction of child abuse. In J. Best (Ed.), *Images of issues: Typifying contemporary social problems* (pp. 5-19). New York: Aldine De Gruyter.

Johnson, J. (1989b, April 6). Images are weapons on abortion battlefield. *New York Times*, p. A14.

Jorgensen, C., Nunnally, B., & Dunmire, R. (1992). *Forging partnerships in public information: State and federal agencies working together in HIV prevention efforts*. Paper presented at the 120th annual meeting of the American Public Health Association.

Kagay, M. (1991, October 20). As candidates hunt the big issue, polls can give them a few clues. *New York Times*, p. E3.

Kelly, M. (1992, July 16). A few workers keep Clinton's campaign on track. *New York Times*, p. A9.

Kinsella, J. (1989). *Covering the plague: AIDS and the American media*. New Brunswick, NJ: Rutgers University Press.

Kitagawa, E., & Hauser, P. (1973). *Differential mortality in the United States: A study in socioeconomic epidemiology*. Cambridge, MA: Harvard University Press.

Klass, P. (1992, December 13). Tackling problems we thought we solved. *New York Times Magazine*, pp. 54-62.

Kotler, P., & Roberto, E. (1989). *Social marketing: Strategies for changing public behavior*. New York: The Free Press.

Kozel, J. (1988). *Rachel and her children*. New York: Crown.

Kreiger, N. (1990). On becoming a public health professional: Reflections on democracy, leadership, and accountability. *Journal of Public Health Policy, 11*, 412-419.

Kurtz, H. (1992, June 21). Networks adapt to changed campaign role: As candidates use other means to deliver messages, big three scramble to find new niche. *Washington Post*, p. A19.

Ladd, E. (1981, June-July). 205 and going strong. *Public Opinion*, pp. 7-12.

Lazarsfeld, P., & Merton, R. (1975). Mass communication, popular taste, and organized social action. In W. Schramm (Ed.), *Mass communications* (pp. 492-512). Urbana: University of Illinois Press. (Original work published 1948)

Lefebvre, C., & Flora, J. (1988). Social marketing and public health intervention. *Health Education Quarterly, 15*, 299-315.

Levin, G. (1990, October 8). PR gives new life to rejected TV ads: Networks' "no" sparks news interest. *Advertising Age*, p. 76.

Levine, H. (1981). Spirits in America: The birth of demon rum. *Public Opinion, 4*, 13-15.

Lipman, J. (1991, August 21). Sobering view: Alcohol firms put off public. *The Wall Street Journal*, p. B1.

Lippmann, W. (1965). *Public opinion.* New York: Free Press. (Original work published 1922)

MADD gets mad. (1991). *Lobbying and Influence Alert, 1*(3), 1-2.

Malt liquor makers find lucrative market in the urban young. (1992, March 10). *Wall Street Journal*, p. A1.

Marinucci, C. (1992, April 6). Alcohol industry draws more fire. *San Francisco Examiner*, p. D1.

Marmot, M., Koqevinas, M., & Elston, M. (1987). Social/economic status and disease. *Annual Review of Public Health, 8*, 111-135.

Massey, D. (1992, September 1). American apartheid: Segregation and the making of the underclass. *Poverty and Race.*

Mayer, N. (1984). *Neighborhood organizations and community development.* Washington, DC: Urban Institute Press.

McCombs, M., & Shaw, D. (1972). The agenda setting function of mass media. *Public Opinion Quarterly, 36*, 176-187.

McGuire, A. (1992). The California alcohol tax initiative. In A. Bergman (Ed.), *Political approaches to injury control at the state level* (pp. 79-88). Seattle: University of Washington Press.

McKeown, T. (1978). Determinants of health. *Human Nature, 1*, 60-67.

McKinlay, J., McKinlay, S., & Beaglehole, R. (1989). Trends in death and disease and the contributions of medical measures. In H. Freeman & S. Levine (Eds.), *Handbook of medical sociology* (pp. 14-45). Englewood Cliffs, NJ: Prentice-Hall.

McKnight, J. (1987, Winter). Regenerating community. *Social Policy*, pp. 54-58.

McKnight, J. (1989, January-February). Servanthood is bad. *The Other Side*, p. 38.

McLoughlin, E., & Clarke, N. (1977). One pediatric burn unit's experience with sleepwear-related injuries. *Pediatrics, 60*, 405-409.

McMillan, D., & Chavis, D. (1986). Sense of community: A definition and theory. *Journal of Community Psychology, 14*, 6-23.

Miller, C. (1976). Societal change and public health: A rediscovery. *American Journal of Public Health, 66*, 54-60.

Miller, M. (1988, Winter). Death grip. *Propaganda Review*, pp. 34-35.

Mills, C. (1959). *The sociological imagination.* New York: Oxford University Press.

Minkler, M. (1978). Ethical issues in community organization. *Health Education Monographs, 6*, 198-210.

Mintz, M. (1990, July-August). No ifs, ands, or butts. *The Washington Monthly*, pp. 30-37.

Montgomery, K. (1989). *Target: Prime time, advocacy groups and the struggle over entertainment television.* New York: Oxford University Press.

Moore, M., & Gerstein, D. (Eds.). (1981). *Alcohol and public policy: Beyond the shadow of prohibition.* Washington, DC: National Academy Press.

Murrow, E. (1958, November 13). A broadcaster talks to his colleagues. *The Reporter* (The Reporter Magazine Company).

Nelkin, D. (1987). *Selling science: How the press covers science and technology.* New York: Freeman.

Neubauer, D., & Pratt, R. (1981). The second public health revolution: A critical appraisal. *Journal of Health Politics, Policy and Law, 6,* 205-228.

Neuman, W. R. (1990). The threshold of public attention. *Public Opinion Quarterly, 54,* 159-176.

O'Malley, P., & Wagenaar, A. (1991). Effects of minimum drinking age laws on alcohol use, related behaviors and traffic crash involvement among American youth. *Journal of Alcohol Studies, 52,* 5.

Olien, C. N., Tichenor, P. J., & Donahue, G. A. (1989). Media coverage and social movements. In C. Salmon (Ed.), *Information campaigns: Balancing social values and social change* (pp 139-163). Newbury Park, CA: Sage.

Oregon bans malt liquor ad. (1991, November 18) *Alcoholic Beverage Control,* p. 1.

Oreskes, M. I. (1990, September 9). For G.O.P. arsenal, 133 words to fire. *New York Times.*

Paletz, D., Pearson, R., & Willis, D. (1977). *Politics in public service advertising on television.* New York: Praeger.

Pertschuk, M., & Schaetzel, W. (1989). *The people rising: The campaign against the Bork nomination.* New York: Thunder's Mouth.

Pertschuk, M., & Wilbur, P. (1991). *Media advocacy: Reframing public debate.* Washington, DC: Benton Foundation and the Center for Strategic Communications.

Pierce, J., Gilpin, E., Burns, D., Whalen, E., Rosbrook, B., Shopland, D., & Johnson, M. (1991). Does tobacco advertising target young people to start smoking? *Journal of the American Medical Association, 266,* 3154-3158.

Postman, N. (1985). *Amusing ourselves to death.* New York: Viking.

Powles, J. (1979). On the limitations of modern medicine. In D. Sobel (Ed.), *Ways of health: Holistic approaches to ancient and contemporary medicine.* New York: Harcourt Brace Jovanovich.

Public Media Center. (n.d.). [Brochure]. San Francisco: Author.

Puska, P., McAlister, A., & Maccoby, N. (1985). Planned use of mass media in national health promotion: The "Keys to health" TV program in 1982 in Finland. *Canadian Journal of Public Health, 76,* 336-342.

Pytte, A. (1989, October 21). Far-reaching smoking ban climaxes 2-year odyssey. *Congressional Quarterly Weekly Report,* p. 2779.

Quinn, J. R. (1991, March 31). [Letter to the editor]. *New York Times.*

Reinhold, R. (1992, July 2). California forced to turn to I.O.U.'s. *New York Times,* p. 1.

Rice, R., & Atkin, C. (Eds.). (1990). *Public communication campaigns.* Newbury Park, CA: Sage.

Rogers, E., & Dearing, J. (1988). Agenda-setting research: Where has it been and where is it going? In J. A. Anderson (Ed.), *Communication yearbook.* Newbury Park, CA: Sage.

Rogers, E., Dearing, J., & Chang, S. (1991). AIDS in the 1980s: The agenda-setting process for a public issue. *Journalism Monographs, 126,* 1-47.

Romano, C. (1987). The grisly truth about bare facts. In R. K. Manoff & M. Schudson (Eds.), *Reading the news* (pp. 38-78). New York: Pantheon.

Rothenberg, R. (1990, January 8). Controversy in commercials used to gain extra publicity. *New York Times,* p. D1.

Ryan, C. (1991). *Prime time activism.* Boston: South End Press.

Ryan, W. (1976). *Blaming the victim*. New York: Vintage.

Ryan, W. (1981). *Equality*. New York: Vintage.

Saffer, H., & Grossman, M. (1987). Beer taxes, the legal drinking age, and motor vehicle fatalities. *Journal of Legal Studies*, 351-374.

Salmon, C. (Ed.). (1989). *Information campaigns: Balancing social values and social change*. Newbury Park, CA: Sage.

Salmon, C. (1990, Spring). God understands when the cause is noble. *Gannett Center Journal*, *18*, 23-34.

Schiller, H. (1973). *The mind managers*. Boston: Beacon.

Schorr, L. (1988). *Within our reach*. New York: Anchor/Doubleday.

Schuftan, C. (1989). Health still for only some by the year 2000? *Journal of Tropical Pediatrics*, *35*, 197-198.

Scribner, R. (1992). *The overconcentration loophole*. Los Angeles: USC School of Medicine, Local Alcohol Availability Database.

Selikof, I. (1991, August 30). *New York Times*, p. B7.

Shales, T. (1988, March 3). Tony Schwartz, on the citizen channel. *Washington Post*, p. D1.

Sharpe, T. (1992a, March 16). Beer ads canned. *Albuquerque Journal (North)*, p. A1.

Sharpe, T. (1992b, March 10). Beer billboards may move. *Albuquerque Journal (North)*.

Shaw, D., & McCombs, M. (1989). Dealing with illicit drugs: The power and limits of mass media agenda setting. In P. Shoemaker (Ed.), *Communication campaigns about drugs: Government, media, and the public* (pp. 113-120). Hillsdale, NJ: Lawrence Erlbaum.

Shoemaker, P., & Mayfield, E. (1987). Building a theory of news content: A synthesis of current approaches. *Journalism Monographs*, *103*, 1-36.

Smikle, K. (1991). "Mandrake," guerrilla activist. *Emerge*, p. 28.

Smith, D., & Egger, M. (1992). Socioeconomic differences in mortality in Britain and the United States. *American Journal of Public Health*, *82*, 1079-1081.

State round-up. (1992, March 17). *USA Today*, p. A6.

Stevenson, R. (1990, June 9). Current events in the world of prime time. *San Francisco Chronicle*, p. C9.

Suess, Dr. (1954). *Horton hears a who!* New York: Random House.

Sullivan, T. J. (1992, March 7). "What kid can resist that?" Students declare war on booze, tobacco ads. *The New Mexican*, p. A1.

Suro, R. (1993, January 11). Weary minorities try civil rights tack. *New York Times*, p. A12.

Taylor, Elizabeth. (1990, September 28). [Letter to the editor]. *Los Angeles Times*, p. B6.

Tesh, S. (1988). *Hidden arguments: Political ideology and disease prevention policy*. New Brunswick, NJ: Rutgers University Press.

Thomas, J. (1991, August 22). 2nd malt liquor cited by protesters. *Chicago Tribune*.

Tuchman, G. (1978). *Making news: A study in the construction of reality*. New York: Free Press.

Tyndall Report. (1991). *1990: The year in review*. New York: ADT Research.

Varied Directions, Inc. (1988). *A citizen's guide to using electronic media for social change: The inside story from Tony Schwartz* [Video]. Camden, ME: Author.

Wagenaar, A., & Farrell, S. (1989). Alcohol beverage control policies: Their role in preventing alcohol-impaired driving. In *Surgeon general's workshop on drunk driving: Background papers* (pp. 1-14). Rockville, MD: U.S. Department of Health and Human Services.

Wallack, L. (1981). Mass media campaigns: The odds against finding behavior change. *Health Education Quarterly*, *8*(3), 209-260.

Wallack, L. (1990a). Improving health promotion: Media advocacy and social marketing approaches. In C. Atkin & L. Wallack (Eds.), *Mass communication and public health: Complexities and conflicts* (pp. 147-163). Newbury Park, CA: Sage.

Wallack, L. (1990b). Mass media and health promotion: Promise, problems, challenge. In C. Atkin & L. Wallack (Eds.), *Mass communication and public health: Complexities and conflicts* (pp. 41-51). Newbury Park, CA: Sage.

Wallack, L. (1990c). Social marketing and media advocacy: Two approaches to health promotion. *World Forum, 11,* 143-154.

Wallack, L., & Dorfman, L. (1992). Television news, hegemony, and health. *American Journal of Public Health, 82,* 125.

Wallack, L., & Sciandra, R. (1990-1991). Media advocacy and public education in the community trial to reduce heavy smoking. *International Quarterly of Community Health Education, 11,* 205-222.

Walzer, M. (1983). *Spheres of justice: A defense of pluralism and equality.* New York: Basic.

Watzlawick, P., Weakland, J., & Fisch, R. (1974). *Change: Principles of problem formation and problem resolution.* New York: Norton.

Wilkinson, R. (1992). National mortality rates: The impact of inequality? *American Journal of Public Health, 82,* 1082-1084.

Winkleby, M., Jatulis, D., Frank, E., & Fortmann, S. (1992). Socioeconomic status and health: How education, income, and occupation contribute to risk factors for cardiovascular disease. *American Journal of Public Health, 82,* 816-820.

Wintemute, G., Teret, S., Kraus, J., Wright, M., & Bradfield, G. (1987). When children shoot children: 88 unintended deaths in California. *Journal of the American Medical Association, 257,* 3107-3109.

Wolfe, S., Wilbur, P., & Douglas, C. (1992). *The congressional addiction to tobacco: How the tobacco lobby suffocates federal health policy.* Washington, DC: Public Citizen's Health Research Group and the Advocacy Institute.

Wong, J. (1989, August 18). Beer promo at A's game causes minor dispute. *The (Oakland) Tribune,* p. D1.

INDEX

ABOUT THE
AUTHORS

Lawrence Wallack is Professor, School of Public Health, University of California at Berkeley. He coedited *Mass Communication and Public Health: Complexities and Conflicts* and has published extensively on health promotion issues. He has been a consultant to the World Health Organization and various other community, philanthropic, and government entities. He is currently Director of the Berkeley Media Studies Group. The group conducts research and works to provide diverse groups with the skills to access the news media, frame public health issues in a policy context, and advance healthy public policy.

Lori Dorfman is Associate Director for the Berkeley Media Studies Group, where she conducts research on mass media and public health and provides media advocacy training for community groups and government agencies. She is also a doctoral candidate in the School of Public Health, University of California at Berkeley. Her dissertation research focuses on how television news frames health issues. She has published articles on television news, advertising, and public health.

David Jernigan is cofounder of the Marin Institute for the Prevention of Alcohol and Other Drug Problems and a media advocate who works primarily on alcohol policy issues. He has developed curricula and led numerous seminars and training sessions on media advocacy, serving as a consultant to community groups and government bodies across the nation. The author of several articles on environmental approaches to the prevention of alcohol-related problems, he is currently pursuing doctoral studies in Sociology at the University of California at Berkeley.

Makani Themba is a veteran in the struggles for neighborhood control and human rights. She has worked with a number of community-based and national organizations. She is currently Associate Director for Media and Policy Analysis at the Marin Institute for the Prevention of Alcohol and Other Drug Problems. She works with policymakers, community organizations, and the media to develop environmental public health approaches that address alcohol and other drug problems. She also provides training and technical assistance to community organizations and government entities on alcohol advertising and availability issues.